3000 80002
St. Louis Community College
D0848392

American Realism and the Canon

American Realism and the Canon

Edited by

Tom Quirk and Gary Scharnhorst

Newark: University of Delaware Press
London and Toronto: Associated University Presses

Associated University Presses
440 Forsgate Drive
Cranbury, NJ 08512

Associated University Presses
25 Sicilian Avenue
London WC1A 2QH, England

Associated University Presses
P.O. Box 338, Port Credit
Mississauga, Ontario
Canada L5G 4L8

The paper used in this publication meets the requirements of the American National Standard for Permanence of Paper for Printed Library Materials Z39.48-1984.

Library of Congress Cataloging-in-Publication Data

American realism and the canon / edited by Tom Quirk and Gary Scharnhorst.
p. cm.
Includes bibliographical references.
Contents: Men of color, women, and uppity art at the turn of the century / Elizabeth Ammons—Nineteenth-century women poets and realism / Cheryl Walker—I can't write a book / Nancy Walker—Reading her/stories against his/stories in early Chinese American literature / Amy Ling—Native American literatures and the canon / Patricia Okker—Romance and realism / Sanford E. Marovitz—Problems of representation in turn-of-the-century immigrant fiction / Susan K. Harris—Three black writers and the anthologized canon / Keneth Kinnamon—Recanonizing the multiple canons of Henry James / Richard A. Hocks—From painful cult to painful realism / Alfred Habegger—Is Huckleberry Finn politically correct? / Tom Quirk—Whatever happened to Bret Harte? / Gary Scharnhorst.
ISBN 0-87413-524-9 (alk. paper)
1. American literature—Minority authors—History and criticism. 2. American literature—Women authors—History and criticism. 3. American literature—History and criticism—Theory, etc. 4. Women and literature—United States—History. 5. Ethnic groups in literature. 6. Minorities in literature. 7. Realism in literature. 8. Canon (Literature) I. Quirk, Tom, 1946– . II. Scharnhorst, Gary.
PS153.M56A42 1994
810.9′920693—dc20 94-11782
CIP

PRINTED IN THE UNITED STATES OF AMERICA

To Jim Barbour,

coeditor and unindicted coconspirator

Contents

Acknowledgements

EARLIER versions of the essays by Elizabeth Ammons, Cheryl Walker, Keneth Kinnamon, Nancy Walker, and Richard A. Hocks originally appeared in *American Literary Realism* 23 (Spring 1991). We are grateful to Robert Franklin of McFarland & Company, Inc., the publisher of *ALR,* for granting us permission to print these essays in the present volume. An earlier version of Tom Quirk's piece originally appeared in his book *Coming to Grips with "Huckleberry Finn": Essays on a Book, a Boy, and a Man* (1993); we thank the University of Missouri Press for permission to print it.

American Realism and the Canon

Introduction

TOM QUIRK and GARY SCHARNHORST

More than a hundred years ago, the red velvet rope was invented in the Palmer House in Chicago. The occasion was hardly frivolous. Hotel visitors night after night had walked past the dining room off the lobby and out onto the streets to seek their suppers. Then some inspired *maître d'* found the way to bring them in: he stretched a red velvet rope across the entrance. The best way to bring people in, he discovered, is to pretend to keep them out. In fact, the night the red velvet rope was invented, people lined up to get into the hotel dining room.

More than thirty-five years ago, Daniel L. Marsh, then president of Boston University, stretched a figurative red velvet rope around the sacred documents that, he believed, upheld a number of cherished American ideals. The American Canon, he wrote, is comprised of "certain American writings so significant, so inspired, so esteemed by Americans, so durably valuable to the American people, so pregnant with the essence of the American spirit, so revelatory of the genius of America, that, taken together, they constitute the authoritative rule of Americanism." Marsh specified the writings he meant: the Mayflower Compact, the Declaration of Independence, the Constitution, Washington's Farewell Address, the Star Spangled Banner, Lincoln's Second Inaugural Address, and Woodrow Wilson's essay "The Road Away from Revolution." It seems that not all of these documents have been as "durably valuable" as Marsh thought. However, the original parchment copies of the Declaration and the Constitution are so revered that, in the event of a nuclear attack on Washington, D.C., they will drop into a lead vault beneath the marble floor of the National Archives. The life of the nation is, by implication, coterminous with the existence of these documents. Meanwhile, however, they are protected only by plexiglass—and a red velvet rope to control the flow of gaping tourists.

The implications of privileging texts are familiar enough to those of us in the academy nowadays. Recall Nathaniel Hawthorne's infamous complaint in a letter he sent William Ticknor in 1855: "America is now wholly given over to a d———d mob of scribbling women." There is no repairing the remark. In fact, twenty-five years earlier, Hawthorne had published without signature a piece in the *Salem Gazette* called "Mrs. [Anne] Hutchinson" and, apropos of nothing at all, observed that the "ink-stained Amazons" in the literary marketplace add only a "girlish feebleness" to the "tottering infancy" of American fiction. In a follow-up to this oft-quoted letter, however, Hawthorne recanted a bit: "In my last, I recollect, I bestowed some vituperation on female authors. I have since been reading [Fanny Fern's] 'Ruth Hall'; and I must say I enjoyed it a good deal. The woman writes as if the devil was in her; and that is the only condition under which a woman ever writes anything worth reading. Generally, women write like emasculated men, and are only to be distinguished from male authors by greater feebleness and folly." He closed by asking Ticknor to let Fanny Fern know how much he admired her. In Nancy Walker's essay in the present volume, by the way, we find more reason to share his admiration of her.

Yet another Hawthorne letter, again to Ticknor, provides a private glimpse at a kind of rough-and-ready canon formation:

> Mr. Monckton Milnes wants me to send him half a dozen good American books, which he has never read or heard of before. For the honor of my country, I should like to do it, but can think of only three which would be likely to come under his description—viz. "Walden," [Julia Ward Howe's] "Passion Flowers," and "Up-Country Letters." Possibly, Mrs. [Anna] Mowatt's Autobiography might make a fourth; and Thoreau's former volume [*A Week on the Concord and Merrimack Rivers*] a fifth. You understand that these books must not be merely good, but must be original, with American characteristics, and not generally known in England.

Like Daniel L. Marsh, Hawthorne is here thrown into the position of enforcing the "authoritative" rule of Americanism and is glad to do so for the honor of his country. His criteria are straightforward—the books he nominates must be "good" literature, original, and thoroughly American. By recommending to a friend (and one supposes by implication a wider circle of English readers) a few good American books, he acts as the dispenser of American culture and taste by virtue of his own literary reputation. And apart from the perhaps surprising fact that two of these five works are by women (the long-since-forgotten *Up-Country Letters* is by a Professor B______, and therefore likely a man), there is the interesting attempt at promoting Thoreau's reputation. Nor was this the only occasion Hawthorne tried to promote his Concord friend—in 1856 he proposed to send copies of Thoreau's works to an editor at the *Illustrated London News* who "might be inclined to draw attention to them." We tend to forget that Thoreau was much more a part of the canon at the end of the century than he was during his lifetime, that before the so-called Melville revival of the 1920s there had been a Thoreau revival in the 1880s—smack in the middle of that period in American literary history we have been taught to regard as the age of realism.

Of course the issues of canon-building and -busting are complicated, far too complicated to be problematized. They are also too political for us to be very polemical about them. We might continue in the apologist vein and point out that W. D. Howells devoted the last months of his life to editing an anthology of short fiction entitled *The Great Modern American Stories*. Of the twenty-four great stories in the volume, nine were by women. The representation of women is insufficient, to be sure, but not altogether discountable. Besides the women authors one might expect (Jewett, Wharton, Freeman) there are included stories by Harriet Spofford, Alice Brown, Edith Wyatt, Madelene Yale Wynne, and Virginia Tracy. Not even the Dean of American Letters could perpetuate their fame, it seems. The anthology also contained a story by Charlotte Perkins Gilman, "The Yellow Wall-paper," which has been rediscovered only within the past generation. It was Howells, incidentally, who (after Horace Scudder refused it for the *Atlantic*, as being "too terribly good to be printed") found that "terrible and too wholly dire as it was" he nevertheless "could not rest until [he] had corrupted the editor of *The New England Magazine* into publishing it."

Having perhaps inflated Howells's stock, it would be no less proper in fine academic fashion to depreciate it by examining another famous comment, this one by Sinclair Lewis: "Mr. Howells was one of the gentlest, sweetest, and most honest of men, but he had the code of a pious old maid whose greatest delight was to have tea at the vicarage." What a nest of ironies the remark and its context reveals. Our first Nobel Laureate takes the occasion of his acceptance speech (a canon-forming occasion if ever there was one) to smash idols left and right. Not Howells merely, but the American

Academy of Arts and Letters epitomized by the "fishing Academician" Henry Van Dyck, the "New Humanism" of Irving Babbitt and the Rotary Club of George Babbitt, even the man who seemed then to occupy the post vacanted by Howells, the new Dean of American Letters, Hamlin Garland. It was Garland, Lewis allowed, who permitted him to see America as he himself saw it; it was Garland's tragedy to become thus canonized and domesticated, "a completely revelatory American tragedy, that in our land of freedom, men like Garland, who first blast the roads to freedom, become themselves most bound."

The ironies proliferate. Lewis recommends several other American writers as perhaps more worthy of the honor he is at the time receiving, most notably Theodore Dreiser (who once described the prize as "a nice piece of change") and Willa Cather. In 1937, just a few years after Lewis observed that Cather had profoundly disturbed the "tedious virtuousness" of Americans, Lionel Trilling would dismiss her as having descended into the "gaudy domesticity of bougeois accumulation gloried in the *Woman's Home Companion.*" Today, happily, Cather's stock is again on the rise, but Lewis is more often taught in history than in English departments. Not even the capacious Heath anthology has made room for poor Lewis. Nor has the Heath, for that matter, made a place for Bret Harte, as Gary Scharnhorst notes in the piece he contributes to this volume.

Having inadvertently introduced the topic, perhaps we should turn to the fact of the anthology itself. It is, after all, one of the leading instruments of canon formation, as Keneth Kinnamon reminds us in his essay on the (in)frequency with which three prominent African American writers have been anthologized. It so happens that several of our contributors have been or are engaged in anthologizing: Nancy Walker with Zita Dressner has edited *Redressing the Balance: American Women's Literary Humor from the Colonial Times to the 1980s*; Kinnamon with Richard Barksdale has edited *Black Writers of America*; Elizabeth Ammons has edited *Short Fiction by Black Women, 1900-1920*; and Cheryl Walker has prepared an anthology of nineteenth-century American women poets. Two others have engaged in a similar process: Richard Hocks with J. Donald Crowley edited the Norton Critical Edition of *The Wings of the Dove* and Elizabeth Ammons edited the Norton Critical Edition of *The House of Mirth*. The firsthand involvement in canon-making does not necessarily mean that the process is user-friendly, however. Even in the case of an extremely successful anthology such as Barksdale and Kinnamon's, commercial interests may thwart scholarly engagement and professional responsibility. We understand that the editors approached their publisher about revising and updating the text. But the book was a going concern, and the publishers preferred profit-making to cultural investment. So now we wait for Henry Louis Gates's overdue Norton edition of African American literature.

It is well to remember that the reading, writing, and production of texts are culturally, politically, and economically conditioned. But that same awareness hardly solves the complexities of the issue at hand. It may well be that the forces at work in the literary marketplace are just as confused as the people who labor under their influence. Some years ago the appearance of a new, revised American literature anthology was delayed by about six months. A salesman representing the publishing company blamed the delay on the tobacco companies in Raleigh-Durham. All the large anthologies are printed on cigarette paper, he explained, and the tobacco companies had been slow in supplying it.

Sometimes, too, anthologizing is both thankless and unprofitable. William Stanley Braithwaite was surely one of the busiest anthologizers on record. He brought out his annual *Anthology of Magazine Verse and Year Book of American Poetry* between 1913 and 1929. This gathering of American poetry, culled yearly from hundreds of magazines, helped to establish and perpetuate the reputations of such poets as Pound, Stevens, Masters, and Eliot. Braithwaite even collected a volume of verse by American nuns. He was, moreover, a self-sponsored anthologist whose publishing venture was conducted on a barely break-even basis; he was also black.

Surely there is some irony in the fact that the reformation of the canon as it appears in ever more frequent editions of American literature textbooks (sometimes, it is true, motivated by a political agenda) should be so gladly welcomed by capitalist publishers, who in their turn have often become subsidiaries to ever larger entrepreneurial concerns. "Make it new" has its American corollary: "Make it obsolete." Every few years, purportedly in the interests of democratization and social responsibility, our anthologies are revised and updated and their prices increased; the used book trade, which after all, by virtue of affordability alone, once served a certain democratic function, is cut out of the process.

Having introduced the topic of the anthology, we turn next to the other recognized instrument of canon formation—the classroom.

Paul Lauter has performed an invaluable service in compiling *Reconstructing American Literature: Courses, Syllabi, Issues* (1983). Among other things, the volume contains a collection of syllabi from several teachers of American literature. There is, or ought to be, genuine interest in seeing how differently other teachers and scholars represent to their students this curious thing we call American literature. Would such a volume as Lauter's have been published before 1980?

The college classroom is the place where the canon is not only most importantly formed and perpetuated through the distribution of texts, but also where the circuit of repetition and perpetuation may be most effectively broken. So the argument runs, our college students bring with them certain expectations, even literary values, they have acquired in high school. Where did their high school teachers acquire these values? From their own college teachers. As a rule, it is the college or university teacher/scholar who prepares the anthologies, writes the criticism and literary histories, and otherwise advances, retards, or maintains the reputations of authors and texts. Not only out of a commitment truly to educate, but to keep us as teachers and critics from becoming too helplessly what we are, it is crucial that we understand our roles and cultural responsibilities in this process. Not that we should write our literary history on ditto paper. Nevertheless, we should ever remember as we write our syllabi that we thereby promote, even in ten or fifteen week increments, the future we mean to occupy.

Wendell V. Harris has likewise performed a useful service in arguing in his *PLMA* essay "Canonicity" (January 1991) the seemingly paradoxical claims that "first, there are no canons and never have been; second, that there have necessarily always been canons; and third, that canons are made up of readings, not of disembodied texts." The apparent confusions and contradictions of these statements result from the differing connotations of the term *canon*. Harris examines Alastair Fowler's list of six kinds of canons—*potential, accessible, selective, official, personal,* and *critical* canons—and adds a few of his own: *authoritative* or *scriptural, pedagogical, diachronic* and *nonce* canons. The list is itself suggestive, and it is unnecessary to elaborate upon it other than to say that several (perhaps all) of these canons often and to widely varying degrees have been shaped by racist and mysogynist forces at the heart of our culture. But it is also true that there is a far less sinister, though perhaps far more threatening, source of resistance to expanding or redefining any or all of the several canons of American literature—habit. The habitual occurs always at the most local level of attention and motor activity.

Habit, wrote William James, at once sardonic and despairing, is "the enormous fly-wheel of society, its most precious conservative agent. It alone is what keeps us within the bounds of ordinance, and saves the children of fortune from the envious uprisings of the poor. It alone prevents the hardest and most repulsive walks of life from being deserted by those brought up to tread therein." A trendy critic nowadays might write that last phrase "to (t)read therein." Habit, of course, has its ethical and pedagogical dimensions, or as James added, "The great thing, then, in all education, is to *make our nervous system our ally instead of our enemy.*" How difficult and painful a task it is to lay down an outworn habit. Our own role in reforming the canon is always cast in terms of the texts we teach, whether we should assign our students, say, *Uncle Tom's Cabin* or *Benito Cereno*, Douglass's *Narrative* or Franklin's *Autobiography*. For while the number of texts to be taught has multiplied considerably in the last several years, the semester calendar remains the same.

In brief, the issue of the canon is probably the most important and certainly the most provocative topic in literary studies right now. The issue would probably be as urgent and as vital—and the discussion of it as heated—had the revolutions known as deconstruction and poststructualism never occurred. Indeed, poststructuralists have so discredited the very idea of "realism" that even the title of this volume will strike some as quaint and provincial. Yet it remains true that the realist era was one of unprecedented literary diversity. The realist mode was flexible enough and of sufficient range, the realist era itself hospitable enough, that a multitude of women writers and minority writers produced and published texts that, albeit at times covertly, gave voice to the most urgent concerns of race and ethnicity, gender, class, section, and region. Among the essayists represented in the present volume, Elizabeth Ammons contends that "women and black men can be seen as the majority, not the minority, of the most important authors" in America around the turn of the century; Cheryl Walker pleads the case for the "surprisingly chilling and tough-minded" verse of such neglected poets as Alice and Phoebe Cary, Lucy Larcom, Ina Coolbrith, and Rose Terry Cooke; Amy Ling resurrects several of the earliest texts by Chinese American writers; Patricia Okker argues the case for including Native American literatures in the canon; Sanford E. Marovitz explores the unique double-consciousness of Jewish American realists; and Susan K. Harris discusses such vexed issues as narrative framing and the debate over cultural assimilation raised by writers of immigrant fiction around the turn of the century. It ought to be noted here, too, that those already canonized writers of the period (Mark Twain, Henry James, Howells, Crane, et al.) were themselves frequently at odds with the prevailing ethos of American culture. As Tom Quirk observes in his article on *Huck Finn*, Twain's most celebrated novel "resists" and "refuses" ideological oversimplification; and Alfred Habegger explains in his piece how Howells's writing of *A Modern Instance* and *The Rise of Silas Lapham* was complicated by the cult-popularity of a now all-but-forgotten novel.

As the reader of this volume will soon discover, there were a great many participants in the literature of the period whose names and works have remained too long in obscurity. Larcom, Coolbrith, Holly, Chesnutt, Mary Roberts Rinehart, Zitkala-Ša, Abraham Cahan, Frances Ellen Harper, Anzia Yezierska, James Weldon Johnson, Emma Lazarus, and Sui Sin Far are but a few of the writers discussed in these essays. Even so familiar an author as James appears in Richard A. Hocks's essay in these pages in a perhaps unfamiliar guise—as the author not only of *The Portrait of a Lady* and *The Ambassadors*, but of *In the Cage* and *The American Scene* as well.

Such diversity is as apt to be as paralyzing as it is invigorating. After all, Spencerian evolutionary theory (defined as the movement from an incoherent homogeneity to a definite heterogeneity) was widely considered to be a value no less than a scientific fact. The same multiplying and divergent interests and energies in the world at large contributed something to the formation of William James's more genial and ample philosophical pluralism as a point of view large enough to contain and encourage them. What we call *literary realism* was in fact composed of a multitude of *isms*: naturalism, impressionism, local colorism, aestheticism, imagism, regionalism, veritism. Each of these *isms*, in turn, has been and will continue to be defined and redefined. The most salient characteristic of the realist era was that in the face of poverty, alienation, confusion, exclusion, and misery, writers retained an abiding sense of human cultural possibility. The materials are there in abundance for our reconstructing literary histories that answer to the interests of the present and the hopes for the future while at the same time remaining faithful to an inherited past. We must choose from this plenty, inevitably—choose our texts, our methods, our concerns, even our hard facts.

Opening up the canon means, relatively, reading and knowing more, not less, and becoming more, not less selective. Those same judgments and decisions need be neither arbitrary nor elitist. Rather, they represent good faith efforts, renewed continually, to connect a vital past with a living present. In our roles as critics, scholars, and teachers, we may confidently hold up our red velvet ropes as tokens of the banquet within. But we must let them down again, without regard to pedigree, for all who desire to enter.

Men of Color, Women, and Uppity Art at the Turn of the Century

ELIZABETH AMMONS

WHEN I teach American realism, my students often ask at the end of the semester: Why haven't I heard of these authors before? I tell them that their high school teachers, almost all of them overworked, have not been irresponsible or dishonest. They have simply taught their students what they themselves learned in high school and college. To which my students respond: Well why didn't they learn about these writers?

My answer to that question is a little longer.

I think that a direct connection exists between the high canonical postition of the mid-nineteenth century and the 1920s as literary periods, on the one hand, and the relatively low status of the turn of the century as a period, on the other. Specifically, I will suggest that this discrepancy has less to do with "objective" literary criteria than with racism and misogyny.

Until recently, there has been ready agreement among literary critics about who the "great" American writers were: Emerson, Thoreau, Hawthorne, Melville, and Whitman in the middle of the nineteenth century, and Hemingway, Fitzgerald, and Faulkner in the third decade of the twentieth. Additions were absorbed into that picture, rather than changing it. Thus, for most scholars, Emily Dickinson joined rather than disturbed F. O. Matthiessen's "American Renaissance." A little trickier was what to do about Twain and James, neither of whom fit chronologically into the two major periods. But both had to be included somehow. So James became, in one artful critical maneuver, a writer in the romance tradition,[1] while Twain, easier to rationalize, became a bridge between the 1850s and the 1920s. He linked the outlawry of Melville, say, and Hemingway. Thus, by the third quarter of the twentieth century, this elaborated picture of the "greats" had become standard: Emerson, Thoreau, Hawthorne, Melville, Whitman, Dickinson, James, Twain, Hemingway, Fitzgerald, and Faulkner.

My quick summary here is not news.[2] I review what is well known to pose the question: If we define the authors listed above as the great figures in American literature and then look at the turn of the century for authors similar to the majority of them—that is, white, male, and American-born—who appears? In addition to James and Twain, both of whom ended their careers in the period, four writers customarily come to mind: Howells, Crane, Norris, and Dreiser. But they present serious problems for inclusion with figures such as Emerson and Faulkner. Although Howells and Crane might initially appear promising, the first wrote so conventionally and the second wrote so little that it is finally difficult even for their most ardent admirers successfully to argue that they merit "major" status. Dreiser and Norris are in crucial ways simply embarrassing. Dreiser's sloppiness as a writer and sentimentality as a thinker and Norris's crude biases and philosophizing disqualify them for inclusion in the great white male writers' tradition, even if only because they expose too nakedly certain attitudes and values more subtly veiled in the work of their artistic superiors.

The result is that the turn of the century fails the standard test of canonization. Except for Twain and James, the work of the white men publishing at the time does not hold its own with that of the white men who came before and after them. As critics, this presents us with two possibilities. One: the turn of the century is a disappointing and relatively uninteresting literary period. Or two: the definitions of authorship and literary greatness that have guided canon-making for most of the twentieth century have been deficient. Most literary criticism and history until quite recently has embraced the first possibility. Here I want to pursue the second.

The authors currently in my American realism course are Zitkala-Ša, Henry James, William Dean Howells, Frances Ellen Harper, Charlotte Perkins Gilman, Charles Chesnutt, Kate Chopin, W. E. B. Du Bois, María Cristina Mena, Edith Wharton, Upton Sinclair, Sui Sin Far, James Weldon Johnson, Willa Cather, and Anzia Yezierska. If the semester were longer, it would be easy to enlarge this list. I would add many other people, and I tell the students that. But I offer these writers as representative. Clearly, they do not represent Matthiessen's American Renaissance updated, nor are they a Lost Generation preview. My list departs radically from both of those traditional models and ways of modeling. I argue instead that the most important characteristic of American realism was its racial, ethnic, sexual, and cultural range. Further (and obviously related), I present the turn of the century as a time in American literary history especially distinguished by these three things: topical issues frequently occupied a central position in the literature; formal experimentation was a primary focus for many writers; and women and black men can be seen as the majority, not the minority, of the most important authors.

It is obvious that turn-of-the-century American literature, reflecting fierce debates and fractures within the society, was deeply engaged with political and social issues. Jim Crow laws, anti-Semitism, urban poverty, lynching, the exploitation of labor, the suffocating effect of white middle-class marriage on women, anti-Chinese immigration policies, unemployment, political corruption, internalized racism, sexual repression and hypocrisy—even a partial list of significant themes in the literature gives some idea of its commitment to social criticism. So too, if we construct turn-of-the-century literature heterogeneously, a broad range of cultural experiences emerges. Writers are African American, Euroamerican, Chinese American, Mexican American, Native American, male, female, heterosexual, homosexual, native born, immigrant, leisure class, middle class, working class, Christian, Jewish, southern, northern, western, expatriate. Published American literature at the turn of the century, both despite and because of rampant injustices in the society, was diverse in subject matter and perspective. As a body of work it is consequently full of tensions, contradictions, conflicts, vitality, risks, and failures. Indeed, it is hard to imagine a period that offers a better window on American multiculturality *and* the attendant power structure in the United States designed to maintain inequalities.

Artistically, the vitality and volatility of the period show up in the formal experimentation of the literature. Often cited are Crane's adaptations of impressionism and the late James's forays into dense psychological narrative. But these manipulations look mild, perhaps even minor, compared with what Gertrude Stein was doing with words themselves or Charles Chesnutt tried with racist Plantation School story-cycle forms. In fact, the turn of the century saw writers stretch, unravel, invert, and invent form to such an extent that multiplicity of form might well be said to be a defining characteristic of literary art in the period. One obvious example of radical formal experimentation can be seen in texts such as Sarah Orne Jewett's *The Country of the Pointed Firs* (1896), Alice Dunbar-Nelson's *The Goodness of St. Rocque and Other Stories* (1899), W. E. B. Du Bois's *The Souls of Black Folk* (1903), and Mary Austin's *The Land of Little Rain* (1903). Although all quite different, each creates out of accumulated short sections an extended narrative that does not conform to familiar, western, climax-oriented, dramatic structure yet does have its own internal drama, rhythm, and coherence. Another obvious example of radical formal rebellion and experiment is James Weldon Johnson's *Autobiography of an Ex-Coloured Man* (1912), a novel so successfully constructed to "pass" as fact that it was years before its real author and its status as fiction became clearly established. Or consider Willa Cather's many experiments with narrative form involving the enclosure of story within story, beginning with the novel she liked to claim was her first, *O Pioneers!*, in 1913.

Most important, however, American realism is a literary period in which women and black men are major writers. On my syllabus they out-number white men because I think that configuration most accurately represents the period. White men are one part of the story, but not the only nor the most important part. If the turn of the century is defined as the period from 1880 to 1920 and we are truly interested in the entire period, James, Twain, and Howells, for example, do not dominate. They figure importantly for a while, and then a number of different kinds of writers emerge. During the 1890s and the opening decades of the twentieth century, four major African American male writers were publishing: Charles Chesnutt, Paul Laurence Dunbar, W. E. B. Du Bois, and James Weldon Johnson. Similarly but even more strikingly, the turn of the century provided the context for a remarkable group of women writers. Between the early 1890s and 1920 just some of the women publishing fiction in the United States were Frances Ellen Harper, Charlotte Perkins Gilman, Sarah Orne Jewett, Kate Chopin, Alice Dunbar-Nelson, Pauline Hopkins, Zitkala-Ša, Edith Wharton, Mary Austin, Ellen Glasgow, Sui Sin Far (also known as Edith Eaton), María Cristina Mena, Willa Cather, Gertrude Stein, Jessie Fauset, May Sinclair, and Anzia Yezierska.

The turn of the century was not a period in which women writers faced few or no obstacles. Yet it was an era unusually friendly to artistically ambitious women writers as a group.[3] It is well known, for instance, that, when asked at a symposium in 1929 to name the leading fiction writers of the day, a group of thirty-two "outstanding critics," as described by Fred Lewis Pattee, placed Edith Wharton and Willa Cather first and second on the list.[4] It is also well known by now that African American women published more novels and short stories in the space of a few decades at the turn of the century than in all previous decades of United States history combined.[5] It is probably less well known that, according to current information, it was during the same period that the first published fiction in English in the United States appeared by Native American, Mexican American, and Asian American women. In 1901 Zikala-Ša (sometimes referred to as Gertrude Bonnin) published *Old Indian Legends*; in the 1910s María Cristina Mena published a series of short stories in *Century* magazine; between 1899 and the mid-1920s Onoto Watanna (also known as Winnifred Eaton) published more than a dozen novels; and in 1912 her sister, Sui Sin Far, who had been publishing in various magazines since the 1890s, brought out her collection of short stories, *Mrs. Spring Fragrance*.[6]

Racism, class bias, and cultural discrimination blighted the careers of many women and of men of color at the turn of the century, as has also been true before and since. Moreover, for all women writers at the turn of the century being a woman and a writer was not easy. The fact remains, nevertheless, that black men and a large number of women at the end of the nineteenth century and the beginning of the twentieth wrote, published, and in fundamental ways shaped the national literature. That fact, in my view, plays an important role in the low status of the period in existing accounts of American literary history.

The struggle to keep American literature white and male has been long and determined. As Paul Lauter explains in "Race and Gender in the Shaping of the American Literary Canon: A Case Study from the Twenties," and Nina Baym describes in "Early Histories of American Literature: A Chapter in the Institution of New England," the racial and sexual character of the American literary canon has resulted from a series of deliberate choices by scholars and other powerful cultural arbiters.[7] Lauter notes that the professionalization of the study of American literature early in the twentieth century meant that the definition of what is "best" and most important in the nation's literary past passed at that time officially and formally into the hands of academicians. University and college professors—a group until quite recently almost exclusively white, male, and privileged (and still largely so)—compiled the anthologies and wrote the scholarly works. Not accidentally, those books systematically minimized or omitted white women and people of color as significant literary figures.[8]

Even a glance at the shelves of an ordinary university library such as my own at Tufts shows the pattern. In the 1930s a little diversity peeks through. In 1934 James McDonald Miller's *An Outline of American Literature*, which begins with "The Literature of Discovery and Exploration" and runs through fiction and poetry published in the 1920s, includes some white women writers. Most show up in the section titled "The Literature of the Gilded Age" under the subheading "Local Colorists." These are Helen Hunt Jackson, Alice French, Harriet Beecher Stowe, Harriet Prescott Spofford, Rose Terry Cooke, Louisa May Alcott, Elizabeth Stuart Phelps, Sarah Orne Jewett, Mary Wilkins Freeman, Alice Brown, Grace King, Kate Chopin, Constance Fenimore Woolson, Mary Noailles Murfree, Mary Hartwell Catherwood, and Margaret Deland. No women appear in the following sections: "The Literature of Humble Life," "The Literature of Cleverness," "The Literature of Realism" (Howells, James, Garland), "The Literature of Naturalism" (Bierce, Crane, Fuller, Herrick, Norris), "The Literature of Revolt," and "The Literature of the Strenuous Life." Mary Johnston figures in the next section, "The Literature of Romance," and Gertrude Atherton, Edith Wharton, Zona Gale, and Dorothy Canfield Fisher in the next, "The Literature of Social Criticism." Some women and two black men appear in "The Artistic Tradition": Emily Dickinson, Emma Lazarus, Celia Thaxter, Lizette Woodworth Reese, Harriet Monroe, Louise Imogene Guiney, Amy Lowell, Paul Lawrence [*sic*] Dunbar, James Weldon Johnson, and Agnes Repplier. A few other black writers are simply named: William Stanley Braithwaite, Claude McKay, Josephine Pinckney, Beatrice Ravenel, and Countee Cullen. Then some other white women who published work at the turn of the century appear in "Today's Tendencies": for example, Ellen Glasgow, Elizabeth Madox Roberts, Willa Cather, Edna St. Vincent Millay.[9]

V. F. Calverton in *The Liberation of American Literature* (1932) largely dismisses white women writers. Cather and Austin, for example, are barely mentioned, and Wharton is not included at all. Yet Calverton is more than ordinarily aware of black writers. He states: "Without question the work of Jean Toomer, Rudolph Fisher, Burghardt Du Bois, and Walter White in fiction; Langston Hughes,

Countee Cullen and Claude McKay in verse; and Abram L. Harris, Alain Locke, Franklin Frazier, James Weldon Johnson, Charles S. Johnson, and George Schuyler in the essay, has been distinguished by fine intelligence and advancing artistic vision. Surely at no other period, and certainly never in so short a time, have so many Negro writers of genuine talent appeared." Calverton is aware of some black women writers; he mentions, for example, Gwendolyn Bennett, Jessie Fauset, and Nella Larsen. Also, he expresses outrage (though in a footnote, it must be emphasized) at the racism that permits whites to write scholarly works that totally omit African American writers:

> *In the sixteen-volume library of Southern Literature, for example, not a single Negro writer's work is included.* . . .Paul Laurence Dunbar is not even mentioned. . . .Needless to add, dozens of Southern writers whose works are greatly inferior to those of Douglass, Washington, and Du Bois are included, with ample space provided for their ofttimes inferior selections. Equally revealing is the fact that Professor Fred L. Pattee in his recent volume, *American Literature Since 1870*, does not even mention a single Negro writer, although he discusses hundreds of white writers, many of whose works are of no more than microscopical importance.[10]

More typical of what was to come than Miller's and Calverton's attempts at a little breadth, however, is the three-volume *Cambridge History of American Literature,* published sequentially in 1917, 1918, and 1921; reissued a number of times throughout the 1920s; and then brought out in a "cheap edition" in 1933.[11] William Peterfield Trent, John Erskine, Stuart P. Sherman, and Carl Van Doren edited the volumes, and a scholar wrote each chapter. Fifty-two different scholars' names appear. Four of them are women—Elizabeth Christine Cook, Ruth Putnam, Louise Pound, and Mary Austin—and none of the fifty-two, as far as I know, is a person of color. Although some white women writers and a very few black writers' names appear in the summaries of chapters provided on the Contents page of each volume, these are clearly minor inclusions. The major inclusions are the figures who receive individual chapters in the prestigious history. They are: Edwards, Franklin, Irving, Emerson, Thoreau, Hawthorne, Longfellow, Whittier, Poe, Webster, Lowell, Whitman, Twain, James, and Lincoln.

This institutionalization of an exclusively white and an entirely or almost entirely male literary canon in the United States proceeded virtually unchecked throughout most of the twentieth century. By the

1950s and 1960s, as is now commonplace to observe, the standard canonical view of American literature encompassed an extremely narrow, homogeneous group of authors. Eleven white men and one white woman are given Table of Contents status in the 1959 volume *Interpretations of American Literature* edited by Charles Feidelson, Jr., and Paul Brodtkorb, Jr.: Hawthorne, Poe, Melville, Edwards, Emerson, Thoreau, Whitman, Dickinson, Twain, James, Hemingway, and Faulkner.[12] Only slightly broader, the 1967 edition of the Penguin *Literature of the United States* adds a few more white people. The Contents page singles out for specific naming: Irving, Cooper, Poe, Emerson, Thoreau, Hawthorne, Melville, Whitman, Twain, Dickinson, Howells, Dreiser, James, Wharton, Henry Adams, and Gertrude Stein. Perhaps more important, the only authors announced on the book's cover—against a backdrop of red and white stripes emblazoned with an eagle carrying in its beak the banner (all too true) "E Pluribus Unum"—are Ernest Hemingway, Ezra Pound, Herman Melville, Mark Twain, Edgar Allan Poe, Henry James, and Walt Whitman.[13] Telling the story very simply, the subtitles on the Contents page of *American Literature: A World View* (1968) proceed without hitch:

Columbus to Franklin
Paine to Cooper
Poe to Whitman
Twain to James
Eliot, O'Neill, Faulkner
Wilbur, Albee, Morris.[14]

In many respects this tradition continues in the 1986 Harvard English Studies volume edited by Sacvan Bercovitch and titled, misleadingly, *Reconstructing American Literary History.* Several of this book's twelve essays do offer useful and provocative critiques of established literary historical premises and practices. But in the entire volume one woman writer is discussed at any length—Emily Dickinson. Moreover, in all but three essays, the only rational conclusion to draw is that the United States is and has been inhabited entirely by white people.[15]

What explains this incredible twentieth-century project in suppression? How is it possible that even after the Harlem Renaissance and after a three-decade period distinguished by the achievements of women writers such as Edith Wharton and Willa Cather (just to name the most incontestably "great" of a large group), critics could nevertheless for decades (and apparently still today) proceed unfazed in the construction of an overwhelmingly or often exclusively white male canon in the United States?

If we look at the turn of the century, some of the emotion motivating at least one part of this project in suppression—the dismissal of white women as serious literary figures—can be found in an essay that Lauter cites, Robert Herrick's lead article for the *Bookman* in March 1929, titled "A Feline World." The essay viciously attacks women writers. They have taken "to story writing in flocks," Herrick says, and the result is alarming. He exclaims: "What women have not done to the novel in a brief twenty years or so!"[16] The essay then sketches the damage.

According to Herrick, women fiction-writers used to write like men:

> In deference to the convention that this was a male world, or because they were new at the game, they did not dare to write about what merely interests women. Such women novelists [for example, George Eliot] wrote of men's interests more or less successfully in men's fashion. . . . Only recently, however, have women taken to writing novels themselves so commonly that quite a half, more likely two-thirds, of the new titles are books written by women. Even more recently have these younger women novelists [May Sinclair and Virginia Woolf are two who are named] disregarded the tradition that this is primarily a man's world and have taken to describing boldly their own primary interests, among themselves, for themselves. (2)

Having space for "only the more obvious features in this change," Herrick must be brief. He asserts that the new generation of "women novelists . . . deal largely in emotions, first of all sex emotions" (3), and explains that those consist of "the neurotic sides of sex, which do not eventuate in either marriage or maternity, as well as what once was called (with a hush) the perverted side, the wooing of one's own sex. A disturbing number of recent stories by women deal with this taboo" (4). Other stories "quite frankly portray women, heroines, too, as polyandrous. My mind recalls a recent story by an excellent young writer that portrays a black woman—an admirable creature, too—with a dozen children, no two of whom have the same father" (4). Next we find: "Another thing they have dared to do, these young women writers, is to paint the slut to life" (4).

Finally, getting close to the top of the list and the root of the problem, Herrick "can't recall any instance in their stories of 'beautiful motherhood,' though doubtless there must be some" (4).

What Robert Herrick sees in work by early twentieth-century women novelists are lesbianism, sexually active heterosexual women, black heroines who shape their lives the way they wish, socially stigmatized women as central rather than peripheral characters, and attacks on the beauty and sanctity of motherhood. What he sees, put another way, are women out of his control. This prospect of female self-determination frightens and angers him. The essay ends with an extended metaphor of women as cats: "cunning and grim and tireless." The cat is able "to sit for hours in the brush or long grass, waiting for its prey to come within reach" (6). Feigning affection, the animal is in fact cruel. The same is true of women, who, we are told in the essay's last and most remarkable turn, will not hesitate to use poison gas in the next war if their power is not checked by men (6).

In six pages, Herrick moves from women taking over the novel to women taking over the world. To allow women to use fiction as they wish is, for Herrick, quite clearly to risk unleashing uncontrollable female sexual energy, anger, and power. Generalized, the (not so) hidden axiom might be stated: To permit people other than straight white men to tell their own stories and tell them on their own terms constitutes a serious threat to fundamental, hegemonic, white male constructions of and rules about sex, race, gender, culture, order and disorder, and subservience and dominance in the United States.

Nina Baym shows in "Early Histories of American Literature" that the institutionalization of the extremely narrow, New England-based canon in American literature with which we are all familiar occurred over a period of time at the turn of the century. "When, in the second decade of the twentieth century, academics defined a field of study called 'American literature,' they did so by appropriating and sophisticating a narrative already constructed in the plethora of American literary history textbooks that had been published between 1882 and 1912." The early twentieth-century histories "were written for the most part by professors of New England origin employed at elite colleges," and the textbook tradition that they drew on had been designed to make "literary works and authors display the virtues and achievements of an Anglo-Saxon United States founded by New England Puritans."[17]

The political agenda of this concerted installation of a white, male, Protestant, New England literary canon at precisely the time that immigrants, non-New Englanders, Jews, Catholics, blacks, Asian Americans, Hispanics, Native Americans, and more and more white women were publishing at an unprecedented rate is not hard to grasp. As Baym points out:

> Conservative New England leaders knew all too well that the nation was an artifice and that no single national character undergirded it. And they insisted passionately that peace and progress called for a commonalty that, if it did not exist, had at once to be invented. By originating American history in New England and proclaiming the carefully edited New England Puritan as the national type, they hoped to create such a commonalty, instilling in all citizens those traits that they thought necessary for the future: self-reliance, self-control, and acceptance of hierarchy.[18]

Obviously, a great deal of the large and important body of fiction published at the turn of the century by women and by men of color contradicted this notion of commonalty, particularly its ideal of accepting hierarchy. Historians and literary scholars at the turn of the century were not fools. Without their dedicated labor to establish, reify, and keep in place a controlled, tidy, white, male version of American literture, what might happen? Chaos—all kinds of different and conflicting narratives about America, Americanness, and American literature could erupt. That is, the multiple possibilities suggested by the contemporary scene in American literature and the unified story that scholars were constucting went, in important respects, in two different directions.

That divergence, of course, is the crucial point. The academic project of canonizing a select collection of white male texts as *the* American tradition intensified at exactly the time in American literary history that white, male hegemony in literature was under heavy attack by women and by men of color. The need to write Du Bois or Wharton or Sui San Far or Jessie Fauset out of the American literary record at precisely the same time they were audaciously writing themselves in was not a historical accident. As my students know, they disrupt the tidy focus. Crack the lens.

Notes

1. See Richard Chase, *The American Novel and Its Tradition* (Garden City, NY: Doubleday, 1957).

2. For excellent analysis of the ideas and motives generating the canon I have sketched, see Nina Baym, "Melodramas of Beset Manhood: How Theories of American Fiction Exclude Women Authors," *American Quarterly* 33 (Summer 1981): 123-39.

3. For extended, detailed discussion, see Ammons, *Conflicting Stories: American Women Writers at the Turn into the Twentieth Century* (New York: Oxford University Press, 1991).

4. John M. Stalnaker and Fred Egan, "American Novelists Ranked: A Psychological Study," *The English Journal* 18 (April 1929): 295-307; quoted in Pattee, *The New American Literature, 1890-1930* (New York: Cooper Square, 1930), 260.

5. See, e.g., the novels in The Schomburg Library of Nineteenth-Century Black Women Writers, General Editor, Henry Louis Gates, Jr. (New York: Oxford University Press, 1988) and, in the same series, *Short Fiction by Black Women, 1900-1920*, ed. Elizabeth Ammons (New York: Oxford University Press, 1991). Excellent critical discussion can be found in Hazel V. Carby, *Reconstructing Womanhood: The Emergence of the Afro-American Woman Novelist* (New York: Oxford University Press, 1987) and Claudia Tate, *Domestic Allegories of Political Desire: The Black Heroine's Text at the Turn of the Century* (New York: Oxford University Press, 1992).

6. The body of critical writing about these authors is at the present time rapidly growing. See, e.g., Amy Ling, *Between Worlds: Women Writers of Chinese Ancestry* (New York: Pergamon, 1990); my analyses in *Conflicting Stories*; and Elizabeth Ammons and Annette White-Parks, eds., *Tricksters in Turn-of-the-Century American Literature* (Hanover, NH: University Press of New England, 1994).

7. Paul Lauter, "Race and Gender in the Shaping of the American Literary Canon: A Case Study from the Twenties," *Feminist Studies* 9 (Fall 1983): 435-63; and Nina Baym, "Early Histories of American Literature: A Chapter in the Institution of New England," *American Literary History* 1 (Fall 1989): 459-88.

8. See Lauter, 435-63.

9. James McDonald Miller, *An Outline of American Literature* (New York: Farrar & Rinehart, 1934).

10. V. F. Calverton, *The Liberation of American Literature* (New York: Charles Scribner's Sons, 1932), 446, 448, 148.

11. William Peterfield Trent et al., eds., *The Cambridge History of American Literature*, 3 vols. (New York: Macmillan Co. and Cambridge: Cambridge University Press, 1933).

12. *Interpretations of American Literature* (New York and London: Oxford University Press).

13. Marcus Cunliffe, *Literature of the United States* (Baltimore: Penguin, 1967).

14. Willis Wager, *American Literature: A World View* (New York: New York University Press, 1968).

15. Sacvan Bercovitch, ed., *Reconstructing American Literary History* (Cambridge: Harvard University Press, 1986).

16. Robert Herrick, "A Feline World," *The Bookman* 69 (March 1929), 2. The following page references refer to this essay.

17. Baym, "Early Histories," 459.

18. Baym, "Early Histories," 460.

Nineteenth-Century Women Poets and Realism

CHERYL WALKER

SINCE the 1940s, poetry has been virtually excluded from most discussions of realism. One argument against including poetry as a vital element in realism asserts that realism usually involves a type of content and an attitude toward that content, whereas poetry is preeminently a matter of form. "No other kind of writing holds its own words up to the light as poetry does," writes Jan Montefiore[1], and it is that same linguistic hypersensitivity that argues against poetry as a mode of realism.

Of course, terms like *realism* are notoriously difficult to define. However, a brief survey of several college anthologies suggests that, where categories like realism are used to organize the texts, prose is what we generally find under the heading of realism. In James E. Miller's *Heritage of American Literature* (vol. 2), there are two such headings. "Regional Realism and Local Color" includes texts by Bret Harte, Ambrose Bierce, George Washington Cable, Joel Chandler Harris, and Charles W. Chestnutt. "Realism in Transition: Society and Psychology" includes Hamlin Garland, Edith Wharton, Frank Norris, Stephen Crane, Theodore Dreiser, and Jack London. It is followed by a separate heading for "Poetry in Transition." McGraw-Hill's anthology, *The American Tradition in Literature* (vol. 2), lists realists and regionalists together: Twain, Howells, James, Harte, Bierce, Cable, and Harris.

Macmillan's *Anthology of American Literature*, whose second volume is subtitled "Realism to the Present," calls the whole late nineteenth century "The Age of Realism" and begins with an essay discussing the social, economic, technological, geographical, and political changes in America that gave rise to it. George McMichael, the general editor, does include Whitman, Dickinson, and a few poems by Crane as part of the Age of Realism but the other choices are all prose writers: Freeman, Jewett, Harte, Cable, Chestnutt, Harris, Twain, Howells, James, Bierce, Garland, Gilman, Chopin, Norris, London, Wharton, Dreiser, and Adams. In his introductory essay McMichael sees realism persisting into the twentieth century and mentions Robinson and Frost as part of the triumph of realist values, but his main focus remains prose. James and Twain are his candidates for America's greatest realists.[2]

Though poets play only a small role in his presentation of realism, McMichael is in fact unusual in including poetry at all. Today, if realism means anything in particular, it is likely to be situated in a realm that does not include poetry. If poetry can be accommodated to realism, it is likely that the understanding of realism in play is more akin to Eric Sundquist's imaginative "country of the blue"[3] than to the naturalist realism of the tough-minded writers of the 1890s, many of whom were nourished by careers in journalism.

Sundquist is surely right that an intelligent exploration of those texts generally associated most closely with realism reveals a bewildering range of attitudes, subjects, settings, and techniques that make difficult any comprehensive definition or any clear demarcation between realism and what is usually taken as its opposite, romanticism. "Which is to say again," Sundquist insists, "that the life of American realism exists, perhaps, either everywhere or nowhere; like 'the real' itself, it resists containment, and for the very good reason that 'the real' in America, like the country itself, has always had a notoriously short life."[4]

My interest in Sundquist's argument is in seeing it as part of our contemporary discourse in which the opposition between fact and figuration, if it hasn't collapsed entirely, is certainly less stringent than it once was. At such a juncture, it is easy enough for poetry to enter the realm of realism (indeed Sundquist includes the ecstatic realism of Whitman's poetry), but it does so at a cost. The political focus, that at one time, for Georg Lukacs and others, was sharpened in the literature belonging specifically to the capitalist era of the late nineteenth and early twentieth centuries, has softened. Confronted by our own political derealization, we are perhaps all too ready to see ourselves "waking in the blue."

It is with some relief, therefore, that one turns back—perhaps anachronistically, certainly nostalgically—to a group of writers for whom poetry was still vital as a medium of political critique, who had no thought for the epistemological abyss, and who were passionately interested in having an effect on their world. I refer here to nineteenth-century women poets. With the exception of Emily Dickinson (a dubious candidate for a realist), these poets are virtually never mentioned in discussions of realism. Yet some of their works might profitably be studied as part of the reaction against the social and economic conditions of their time, conditions they saw as contributing to injustice, greed, political mismanagement, and cultural mystification.

If we understand realism in America as a movement whose first objective was to portray American life accurately and in detail, especially in its ordinary and local manifestations, then these women can certainly be classified as early realists whose work foreshadows the rise of local color writers like Sarah Orne Jewett and Mary E. Wilkins Freeman. If, for the sake of argument, we use the definition of realism provided by the *Princeton Encyclopedia of Poetry and Poetics*, [5] we can recognize in this poetry the three critical ingredients of poetic realism: descriptions of normal situations and average characters, often with an emphasis upon those in the lower stata of society; a preference for common language and homely images over high-flown rhetoric or esoteric literary allusions; and a tendency to try to approximate actual speech rhythms, even to reproduce dialogue as a basic ingredient of the poem.

Though no specific attitudes can necessarily be linked to realism broadly understood, I have further restricted my choice of precursors to those poems that include no overt moralizing. Though a moral (and political) perspective is certainly implied in many of these works, the ability to link them with later literary developments is strengthened, it seems to me, when one excludes poems that turn to the reader to spell out the moral point. It goes without saying that a "point of view" (or several) about what is being presented is an aspect of every literary text. Indeed, it has been suggested by Donald Pizer that American realism is *especially* "ethically idealistic,"[6] although numerous contemporary interpreters of realism have shown that the ethics (or politics) of the text may differ from, even contradict, the conscious intentions of the writer.[7] Nevertheless, if we wish to separate the examples of early realism provided by nineteenth-century women poets from typical American jeremiads, it seems well to concentrate on those poems that in some way violate our stereotypes of such women. The poems that follow, therefore, are *not* especially precious, pious, sentimental, or sweet. In fact, many of them are surprisingly chilling and tough-minded.

One might, for instance, look at three poets from the middle of the nineteenth century: Alice (1820–1871) and Phoebe (1824–1871) Cary and Maria White Lowell (1821–1853). All of them were politically engaged feminists and abolitionists: Lowell was a member of Margaret Fuller's circle; the Cary sisters worked for a time with Susan B. Anthony.

Maria Lowell's poem "The Slave-Mother"[8] portrays the agony of a woman who knows that her daughter is destined for a life of shame and degradation. Lowell refuses the gambits of two conventions of nineteenth-century women's poetry: the poem about a child's death (usually consoling) and the poem that celebrates the mother-child relationship as nurturing. Here Lowell (like Toni Morrison in *Beloved*) describes a woman whose most earnest prayer is that her child should die. Nowhere does the poem criticize this mother or suggest that some other position regarding her daughter's fate would have been preferable. Neither does the poem provide religious consolation. It simply ends:

> She cannot bear to know her child must be as she hath been,
> Yet she sees but one deliverance from infamy and sin,—
> And so she cries at midnight, with exceeding bitter cry,
> "God grant my little helpless one in helplessness may die!"

A number of women's poems from this period assume the persona of a simple character (often in a rural setting) whose concerns, like the slave mother's, represent a critique of the larger society. Alice Cary's "Growing Rich" is an example of an attack on industrial capitalism and the mercantile values it produced.

> And why are you pale, my Nora?
> And why do you sigh and fret?
> The black ewe had twin lambs to-day,
> And we shall be rich folk yet.
>
> Do you mind the clover-ridge, Nora,
> That slopes to the crooked stream?
> The brown cow pastured there this week,
> And her milk is sweet as cream.
>
> The old grey mare that last year fell
> As thin as any ghost,
> Is getting a new white coat, and looks
> As young as her colt, almost.

And if the corn-land should do well,
 And so, please God, it may,
I'll buy the white-faced bull a bell,
 To make the meadows gay.

I know we are growing rich, Johnny,
 And that is why I fret,
For my little brother Phil is down
 In the dismal coal-pit yet.

And when the sunshine sets in th' corn,
 The tassels green and gay,
It will not touch my father's eyes,
 That are going blind, they say.

But if I were not sad for him,
 Nor yet for little Phil,
Why, darling Molly's hand, last year,
 Was cut off in the mill.

And so, nor mare nor brown milch-cow,
 Nor lambs can joy impart,
For the blind old man and th' mill and mine
 Are all upon my heart.[9]

In addition to its unveiling of several social evils—child labor, the conditions in the mines, mill accidents—this poem introduces a form that reappears in many of these early realists' works: the dialogue between husband and wife. Neither Alice nor her sister Phoebe married. They maintained a very close relationship, sharing a house in New York they bought with the proceeds from their writings, until the deaths of both in the same year (1871), Alice from tuberculosis, Phoebe from hepatitis. Apparently, Phoebe had a number of proposals of marriage that she rejected, preferring to preserve her freedom and remain with her sister. Though both sisters maintained a deep appreciation for marriage as an ideal, they were well aware that few real marriages even approximated that ideal. As feminists, they were particularly attuned to the way nineteenth-century marriages placed unequal burdens upon the woman. Of the two sisters, Phoebe was the one more given to satire in her presentation of marriage, as the following poem, "Dorothy's Dower," illustrates.

Part I.

"My sweetest Dorothy," said John,
Of course before the wedding,
As metaphorically he stood,
His gold upon her shedding,
"Whatever thing you wish or want
Shall be hereafter granted,
"For all my worldly goods are yours."
The fellow was enchanted!
"About that little dower you have,
You thought might yet come handy,
Throw it away, do what you please,
Spend it on sugar-candy!
I like your sweet, dependent ways,
I love you when you tease me;
The more you ask, the more you spend,
The better you will please me."

Part II.

"Confound it, Dorothy!" said John,
"I haven't got it by me.
You haven't, have you, spent that sum,
The dower from Aunt Jemima?
No; well that's sensible for you;
This fix is most unpleasant;
But money's tight, so just take yours
And use it for the present.
Now I must go—to—meet a man!
By George! I'll have to borrow!
Lend me a twenty—that's all right,
I'll pay you back tomorrow."

Part III.

"Madam," says John to Dorothy,
And past her rudely pushes,
"You think a man is made of gold,
And money grows on bushes!
Tom's shoes! your doctor! Can't you now
Get up some new disaster?
You and your children are enough
To break John Jacob Astor.
Where's what you had yourself when I
Was fool enough to court you?
That little sum, till you got me,

'T was what had to support you!"
"It's lent and gone, not very far;
Pray don't be apprehensive,"
"*Lent!* I've had use enough for it:
My family is expensive.
I didn't, as a woman would,
Spend it on sugar-candy!"
"No, John, I think the most of it
Went for cigars and brandy!"[10]

Of course, this poem is meant to be a humorous rather than serious polemic. Cary even gives the woman more power than was often possible in the real world where a man usually had full access to his wife's money after marriage and need not consult her about its use. Here Dorothy is able to protect a little of her dower, at least, and Cary gives her the last word. Her linguistic force is conveyed by the paucity of her words. Cary undoubtedly implies a link between language and money in Dorothy's ability to save her words and spend them only when necessary, a skill that emerges in high contrast to her husband's clear pattern of both linguistic and economic extravagance.

Though this poem is meant to be light, the problem it unveils was one that several nineteenth-century women poets knew to their sorrow. Elizabeth Oakes-Smith, Rose Terry Cooke, and Celia Thaxter all found that their little personal incomes were recklessly spent by their husbands. Though Lucy Larcom (1824–1893) was another poet, like Cary, who preferred not to marry and rejected a suitor's proposal in order to protect her independence, she created a poem quite subtle and powerful in its way about a wife whose husband has married her for her money. This poem may be a precursor to Robinson's beautiful "Eros Turannos." Larcom's homelier poem, "Getting Along," begins:

We trudge on together, my good man and I,
Our steps growing slow as the years hasten by;
Our children are healthy, our neighbours are kind,
And with the world round us we've no fault to find.

'T is true that he sometimes will choose the worst way
For sore feet to walk in, a weary hot day;
But then my wise husband can scarcely go wrong,
And, somehow or other, we're getting along.

The success of these first two stanzas lies in the way the original picture of marital unity is modified, only to be reasserted once again. Going back to the initial two lines, however, one sees that the language used already contains a foreshadowing of darker things to come. The trudging and slowing that at first suggest a shared experience of aging ("getting along") are also a description of the speaker's mental pattern as she doubles back on her own assertions of happiness, slowing down to reconsider.

Actual disharmony in the marriage comes through sharply in the fifth and sixth stanzas:

> The blackbirds and thrushes come chattering near;
> I love the thieves' music, but listen with fear:
> He shoots the gay rogues I would pay for their song;—
> We're different, sure; still, we're getting along.
>
> He seems not to know what I eat, drink or wear;
> He's trim and he's hearty, so why should I care?
> No harsh word from him my poor heart ever shocks:
> I wouldn't mind scolding,—so seldom he talks.

Perhaps the poem would be more successful if it ended shortly after these reflections, leaving the wife uncertain about how to evaluate the differences that are becoming clearer to her in the very process of analyzing her marriage.

However, the last four stanzas introduce the issue of a financial motive, a commonplace in Victorian literature.

> It is true I was rich; I had treasures and land;
> But all that he asked was my heart and my hand:
> Though people do say it, 't is what they can't prove,—
> "He married for money; she—poor thing! for love."
>
> My fortune is his, and he saves me its care;
> To make his home cheerful's enough for my share.
> He seems always happy our broad fields among;
> And so I'm contented:—we're getting along.
>
> With stocks to look after, investments to find,
> It's not very strange that I'm seldom in mind:
> He can't stop to see how my time's dragging on,—
> And oh! *would* he miss me, if I should be gone?

> Should he be called first, I must follow him fast,
> For all that's worth living for then will be past.
> But I'll not think of losing him: fretting is wrong,
> While we are so pleasantly getting along.[11]

"Getting Along" is effective as an example of early realism not because it is about money, nor even because it exposes some truth about nineteenth-century marriage, but because it captures so well the kind of self-deception women who were economically and emotionally dependent upon their husbands must have engaged in. This self-deception, of course, is comprehensible in part because we know that the actualities of nineteenth-century life made submission in marriage necessary for most women. Even where the marriage was degrading, divorce remained generally "unthinkable."

A number of women's poems detail—sometimes happily, sometimes irritably—the tasks a good housewife was called upon to perform. The black poet Mary E. Tucker (1838– ?) composed a poem "Upon Receipt of a Pound of Coffee in 1863" that emerges as a delightful example of this genre. I will quote only the first three (of six) stanzas in order to demonstrate the lively specificity of some of these poems.

> The sight of the coffee was good for sore eyes,
> For I have not learned yet its worth to despise;
> I welcomed each grain as I culled with care o'er,
> And in fancy increased it to ten thousand more.
>
> I put it on fire, and stirred round and round,
> Then took it off gently when it was quite browned;
> When cool I proceeded to fill up my mill,
> And ground up a boiling with very good will.
>
> I measured three spoons full, you see, for us three—
> The old Lady Lane, my Grand-mother and me;
> I added some water, then put it to boil,
> And stood close by, watching, for fear it might spoil.[12]

Mary Weston Fordham's poem, "The Coming Woman," may seem an odd candidate for entry under realism, for it is actually a futurist fantasy in which roles between husband and wife are reversed. However, in the process of detailing the activities that now the husband instead of the wife must perform, "The Coming

Woman" gives us a picture of middle-class married life in the 1890s. Fordham, another black poet whose birth and death dates are unknown, published *Magnolia Leaves* in 1897, but she avoids using black dialect as some other poets of this period did; perhaps imitating Paul Laurence Dunbar.

Just look, 'tis a quarter past six, love—
  And not even the fires are caught;
Well, you know I must be at the office—
  But, as usual, the breakfast'll be late.

Now hurry and wake up the children;
  And dress them as fast as you can;
"Poor dearies," I know they'll be tardy,
  Dear me, "what a slow, poky man!"

Have the tenderloin broiled nice and juicy—
  Have the toast browned and buttered all right;
And be sure you settle the coffee:
  Be sure that the silver is bright.

When ready, just run up and call me—
  At eight, to the office I go,
Lest poverty, grim, should o'ertake us—
  "'Tis bread and butter," you know.

The bottom from stocks may fall out,
  My bonds may get below par;
Then surely, I seldom could spare you
  A nickel, to buy a cigar.

All ready? Now, while I am eating,
  Just bring up my wheel to the door;
Then wash up the dishes; and, mind now,
  Have dinner promptly at four;

For tonight is our Woman's Convention,
  And I am to speak first, you know—
The men veto us in private,
  But in public they shout, "That's so."

So "by-by"—In case of a rap, love,
  Before opening the door, you must look;

O! how could a civilized woman
Exist, without a man cook.[13]

One might puzzle over the politics of both of these poems, of course. In the case of Tucker's coffee poem, there is no hint that this coffee may well have been imported from slave-driven coffee plantations in the Caribbean. We know very little about Mary Eliza Perine Tucker Lambert who published her *Poems* in 1867 under the name Mary E. Tucker except that, according to Joan Sherman, she was black. Mary Weston Fordham remains equally mysterious.

In "The Coming Woman" it seems clear at the beginning that what is being satirized is the overbearing nineteenth-century autocrat of the breakfast table with his numerous demands, his superficial concern for the children, his patronizing praise, etc. However, the reference to the "Woman's Convention" in the penultimate stanza raises some questions. No inversion supplies a ready masculine target. Where Fordham says: "The men veto us in private, / But in public they shout, 'That's so,'" she seems to wish to introduce an accurate picture of 1890s' responses to the New Woman. Is it, then, the coming woman who is the target of this satire? Or, more accurately, is it the fearsome Titaness of 1890s reform movements, frequently held up to ridicule, whom Fordham wishes us to disdain? As a third possibility, is Fordham suggesting that the tyrannical behavior of certain husbands may indeed create this grotesque reversal? Her portrayal of this duplicitous male response to early feminism is both shrewd politically and the one instance in which the speaker seems something other than a grotesque.

The fact that the politics of these poems is not always clear does not, of course, make them any less interesting as part of the school of realism. Most of the major male writers from Twain to Dos Passos have been queried and multiply interpreted in much the same way. Sundquist specifies the challenge of realism as the task of representing social injustice without recuperating its structural properties. Many of these women poets choose an empathetic identification with the oppressed as a means of creating a political response, preferring an alliance with powerlessness to a contaminated assertion of power.

In "The Captive of the White City," the western poet Ina Coolbrith (1841–1928) attacks the contradictions implicit in the vision of civilization purveyed at the 1892 Columbian Exposition in Chicago, where Chief Rain-in-the-Face (supposedly General Custer's killer) was brought from Montana along with his teepee for purposes of display. Like a great many nineteenth-century women poets, Coolbrith was sympathetic to the plight of Native Americans. In her poem she insists:

From the wrongs of the White Man's rule
Blood only may wash the trace.
Alas, for the death-heaped plain!
Alas, for slayer and slain!
Alas for your blood-stained hands,
O Rain-in-the-Face!

The poem ends with a powerful acknowledgment of the silence at the heart of Progressive America on the subject of the disenfranchised and murdered populations on which American cultural prosperity had been built. Though the marveling crowds wander up and down the streets of the White City,

there, in the wild, free breeze,
In the House of the Unhewn Trees,
In the beautiful Midway Place,
The captive sits apart,
Silent, and makes no sign.
But what is the word in your heart,
O man of a dying race?
What tale on your lips for mine,
O Rain-in-the-Face?[14]

As is frequently the case in the poems I have included here as examples of nineteenth-century female realism, the poet leaves the question hanging, leaves the answer to be supplied by an engaged reader, whose energies ideally will be directed toward ameliorating the social evil described.

Julia Ward Howe's (1819–1910) fascinating poem "The Telegrams" is a series of vignettes strung together as though each were the substance of a telegram conveying vital information. All but the last stanza end with a question: What next? Many like this first one are darkly suggestive of a modern world gone awry and in need of a vision able to provide a more satisfactory direction for social progress.

Bring the hearse to the station,
When one shall demand it, late;

For that dark consummation
  The traveler must not wait.
Men say not by what connivance
  He slid from his weight of woe,
Whether sickness or weak contrivance,
  But we know him glad to go.
    On and on and ever on!
      What next?

The fifth stanza gestures toward the economic woes connected to fluctuating economic cycles and the gold standard controversy.

Be rid of the notes they scattered;
  The great house is down at last;
The image of gold is shattered,
  And never can be recast.
The bankrupts show leaden features,
  And weary, distracted looks,
While harpy-eyed, wolf-souled creatures
  Pry through their dishonored books.
    On and on and ever on!
      What next?

Nevertheless, this poem is less political than philosophical in a broad sense, as it concludes:

Thus the living and dying daily
  Flash forward their wants and words,
While still on Thought's slender railway
  Sit scathless the little birds:
They heed not the sentence dire
  By magical hands exprest,
And only the sun's warm fire
  Stirs softly their happy breast.
    On and on and ever on!
      God next![15]

Despite the attempt at a religious resolution, however, the soul of the poem remains its depiction of a highly mobile, urban society whose technology has not supplied it with stable values. "The Telegrams" is a piece of social criticism very much in the spirit of late nineteenth and early twentieth-century realism. The fact that Howe seeks to capture in this poem a world riddled by social ills such as suicide, bankruptcy, murder, and syphilis, suggests that women were not always fastidious about the way they characterized this world any more than their male counterparts were.[16]

One of the most tantalizing women poets of the nineteenth century is Rose Terry Cooke (1827–1892), who is the only one of these women to make an appearance in the volume on *American Realists and Naturalists* in the *Dictionary of Literary Biography*.[17] This volume, published in 1982, typically confines itself to prose writers, finding space for Cooke only as an early realist in fiction whose New England stories foreshadow those of Jewett and Freeman. What has been overlooked is that Cooke was also a fine, if uneven, poet, poetry being her preferred genre.

"In the Hammock" provides an illustration of what makes some of Cooke's poems so interesting. More of a romantic than a realist in most of her poems, she still deserves consideration here for her ability to provide a convincing portrait of a figure from the lower strata of society, whose values are at odds with those of the Victorians yet inspire no critical commentary from Cooke. This poem shows the influence of Western literature, much of it in the realist mode, on writers born and bred in the East.

How the stars shine out at sea!
Swing me, Tita! Faster, girl!
I'm a hang-bird in her nest,
All with scarlet blossoms drest,
Swinging where the winds blow free.

Ah! how white the moonlight falls.
Catch my slipper! there it goes,
Where that single fire-fly shines,
Tangled in the heavy vines,
Creeping by the convent walls.

Ay de mi! to be a nun!
Juana takes the veil to-day,
She hears mass behind a grate,
While for me ten lovers wait
At the door till mass is done.

Swing me, Tita! Seven are tall,
Two are crooked, rich, and old,
But the other—he's too small;

Did you hear a pebble fall?
And his blue eyes are too cold.

If I were a little nun,
When I heard that voice below,
I should scale the convent wall;
I should follow at his call,
Shuddering through the dreadful snow.

Tita. Tita. hold me still!
Now the vesper bell is ringing,
Bring me quick my beads and veil.
Yes, I know my cheek is pale
And my eyes shine—I've been swinging.[18]

This poem is modern in two ways: it leaves a lot of gaps in the story and it suggests a very unconventional attitude toward female sexuality. The speaker's fantasy of following her small cold-eyed lover, "shuddering through the dreadful snow," her delight in swinging and the physical exuberance it represents, are hardly consistent with nineteenth-century views of female passionlessness.[19] Furthermore, the speaker is an attractive figure despite the fact that she tolerates lovers "crooked, rich and old." She remains sympathetic, even more so than Edith Wharton's Undine Spragg, and she conveys more warmth than most of Sherwood Anderson's Winesburg, Ohio heroines.[20] She's the product of a realist sensibility without the grimness of some realists.

Many products of American realism are informed by the insights of Marx, Darwin, and finally Freud. Cooke's poem predates Freud but foreshadows his view of the essentially amoral character of desire. Sarah Helen Whitman's (1803–1878) late poem "Science" (1877) is an index of the impact of Darwinism on American culture, an impact usually traced first to the 1880s. Like the naturalist writers of a later era, Whitman creates a desolate picture of human life.

Earth's long, long dream of martyrdom and pain;
No God in heaven to rend the welded chain
Of endless evolution!

One expects from Whitman, who was a deeply spiritual woman, some rejoinder to this dismal perspective but it remains to be supplied by the reader. The poem simply ends:

Is this *all*?
And mole-eyed "Science," gloating over bones,
The skulls of monkeys and the Age of Stones,
Blinks at the golden lamps that light the hall
Of dusty death, and answers: "It is all."[21]

Until recently it was assumed that women were silent until a much later period about matters such as sex and evolution. Poems such as Whitman's and Cooke's help us to see, as Sharon Harris has also suggested, that the forces of realism were beginning to have an impact on women well before the dominance of Howells. Poetry is one locus of that impact.

As historical scholarship reveals greater complexity in the worlds we have lost, it comes to seem more and more indefensible to exclude poetry from discussions of nineteenth-century realism, especially since we must recognize that this exclusion is of comparatively recent origin. Indeed, as late as the 1930s critics were still considering poetry a branch of realist literature. A 1932 work, *American Literature and Culture* by Grant C. Knight, devotes a whole section to "The Literature of Realism," with subsections analyzing "Poetry" along with "The Novel" and "Drama."[22] For those who wrote of realism in the twenties and thirties, of course, realist poems were typically those of late nineteenth and early twentieth-century male writers: Edwin Markham's "The Man with the Hoe," Edwin Arlington Robinson's Tilbury Town portraits, Edgar Lee Masters' *Spoon River Anthology*, Robert Frost's poems about New England, Carl Sandburg's poems of the Midwest.

Without blurring the general outlines of realism entirely, it may be useful now to consider particular poems by nineteenth-century women poets as part of the early realist reaction to social, economic, intellectual and political changes. To do so helps revise the notion that nineteenth-century women poets were incapable of taking a hard look at social and psychological realities. Since most of these women also wrote more conventional verses, many of them pious and sentimental, the exposure of occasional realistic moments in their work also reveals that their role as "authors" was more complex than it has often been assumed to be. Such writers were able to present themselves in many guises: romantic, sentimental, realist, etc.

We do not need to argue that the primary value of these examples of nineteenth-century realism lies in their historical accuracy. More useful to us is the perspective that poems like Lucy Larcom's "Getting Along," Julia Ward Howe's "The Telegrams" and the works of the Cary sisters had strong representational value for the nineteenth-century readers who bought their books by the thousands. The politics of literary scholarship that once hid them from view may now serve to reveal that nineteenth-century women poets were just as intensely involved in the process of America's self-representation as their better remembered male counterparts. Their social commentary adds to our sense of what realism meant in the nineteenth century and what poetry may contribute to a gendered and historical understanding of the Real.

Notes

1. *Feminism and Poetry* (London: Pandora Press, 1987), 6.
2. James E. Miller, Jr., ed., *Heritage of American Literature* (San Diego: Harcourt Brace Jovanvich, 1991), vol. 2: George Perkins, et al., eds., *The American Tradition in Literature* (New York: McGraw-Hill, 1990), vol. 2: George McMichael, ed., *Anthology of American Literature* (New York: Macmillan, 1989), vol. 2.
3. Eric Sundquist defines the "country of the blue" as the realm of imagination and art, immediately identifiable as the territory of American romance but, in Sundquist's hands, equally the territory of American realism. See "Introduction: The Country of the Blue" in Eric J. Sundquist, ed., *American Realism: New Essays* (Baltimore: Johns Hopkins University Press, 1982).
4. Sundquist, "Introduction," 6–7. For a helpful article on the distinctions between realism and a concern for "the Real," see also Tom Quirk, "Realism, the 'Real,' and the Poet of Reality: Some Reflections on American Realists and the Poetry of Wallace Stevens," *American Literary Realism* 21, ii (Winter 1989), 34–53.
5. *Princeton Encyclopedia of Poetry and Poetics*, Alex Preminger, et al., eds., rev. ed. (Princeton: Princeton University Press, 1984).
6. See Donald Pizer, *Realism and Naturalism in Nineteenth-Century American Literature*, rev. ed. (Carbondale: Southern Illinois University Press, 1984), 2.
7. See, for example, *The Gold Standard and the Logic of Naturalism: American Literature at the Turn of the Century* (Berkeley: University of California Press, 1987), in which Walter Benn Michaels suggests that the works of both Charlotte Perkins Gilman and Theodore Dreiser end up fortifying precisely the positions both writers thought they were attacking.
8. Dates of composition for Maria Lowell's poems are not precise. This work was first published in 1846 in an abolitionist journal, but an edition of poetry was not published until 1855, when James Russell Lowell had fifty copies privately printed to commemorate his wife. A complete edition of her poetry was not published until 1936. See *The Poems of Maria White Lowell*, ed. Hope Jillson Vernon (Providence: Brown University Press, 1936).
9. *The Poetical Works of Alice and Phoebe Cary* (Boston: Houghton Osgood, 1880), 98. Like the Lowell poem above, this and other poems quoted in this article are also available in *American Women Poets of the Nineteenth Century*, ed. Cheryl Walker (New Brunswick, NJ: Rutgers University Press, 1992).

10. *Poetical Works*, 300.
11. *The Poetical Works of Lucy Larcom* (Boston: Houghton Mifflin, 1884, 25–26.
12. *Poems* (1867) rpt. in *Collected Black Women's Poetry*, ed. Joan R. Sherman (New York: Oxford University Press—Schomburg Library of Nineteenth-Century Black Women Writers, 1988), 1:105–06. According to Gwenn Davis and Beverly Joyce, Tucker Lambert also published "Cogitots" in Oakland (no date) and "La Rabida: A California Columbian Souvenir Poem" in San Francisco, 1893. See Gwenn Davis and Beverly Joyce, *Poetry By Women to 1900: A Bibliography of American and British Writers* (Toronto: University of Toronto Press, 1991), 285.
13. Sherman supplies the dates for Fordham's grandmother Mary Furman Weston Byrd (1792–1884) but there are no dates for Fordham herself. *Magnolia Leaves* (1897) rpt. in *Collected Black Women's Poetry*, ed. Joan R. Sherman (New York: Oxford University Press, 1988), 2: 74–75.
14. *Songs from the Golden Gate* (Boston: Houghton Mifflin, 1895), 57–60.
15. *From Sunset Ridge: Poems Old and New* (Boston: Houghton Mifflin, 1898), 22–24.
16. For a similar argument about Rebecca Harding Davis, see Sharon M. Harris, *Rebecca Harding Davis and American Realism* (Philadelphia: University of Pennsylvania Press, 1991), 1–19. Like me, Harris is asking for a reconceptualization of American realism, one that recognizes the contributions of women writers in more detail.
17. Perry D. Westbrook, "Rose Terry Cooke" in *American Realists and Naturalists*, ed. Donald Pizer and Earl N. Harbert, *Dictionary of Literary Biography* (Detroit: Gale Research Co., 1982), 12: 95–98.
18. *Poems* (New York: Gottsberger, 1888), 296–97.
19. See Nancy Cott, "Passionlessness: An Interpretation of Victorian Sexual Ideology" in *A Heritage of Her Own: Towards a New Social History of American Women*, ed. Nancy Cott and Elizabeth H. Pleck (New York: Simon & Schuster, 1979), 162–81.
20. Undine Spragg appears in Edith Wharton's *The Custom of the Country* (1913). Anderson's *Winesburg, Ohio* (1919) is sympathetic to the frustrations of its female characters but none of them seems comfortable with her own sexuality.
21. *Poems* (Boston: Houghton Osgood, 1879), 190–91.
22. *American Literature and Culture* (New York: Ray Long and Richard K. Smith, Inc. 1932).

"I cant write a book": Women's Humor and the American Realistic Tradition

NANCY A. WALKER

THE period of the ascendance of realism as the dominant mode in American fiction is associated historically with some grim realities: corruption and scandal in business and politics, dangerous working conditions in the growing heavy industries, urban congestion and the ghettoization of immigrant groups. Writers as diverse as Twain, Howells, Dreiser, Norris, and Sinclair addressed directly the human costs of these social trends in works of fiction that at times seemed interchangeable with the newspaper headlines and stories of the day—a possibility that Dos Passos was later to employ deliberately as a narrative device in his *U.S.A.* trilogy. Yet the period during which documentary realism established one kind of link between literature and social reality was also a period in which humorous writing flourished. In the years between 1885, when *Huck Finn* was published, and 1925, when *The New Yorker* was established, humor provided a different but no less significant index of changes in American concerns and values.

By its very nature, humor would seem the antithesis of the realist impulse. It refuses—or so we assume—to take life seriously, and the devices of humorous expression—hyperbole, understatement, and absurdity, among others—are determined to bend and alter observable reality rather than to document it. The natural impulse of the humorous writer appears to be to draw our attention away from rather than toward the everyday events and situations that surround us, and to amuse rather than to stir our concern. But the tradition of satire alone proves that precisely the opposite is true. From Jonathan Swift to Mark Twain and into this century, the most grim and shocking of human realities and the largest of life's absurdities have been drawn most forcefully in a mode that tricks us into a realization of deep seriousness. Women writers of humor from the late nineteenth century through the early twentieth, much like their male counterparts, reflect such trends as the shift from rural to urban life, and from dialect humor to the witty urbanity of magazines such as *Vanity Fair* and *The New Yorker*; but more importantly they are united by the common purpose of overturning the genteel stereotype of the woman as pious, sentimental and dependent, and coming to terms with actual changes in women's lives. From the down-home common sense of Marietta Holley (1836–1926) to the sophisticated modernism of Gertrude Stein (1874–1946), women's humor of the period details the struggle for political rights and personal autonomy that was one of the most important social movements of the period.

The first step for the writer who wishes to disassociate herself from a limiting cultural stereotype necessarily takes place on the level of literary form. From the late eighteenth century onward, women authors had been primarily associated with the sentimental romance or the "domestic novel"—genres that reinforced the image of women as frail, emotional, and nonintellectual. By the 1850s these fictional genres and the identification of women as their primary creators had become sufficiently popular to lead to Hawthorne's famous outburst about the "d———d mob of scribbling women" that he considered his chief competitors for the reading public. But some women writers were already beginning to disassociate themselves from this tradition. As early as 1854, "Fanny Fern" (pseudonym of Sara Willis Parton [1811–1872]) announced in the preface to *Ruth Hall* that she did not wish the book to be considered a novel, lest her work—and thus her heroine—be case in the stereotypical mold. *Ruth Hall*, Fanny Fern writes, is "entirely at variance with all set rules for novel-writing. There is no intricate plot; there are no startling developments, no hair-breadth escapes." In fact, *Ruth Hall* often displays the interests of the realistic novel, and by design enters directly into the lives of its invented characters. "I have avoided long introductions and descriptions," Fern writes in her preface, "and have entered unceremoniously and unannounced, into people's houses, without stopping to ring the bell."[1]

Similarly, in the preface to *My Opinions and Betsey Bobbet's* (1872), Marietta Holley disassociates herself from the sentimental novel tradition, but Holley's is a vernacular and overtly comic disassociation that lampoons the romantic adventure by announcing the author's supposed inadequacies:

> I cant write a book, I don't know no underground dungeons, I haint acquainted with no haunted houses, I never seen a hero suspended over a abyss by his gallusses, I never beheld a heroine swoon away, I never see a Injun tommy hawked, nor a ghost; I never had any of these advantages; I cant write a book.[2]

This passage not only sets forth—and sets Holley apart from—some of the conventions of the popular romance; it also reveals her assumption that one writes from experience rather than by borrowing plot devices from other books. In short, it endorses the realist premise that literature should depict actual or probable human life.[3] The life that Holley rendered in her more than twenty humorous books, published between 1872 and 1914, is that of sensible, hard-working Samantha Allen in rural New York, who makes known her views on fads, fashions, and issues of the day—especially the need for equal rights for women—while she churns butter, makes preserves, and raises two children. The robust figure of Samantha Allen not only has never watched a heroine "swoon away"; her busy life as a homemaker marks the distance between romantic fiction and the actual lives of ordinary women.

It was not only the women fiction writers of the period who reacted against the tradition of the popular romance, though they had a particular stake in being viewed apart from this tradition. As Diva Dains has pointed out, a number of feminist social commentators of the era expressed concern that literature intended for women typically emphasized an idealized, romantic love that urged upon women unrealistic expectations of marriage and motherhood. In *Why Women Are So* (1912), for example, Mary Coolidge remarks that "In this dream there were no puzzling and inevitable facts of nature—the lover was always pure and brave and considerate; the heroine beautiful and adored. There was no baby, even, as in real life." Charlotte Perkins Gilman (1860–1935) was even more blunt about romance fiction in *The Man-Made World or Our Androcentric Culture* (1911): "It is the Adventure of Him in Pursuit of Her—and it stops when he gets her! Story after story . . . this ceaseless repetition of the Preliminaries." Such observers, Dains points out, thus functioned as early feminist literary critics,[4] and often at the same time provided in their own fiction a literary alternative to the sentimental romance.

Even more obvious than their resistance to forms of literature that reinforced women's dependence and submissiveness is the authors' creation of central characters who manifest strength and autonomy, even while in some cases (such as that of Samantha Allen) they occupy the culturally-sanctioned role of homemaker. The humor in such fiction frequently arises from the contrast between the strong or at least sympathetic character and other characters who either exemplify feminine dependence or seek to deny the central character's autonomy. Although one result of such contrast is sometimes the creation of stereotypes or even caricature, the exaggeration serves effectively to underscore actual social roles and attitudes.[5]

One of the earliest and most overt examples of the independent-minded character in women's humor of this period is Holley's Samantha Allen, who is contrasted to both her traditional husband, Josiah, and—in Holley's first book—Betsey Bobbet, a neighbor who represents the extreme of the husband-hunting spinster and sentimental believer in the romantic ideal. Samantha is significant in part because of a combination of characteristics unusual in the literature of the period, but very likely common in actuality. On the one hand she is an outspoken, argumentative feminist who is knowledgeable about the issues of the day—not only the central issue of female suffrage, but also the temperance movement, equality in child-rearing and church leadership, and equal pay for equal work. Yet Samantha is not portrayed as the usual stereotype of the late-nineteenth-century women's rights advocate, such as Miss Birdseye in Henry James' *The Bostonians* (1886): a grim single woman who spends her time making speeches and converting others to her cause. Instead, Samantha is a devoted wife and mother and a dedicated homemaker who is proud of her housekeeping skills. Indeed, her industry is frequently contrasted to the idleness of Betsey and Josiah, who tend to spend their time, respectively, writing sentimental poetry and whittling. When, for example, Betsey arrives for a morning visit, Samantha is simultaneously washing Josiah's shirts, making preserves, and baking a pudding; and when Betsey makes her standard pronouncement that "it is woman's greatest privilege, her crowning blessing, to soothe lacerations, to be a sort of a poultice to the noble, manly breast when it is torn with the cares of life," Samantha responds with impatience:

> "Am I a poultice, Betsey Bobbet, do I look like one?—am I in the condition to be one? . . . What has my sect done," says I, as I wildly rubbed [Josiah's] shirt sleeves, "that they have got to be lacerator soothers, when they have got every thing else under the sun to do?" Here I stirred down

> the preserves that was a runnin' over, and turned a pail full of syrup into the sugar kettle. "Everybody says that men are stronger than women, and why should they be treated as if they was glass china, liable to break all to pieces if they haint handled careful."[6]

Samantha, like her creator, understands that the assumed dichotomy between man's strength and woman's weakness is in large part the result of economic disparity, and despite her exasperation with Betsey's extreme attempts to assume genteel femininity, Samantha sees clearly that Betsey, as a single woman, sees no choice but to adopt whatever behavior she believes will make her marriageable, and therefore economically and socially secure. Thus, although she participates in comic confrontations with Betsey, Samantha's satiric thrust is directed at those who have perpetuated women's dependence by insisting that woman's only proper sphere is the domestic, and who therefore contribute to a cultural climate that limits their economic and social independence. To address this issue humorously, Holley makes exaggerated use of the traditional metaphors of the clinging vine and the sturdy oak tree, advising the single men she knows that if women are to be vines, men must provide the support for them to grow on. When the Methodist minister, a widower, preaches a sermon about woman's "holy mission," Samantha muses, "I love to see folks use reason. And I say again, how can a woman cling when she haint got nothin' to cling to?" Ultimately, she asks the minister directly, "*Are you willin' to be a tree?,*" whereupon he changes the subject.

Not all of the images of the single woman in women's humorous fiction of the period are, like Betsey Bobbet, eager to be clinging vines; some, like Anne Warner French's (1869–1913) Susan Clegg and Mary Roberts Rinehart's (1876–1958) Letitia Carberry, are quite content to be unmarried, and, provided by their authors with a measure of economic security, they demonstrate varying degrees of autonomy. Both French's stories about Susan Clegg, published in several collections between 1904 and 1920, and Rinehart's "Tish" stories, published between 1911 and 1937, were enormously popular, and the differences between Susan and Tish help to chart some of the changes in cultural attitudes toward women from the turn of the century through the 1920s and 1930s. The Susan Clegg stories are set in a small town not unlike that which Holley's Samantha Allen inhabits; and Anne French, like Holley, uses dialectical speech to locate her characters in the world of the village rather than in the growing urban centers. Like Samantha, Susan Clegg is a meticulous housekeeper whose life revolves around domestic chores. Rinehart's Tish Carberry, on the other hand, is an adventurous spirit who travels widely, owns—and repairs—an automobile, and engages life quite outside the domestic sphere.

The figure of Susan Clegg works within, at the same time that it resists, several traditional female stereotypes. Most of the stories consist primarily of conversations between Susan and her neighbor, Mrs. Lathrop. The fact that the latter can scarcely get a word into the dialogue marks Susan as the stereotypically talkative woman, and indeed she is, but her talk reveals her to be a practical—at times even cynical—observer of human nature, while Mrs. Lathrop, a widow with one son, is presented as a lazy housekeeper who willingly abandons any chore to chew clover and listen to Susan over the back fence. The chief reason for Susan's single state is that she cares for her invalid father, but far from being a martyr to this responsibility, she often refers to her father in terms that suggest he is little more than another piece of furniture to dust. On Saturday mornings, for example, Susan tells Mrs. Lathrop with unintentional humor that she cannot talk any longer because "this 's father's day to be beat up and got into new pillow-slips."[7] And Susan maintains a healthy skepticism about marriage, based on her observations of those around her. Rather than viewing marriage as the beginning of "happily ever after," she sees it as the end of a pleasant uncertainty: "Once you take a man, nothin' is ever sudden no more." To Deacon White, who has expressed interest in marrying Mrs. Lathrop, Susan observes, "there's lots worse things 'n bein' unmarried, and if you marry Mrs. Lathrop you'll learn every last one of 'em."[8] Instead if viewing married women wistfully, Susan's reasonable nature is struck by a contradiction in their behavior:

> I won't say as married women strike me more and more as fools, for it wouldn't be kindly, but I will say as the way they revel in being married and saying how hard it is, kind of strikes me as amusing. *I* wouldn't go into a store and buy a dress and then, when every one knew as I picked it out myself, keep running around telling how it didn't fit and was tearing out in all the seams.[9]

Such common-sense logic is worthy of Susan's humorous ancestor Samantha Allen.

Only once does Susan Clegg actively pursue marriage, and she is quickly disillusioned by the experience. In the ironically-titled story "The Marrying of Susan Clegg," French shows Susan at the point of realizing that the longer her father lives, the older she will become, and thus the more remote her chances of marrying. Her remarks to Mrs. Lathrop once again have a practical edge that strikes the reader as amusing:

> I've always meant to get married 's soon 's father was off my hands. I was countin' up today, though, 'n' if he lives to be a hundred, I'll be nigh onto seventy 'n' no man aint' goin' to marry me at seventy. Not 'nless he was eighty, 'n' Lord knows I ain't intendin' to bury father jus' to begin on some one else, 'n' that's all it'd be. (5)

Rather than flirting and writing sentimental poetry, in the manner of Betsey Bobbet, Susan Clegg makes straightforward, businesslike proposals to several single men in her town, starting with the minister ("it struck me 's polite to begin with him"). Rebuffed by all of them, Susan is distracted from her search by the death of her father, and her consequent inheritance of some government bonds makes the single life seem quite appealing again. As she tells Mrs. Lathrop, "After all, the Lord said, 'It is not good for a man to be alone,' but he left a woman free to use her common sense, 'n' I sh'll use mine right now" (41).

The emphasis on common sense and reason that Samantha Allen and Susan Clegg illustrate in their dialogue and behavior is a direct counter to the subjectivity associated with the sentimental, dependent female. By making the intellect ascendant over emotion, Holley and French claim for their characters a capacity for self-determination that has its political parallel in the campaign for female suffrage during this period. Unlike Samantha Allen, Susan Clegg would not dream of arguing overtly for gender equality, but her perfect assurance that she is in control of her own life stands as a precondition for such equality. Even while fulfilling the traditional role of the dutiful daughter, Susan displays a firm consciousness of her own worth as an individual.

Rinehart's Letitia Carberry similarly represents a combination of traditional and nontraditional roles and attitudes. While she is in many ways the figure of the somewhat meddlesome maiden aunt who enjoys intervening in the affairs of others, she is also a woman of high principle who confronts directly any authority that opposes her. In creating Tish, Rinehart borrowed from the turn-of-the-century image of the "New Woman," providing her character with mobility and a sense of adventure. Not tied, like Susan Clegg, to the domestic life of small-town America, Tish represents a shift from the nineteenth-century emphasis on woman's "separate sphere" to the modernist critique of fixed roles that characterized the post–World War I years. Interestingly, French's Susan Clegg has observed this transition from her own distance. In the story "Susan Clegg and the Olive Branch," the daughter of a local minister moves to the city and writes a successful book, prompting Susan to comment that whereas she has no interest in earning her own living, "some has to, and some wants to be around men, and there ain't no better way to be around with men nowadays than to go to work with 'em" (86). While Susan sees economic necessity and a desire to be "around men" as the motives for young women to leave the domestic arena, Tish is activated by a spirit of adventure, and the men she encounters are more likely to be adversaries than the objects of romantic interest.

In her stories about Tish Carberry, Rinehart departs further than Holley and French from traditional gender-role expectations by locating Tish within a community of women. Whereas Samantha Allen cooks and washes for Josiah and their children, and Susan Clegg cares for her elderly father, the network of female friends of which Tish is a part recalls the largely female worlds depicted in the work of the New England local-color writers such as Sarah Orne Jewett and Mary Wilkins Freeman. In the Tish stories as in the stories of Jewett and Freeman, women rely on each other for support and advice, but at the same time exist as strong, independent individuals who determine their own life patterns and values. Lizzie, who narrates the Tish stories, and their friend Aggie form with Tish a trio of quite different women who share adventures that reflect Rinehart's own experience as a correspondent for the *Saturday Evening Post,* in which many of the Tish stories first appeared. Not only did the *Post* enjoy a wide circulation among middle-class readers, but Rinehart was herself one of the most popularly successful authors of the period between 1910 and 1940. James D. Hart, in *The Popular Book*, notes that sales of Rinehart's works averaged 300,000 copies annually during the 1920s.[10] In both her mystery novels and the comic Tish stories, Rinehart displayed a shrewd understanding of the tensions between tradition and modernism that affected the taste of her readers. As Hart comments, she was able to give the public "stories about the breaking of old standards, the failure of old beliefs, and the coming of new mores" in the postwar years.[11]

One of these tensions arose from the variety of attitudes toward feminism in the early decades of the century, when, as is often the case now, middle-aged women who had fought for women's equality were confronted by a younger generation who represented a conservative reaction against such activism. In the story titled "Mind Over Motor," Rinehart uses humor to point up this confrontation of values. Lizzie, Tish, and Aggie respond to the plea of Lizzie's cousin Eliza that they serve as live-in chaperones to her college-age daughter, Bettina, while Eliza is in London—not to protect Bettina from youthful wildness, but rather to prevent her from marrying the boy next door: "She believes a woman should marry and rear a large family!" Eliza writes Lizzie with horror.[12] Rinehart contrasts the independence and adventurous spirit of the three older women to the conventionally feminine behavior of Bettina. When the three arrive at Eliza's house, Bettina's suggestion that they "go right upstairs and have some tea and lie down" is met with Tish's determination to lubricate her automobile engine; again offered tea, Aggie responds to a shocked Bettina that they have refreshed themselves with blackberry cordial after changing a tire on the road. And while Bettina becomes involved in a traditional love triangle, Tish becomes involved in automobile racing. This generational role-reversal is accompanied by a reversal of gender roles in which the "boy next door" supports female suffrage while Bettina does not.

Although Rinehart, like other writers of the period, does not overtly denigrate marriage, she does equate the single state with characteristics and values diametrically opposed to Betsey Bobbet's "clinging vine" behavior. After the turn of the century, marriage is presented more frequently as a choice than as an economic necessity. Indeed, Rinehart's Aggie had once been engaged, but her fiancé died in an accident, and the narrator, Lizzie, explains her own status as a single woman merely by commenting that "the Lord never saw fit to send me a man I could care enough about to marry, or one who cared enough about me."[13] Provided with unspecified but clearly sufficient sources of income, Rinehart's single women are thus freed from the stereotype of the husband-hunting spinster.

But even though the image of the single woman had become a more positive one by the early part of the twentieth century, the work of other female humorists of the period reveals that the combination of marriage and career for women was viewed as quite problematic in the popular imagination; women may have gained more freedom of choice, but the choice of either marriage or a career seemed to preclude the other. The independence—economic and otherwise—associated with the professional woman was not easily accommodated to the concept of a woman's dependent, subordinate status within the institution of marriage. In the years immediately before and after passage of the suffrage amendment, writers such as Edna St. Vincent Millay (1892–1950) and Florence Guy Seabury (1881–1951) pointed up the absurdity of this dichotomy of images. Millay, writing humorous sketches under the name "Nancy Boyd" for magazines such as *Vanity Fair*, focuses frequently on men's continuing tendency to categorize and stereotype women and to resent women's professional success. "The Implacable Aphrodite," for example, takes the form of a conversation featuring a man who initially expresses admiration for the independence of his sculptress-companion, but who ultimately reveals his assumption that she is essentially a marriageable object. The man, Mr. White, begins by professing his delight that the two of them can simply be friends: "Oh, if you only knew what a relief you are, what a rest!—a woman who is not married, who has never been married, and who does not insist that I marry her."[14] He professes also to support her freedom to pursue her art: "I want you to go on—to grow—to grow—and to be free!" (47). The woman, Miss Black, also celebrates her single state. Speaking of her love of tea, she observes, "Fortunately, its connotation, as being the accomplice of spinsterhood, is not so offensive to me as it is to most women. If it will help me to remain a spinster, then it is my staunchest ally!" (49). But when Miss Black announces her intention to leave for Europe for the sake of her art, Mr. White becomes angry at what he perceives as her desertion of him, and proposes marriage, at the same time denigrating her professionalism by stating that, as his wife, she could continue to practice her art because "A man's wife *ought* to have some little thing to take up her time" (52). Rejected, Mr. White leaves in a huff. Millay's choice of the names "Miss Black" and "Mr. White" suggests the oversimplification and strict dichotomies of traditional views of woman's role, and also conjures up echoes of the master/slave relationship.

In "The Delicatessen Husband," Florence Guy Seabury approaches the same issue somewhat differently by describing a dual-career marriage. Published in 1926, Seabury's sketch reflects the brief, optimistic flurry of women's entry into the professions in the decade following the suffrage amendment. Ethel, the wife, described as a "modern, self-supporting woman," is a chemist; "like eight million others of her sex," Seabury writes, "she spends her days in gainful occupation out of the home."[15] Ethel hates housework and does it poorly; Seabury speculates that "if she had lived a hundred years ago, with no outlet for the forces of her nature, nothing to exist for except a domestic routine, she would probably have been one of those irritable, inefficient wives and tart mothers who made an entire family miserable, seeing their duty and doing it" (35). The point of view in the sketch is that of Ethel's husband, Perry, who longs for the home-cooked meals of his childhood while he shops unhappily for food at the neighborhood delicatessen. For Perry, the very existence of delicatessens threatens his traditional values, a reaction that Seabury reports with comic hyperbole:

> They were emblems of a declining civilization, the source of all our ills, the promoter of equal suffrage, the permitter of the business and professional woman, the destroyer of the home. (28–29)

Seabury's career and her approach to gender equality exemplify the transition from rural to urban culture and from tradition to modernist critique. A graduate of Columbia University and the New York School of Social Work, she was active in the settlement house movement on New York's Lower East Side before becoming the editor, in 1912, of *The Woman Voter*, the official publication of the Woman's Suffrage Party. Influenced by socialism and by the psychological theories of Carl Jung, Seabury addressed the negative implications of strict gender-role distinctions for both women and men. The maternal nurturance for which Perry Winship yearns is evidence, Seabury believes, of man's essential dependence on women—a dependence that makes men reluctant to free women from the role of caretaker to pursue other interests. Men's dependence on women is not limited to the domestic care of mothers and wives, but extends to the workplace, where receptionists and secretaries protect and buffer the lives of the men for whom they work. In significant ways, then, men rather than women are "the sheltered sex," to use the title of one of Seabury's essays. The magazines for which Seabury wrote in the 1920s—*The Nation*, *Harper's*, and *The New Republic*—represented an earnest urban liberalism that was quite distinct from the middle-America cosiness of *The Saturday Evening Post*, in which Rinehart's "Tish" stories appeared, and the urbane skepticism of *Vanity Fair* and *The New Yorker*, which published Millay and Dorothy Parker. The coexistence of all three types of magazines testifies to the intellectual pluralism that characterized modernist American culture.

In her 1935 book *Love Is a Challenge*, Seabury echoed the common sense of Marietta Holley when she wrote of the sexually repressive raising of children:

> In place of the understanding of human contacts we load young people with don'ts of behavior. Even worse, we bequeath them a set of ancient patterns of emotion, equipping them with stereotypes which belong to other days, encouraging a romanticism which wars with reality.[16]

The stereotype of the nurturing woman, which Holley had made ridiculous in Betsey Bobbet's desire to be a "poultice to the noble, manly breast," is at odds with the image of the career woman such as Ethel Winship, and Seabury was not alone in pointing to this conflict. Charlotte Perkins Gilman, who shared with Seabury a commitment to feminist activism, and who was considered "unnatural" when she gave custody of her daughter to her former husband, wrote frequently of women who resisted definition as homemakers long before Betty Friedan coined the term "the feminine mystique." The stories that Gilman wrote for her magazine *The Forerunner* and for other publications such as *Physical Culture* have a tone of amused skepticism regarding "proper" gender roles.

Julia Gordins, in Gilman's "Making a Change," tries against her nature to care for her infant son: "The child was her child, it was her duty to take care of it, and take care of it she would."[17] Suppressing her desire to follow a career as a musician, Julia attempts to do her "duty" to her child and in the process makes herself and her family miserable. The solution—the "change" of the title—is to turn the care of the child over to Julia's mother-in-law, for whom child care is a natural and rewarding activity, while Julia happily teaches music lessons. But the most telling part of the story is the fact that Julia's husband remains remote from these and all household arrangements. At the beginning of the story he insists that something be done about the baby's crying, but fails to see the desperation his wife feels: "his work lay in electric coils, in dynamos and copper wiring—not in women's nerves—and he did not notice it" (68). Yet once the household is running more smoothly, he is not above taking credit for the change, and remarks to his friends that "this being married and bringing up children is as easy as can be—when you learn how!" (74). Gilman thus makes the husband the butt of her satire.

Another of Gilman's stories suggests that only in fantasy can such rigid divisions in gender-role be bridged. In "If I Were a Man" (1914), Mollie Mathewson is described, somewhat sarcastically, as the epitome of the dutiful wife and homemaker:

> Mollie was "true to type." She was a beautiful instance of what is reverentially called "a true woman." Little, of course—no true woman may be big. Pretty, of course—no true woman could possibly be plain. Whimsical, capricious, charming, changeable, devoted to pretty clothes and always "wearing them well," as the esoteric phrase has it.[18]

Yet this "loving wife and . . . devoted mother" wishes so hard that she were a man that her consciousness enters the body of her husband Gerald one morning as he leaves for work. Provided with the dual awareness of male and female, Mollie/Gerald occupies a unique perspective from which to recognize the realities that lie behind gender stereotyping. To Mollie, women's hats begin to look as frivolous as men have characterized them: "these squirts of stiff feathers, these violent outstanding bows of glistening ribbon, these swaying, projecting masses of plumage which tormented the faces of bystanders" (34). Gerald, for his part, finds himself bristling when his male companions denigrate women; much to his own surprise, he makes a speech in which he identifies men as the source of women's fashions as well as of their economic dependence:

> We invent all those idiotic hats of theirs, and design their crazy fashions, and, what's more, if a woman is courageous enough to wear commonsense clothes—and shoes—which of us wants to dance with her?
>
> Yes, we blame them for grafting on us, but are we willing to let our wives work? We are not. It hurts our pride, that's all. (38)

By presenting the fantasy of Mollie and Gerald's merged consciousness, Gilman implies that the perpetuation of rigid gender definitions results precisely from a lack of mutual understanding. In sharp contrast to the use of fantasy in her story "The Yellow Wallpaper," in which enforced passivity leads to madness, Gilman here uses fantasy as an element of domestic comedy, and in doing so prefigures the work of James Thurber and others who in the 1920s engaged in a comic "war between the sexes."[19]

If earlier writers, such as Fanny Fern and Marietta Holley, had disavowed literary forms that threatened to identify them with stereotypical female roles and characteristics, Gertrude Stein addressed the issue of such identification even more fundamentally—on the level of language itself. By challenging our assumptions about meaning, grammar, and syntax, Stein moved beyond convention in literary composition just as she moved beyond America and its early-century concern with the issue of gender equality. A self-conscious iconoclast, Stein understood clearly both the joy and the perils of breaking with tradition; in "Composition as Explanation," she writes with her characteristic wit that "the creator of the new composition in the arts is an outlaw until he is a classic," and that "classic" status occurs only after the creator is dead.[20] In 1898, nearly thirty years before this essay was published, Stein, while still an undergraduate student, was influenced by Charlotte Perkins Gilman, and borrowed some ideas from Gilman's *Women and Economics* in a speech on the benefits of college education for women delivered to a group of Baltimore women. One of Stein's arguments for women's higher education, in fact, was that the consequent ability to be self-supporting would free women from economic dependence on men—the kind of dependence that created stereotypes of the desperate spinster such as Betsey Bobbet.

As Elyse Blankley has pointed out, Stein later repudiated the stance she took in this early speech, having come to believe in a more radical independence than that represented by women competing with men in the economic marketplace: "She was pleased with her decision to snub the cause of women in favor the demands of her own fierce independence, which ironically excluded her from the ranks of New Women who so desperately wanted her to succeed and hence to serve as a model."[21] In both *The Autobiography of Alice B. Toklas* and *Fernhurst*, Stein rejects the idea that women educated according to the male paradigm will have claimed their own identify as females. As Blankley puts it, "in order to engender herself through language, Stein had to sacrifice the college girl on the altar of her imagination."[22] She was sufficiently prescient to see that merely learning the rules and codes of the patriarchal culture would not break down either the prejudice against female professionalism or assumptions of male superiority—both of which were later the subject of humorous treatment by writers such as "Nancy Boyd" and Florence Guy Seabury.

Rather than addressing the issues of gender identity and gender equality in her work, Stein instead calls into question the very concept of identity and subjectivity through a use of language that denies sequential logic and fixed meaning. Frequently in her writing *about* writing she examines the nature and functions of the parts of speech; she views the noun as inflexible, preferring the parts of speech—conjunctions, adverbs, verbs—that *do* something in a sentence rather than simply stand as the name of something. Thus she told the audience in one of her lectures that "in *Tender Buttons* and then on I struggled with the ridding of myself of nouns. I knew that nouns must go in poetry as they had gone in prose if anything that is everything was to go on meaning something."[23] The method of "ridding" herself of nouns in *Tender Buttons* consists of teasing metaphors that question the nouns' authority of meaning: "Sugar is not a vegetable," "The sister was not a mister," "Any little thing is water." As Neil Schmitz characterizes Stein's process in *Of Huck and Alice*, she changes "the work of definition into the play of metaphor."[24] It is such irreverent "play" that Schmitz correctly identifies as Stein's humorous method—a method that frees her to create not merely meaning but her own relation to meaning, and hence to define herself without the restrictions of gender:

> As a subtle grammarian, Gertrude Stein knew the functions of the parts of speech, the power of classification, and the consequence of gender. She knew, in brief, how politicized were the prevalent modes of scientific and imaginative discourse, how prejudicial to her experience, and knew this as a fate . . . . Her struggle was desperate, its resolution humorous. She would move back and forth between different symbolic orders, different discursive systems, in language, between a figurative identification with the Father and a figurative identification with the Mother, between scientific discourse and chatter, and retain a perfect, playful balance.[25]

The impulse toward androgyny, manifested on the level of plot in Gilman's story of Mollie and Gerald Mathewson (published the same year as *Tender Buttons*), inheres in Stein's work on the more essential level of language itself.

Humor, as it is used by women writers of the period before and after the turn of the century, represents a refusal to be bound, classified, defined by cultural norms and stereotypes. By attending to issues of gender on the levels of plot, characterization, and language, these writers use the methods of humor to reject both the female models of sentiment and dependence and the male models of scientific authority. The year 1914 saw the publication of both *Tender*

Buttons and Marietta Holley's last "Samantha" book. Holley's homespun wisdom and dialectical style could scarcely be further from Stein's modernist skepticism and sophisticated word play; indeed, as Schmitz points out, Holley's use of conventional dialect and her character Samantha's overwhelmingly maternal nature serve to blunt the sharpness of her feminist critique.[26] Yet even these two such disparate writers share a revisionist agenda, and it seems fittingly symmetrical that just as "Josiah Allen's Wife," amidst her myriad domestic duties, declares that she "cant write a book" and then proceeds to do so, Gertrude Stein's Alice, at the end of *The Autobiography of Alice B. Toklas*, declares that she "found it difficult to add being a pretty good author" to the list of her other—decidedly domestic—duties, so that Stein had to write her autobiography for her.[27] Both jokes turn upon the claiming of authorship, just as both texts bring women to the center and insist upon their intellectual power.

Notes

1. Fanny Fern, *Ruth Hall & Other Writings*, ed. Joyce W. Warren (New Brunswick, NJ: Rutgers University Press, 1986), 3.
2. Marietta Holley, *My Opinions and Betsey Bobbet's* (Hartford, CT: American Publishing Co., 1872), v–vi.
3. In Holley's case, the emphasis should be on the word "probable." Although the central *persona* in Holley's more than twenty books is married to Josiah Allen, Holley remained single throughout her life. Further, although several of Holley's books are set in locations far from her central character's small New York State town, such as Europe, Holley herself did not travel to these places, but instead used guidebooks for her research. See Kate H. Winter, *Marietta Holley: Life with "Josiah Allen's Wife"* (Syracuse, NY: Syracuse University Press, 1984).
4. Diva Daims, "A Criticism of Their Own: Turn-of-the-Century Feminist Writers," *Turn-of-the-Century Women* 2, no. 2 (Winter 1985): 22–23.
5. Jane Curry, who performs nationwide as Marietta Holley's Samantha Allen, prefers in her Samantha monologues to omit Samantha's bitingly satiric description of Betsey Bobbet that appears in the following discussion, because without context or interpretation—which is impossible in the performance setting—Holley could seem merely to be perpetuating the negative image of the spinster common in nineteenth century literature. (Conversation with Jane Curry at Vanderbilt University, 27 March 1990.)
6. Holley, *Opinions*, 62–63.
7. Anne Warner [French], "The Marrying of Susan Clegg," *Susan Clegg and Her Friend Mrs. Lathrop* (Boston: Little, Brown, 1904), 4.
8. Anne Warner [French], "Mrs. Lathrop's Love Affairs," *The Century Magazine* 69, no. 6 (April 1905): 839.
9. Anne Warner [French], "Susan Clegg and the Olive Branch," *Susan Clegg and Her Love Affairs* (Boston: Little, Brown, 1916), 85.

10. James D. Hart, *The Popular Book: A History of America's Literary Taste* (Berkeley: University of California Press, 1950), 245.
11. Hart, *Popular*, 231.
12. Mary Roberts Rinehart, "Mind Over Motor," in *Tish: The Chronicle of Her Escapades and Excursions* (New York: A. L. Burt, 1916), 4.
13. Rinehart, *Tish*, 23.
14. Nancy Boyd, *Distressing Dialogues* (New York: Harper & Brothers, 1924), 42–43.
15. Florence Guy Seabury, "The Delicatessen Husband," *The Delicatessen Husband and Other Essays* (New York: Harcourt, Brace, 1926), 32.
16. Florence Guy Seabury, *Love Is a Challenge* (New York: McGraw-Hill, 1935), 8.
17. Charlotte Perkins Gilman, "Making a Change," in *The Charlotte Perkins Gilman Reader*, ed. Ann J. Lane (New York: Pantheon, 1980), 67.
18. Charlotte Perkins Gilman, "If I Were a Man," in *The Charlotte Perkins Gilman Reader*, 32.
19. For an analysis of some of the skirmishes in this war, see Nancy Walker, "'Fragile and Dumb': The 'Little Woman' in Women's Humor, 1900–1940," *Thalia: Studies in Literary Humor* 5, no. 2 (Fall & Winter 1982–83): 24–29.
20. Gertrude Stein, "Composition as Explanation," in *Selected Writings of Gertrude Stein*, ed. Carl Van Vechten (New York: Random House, 1946), 454.
21. Elyse Blankley, "Beyond the 'Talent of Knowing': Gertrude Stein and the New Woman," in *Critical Essays on Gertrude Stein*, ed. Michael J. Hoffman (Boston: G. K. Hall, 1986), 197.
22. Blankley, *Beyond the Talent*, 198.
23. Stein, *Selected Writings*, 406.
24. Neil Schmitz, *Of Huck and Alice: Humorous Writing in American Literature* (Minneapolis: University of Minnesota Press, 1983), 176.
25. Schmitz, *Huck*, 178.
26. Schmitz, *Huck*, 136–37.
27. Gertrude Stein, *The Autobiography of Alice B. Toklas* in *Selected Writings*, 208.

Reading Her/stories Against His/stories in Early Chinese American Literature

AMY LING

THOUGH realism as a literary phenomenon of the late nineteenth and early twentieth centuries was a rejection of romanticism and of representations of the unlikely, the idealized, and the fabulous in favor the real, the ordinary, the everyday, the Chinese, a race generally perceived as alien and unassimilable, were anything but ordinary and everyday for the majority of Euroamericans. While Chinese luxury products—porcelain, silks, fine carpets, ivory and jade carvings—had been prized since the eighteenth century as symbols of wealth and status, Chinese people themselves were regarded as curiosities or as cheap labor from a weak, anachronistic nation. A shocking entry from Ralph Waldo Emerson's 1824 journal makes this attitude clear:

> The closer contemplation we condescend to bestow, the more disgustful is that booby nation. The Chinese Empire enjoys precisely a Mummy's reputation, that of having preserved to a hair for three or four thousand years the ugliest features in the world. I have no gift to see a meaning in the venerable vegetation of this extraordinary (nation) people. They are tools for other nations to use. Even miserable Africa can say I have hewn the wood and drawn the water to promote the civilization of other lands. But China, reverend dullness! hoary ideot!, all she can say at the convocation of nations must be—"I made the tea."[1]

Barnum's Chinese Museum flourished in the mid-1800s by displaying Chinese people as exotic sights, a living anthropological exhibit.[2] Since African slave labor had been abolished by the Emancipation Proclamation, Chinese workers were found to be useful for the completion of the difficult mountainous western portion of the transcontinental railroad, and some 120,000 Chinese men were imported for this purpose in the late 1860s. During the economic depression of the 1870s, the Chinese became scapegoats for the nation's economic ills, and to Bret Harte's later embarrassment, his 1870 poem "Plain Language from Truthful James," known as "The Heathen Chinee," achieved immense popularity and contributed greatly to the stereotyping of the Chinese as deceptive and "peculiar." Asian American historian Ronald Takaki has called this poem "the most powerful articulation of anti-Chinese fears and anxieties."[3] One political cartoon of the period depicts a buck-toothed slant-eyed creature with a dozen arms radiating from his shoulders, each busily at work; the uppermost arm is prominently raising aloft a sack of money labeled "For China," while a group of well-dressed white gentlemen stand unoccupied on the other side of a wall.[4] San Francisco declared a special holiday to bolster attendance at anti-Chinese rallies. Inflamed by Dennis Kearney's slogans, "The Chinese must go. They are stealing our jobs!," crowds became mobs attacking Chinatowns. Up and down the western coast of the United States, Chinese were harassed, driven en masse out of town, and even murdered. A Montana journalist spoke for many when he wrote: "We don't mind hearing of a Chinaman being killed now and then, but it has been coming too thick of late . . . soon there will be a scarcity of Chinese cheap labor in the country . . . . Don't kill them unless they deserve it, but when they do—why kill 'em lots."[5] Sinophobia became part of the platform of both political parties, culminating in the Chinese Exclusion Act of 1882,[6] which was in force until 1943. African Americans were given the vote in 1870, women in 1920, American Indians in 1924, and Asians not until 1954. From 1924 until 1954, any American who married a Chinese lost his or her citizenship. Thus, among the racial minorities in the United States, the Asian was apparently perceived as the most threatening, the most alien.

Synchronous with the racist thinking of the late nineteenth century was a populist desire to give a voice to hitherto silent peoples, to shift the focus from the upper and middle classes to the lower classes, among whom were ethnic and immigrant minorities. Because the majority of Chinese in the United States then were laborers, many lacked the education and the English language skills, and most lacked the leisure, to write in order to counteract the stereotyping and ignorance in the popular press. Nonetheless, between 1887 and 1915, we find the first texts written in English by people of Chinese ancestry, the earliest attempts by Asian subalterns to speak for themselves. Two of these writers were men, who wrote only autobiography and nonfiction; the other two were women, who wrote predominantly fiction, but who also published autobiographical texts. This paper will focus on the autobiographical writings of these four progenitors of Asian American literature since autobiography is an accessible genre necessarily tied to lived experience and to the social context shaping that experience.

When reading the four autobiographical texts in close succession, I was struck by how they clearly they separated themselves along gender lines. Their differences in tone, subject matter, treatment, and themes—seem directly linked to the gender of the authors. Though generalizations are always risky, and especially explosive in the area of gender studies, they are also of great interest. In the past ten or twelve years, research in women's autobiography has mushroomed. The books assembled and edited or written by Estelle Jelinek, Sidonie Smith, Shari Benstock, Celeste Schenck and Bella Brodzki, Valerie Sanders and Carolyn Heilbrun, Susan Bell and Marilyn Yalom, bear witness to this increased interest. My contribution to this discussion comes from a close analysis of four texts, named in chronological order: *When I Was a Boy in China* by Lee Yan Phou (Boston: Lothrup, Lee & Shepard Co., 1887); "Leaves From the Mental Portfolio of an Eurasian" by Sui Sin Far (*The Independent*, 21 January 1909); *My Life in China and America* by Yung Wing (New York: Henry Holt, 1909); and *Me, A Book of Remembrance* by Winnifred Eaton but published anonymously (New York: Century, 1915). Since I previously discussed the two women's writing in my book *Between Worlds: Women Writers of Chinese Ancestry*, I will focus this essay more closely on the texts of the male authors.

Though four texts is undoubtedly too small a sample from which to draw large generalizations, certain points of comparison—what Jelinek called "patterns"—become readily apparent when the texts are juxtaposed: the male writers seem more concerned with expressing what they have done, while the female writers are more concerned with expressing who they are. The men describe how they have acted upon the world; the women explain how they have been acted upon. The men assume what seems to them an appropriate public posture, for it is clear that they are addressing the world; the women, on the other hand, unafraid of the personal and the intimate, seem to be speaking either to themselves or to a relative or close friend and allow us as readers to look over their shoulders. Not surprisingly, these points accord well with the patterns that Jelinek remarked on more than a decade ago when she wrote:

> many male autobiographies . . . concentrate on chronicling the progress of their authors' professional or intellectual lives, usually in the affairs of the world, and their life stories are for the most part success stories . . . . On the other hand, women's autobiographies rarely mirror the establishment history of their times. They emphasize to a much less extent the public aspects of their lives, the affairs of the world, or even their careers, and concentrate instead on their personal lives—domestic details, family difficulties, close friends, and especially people who influenced them.[7]

A closer examination of these four texts will make my points clearer. But first, we need to establish the identities of the writers.

As far as our research has uncovered, the first Asian to graduate from a major American university (Yale class of 1854) was Yung Wing (1828–1912). He did not publish his autobiography until 1909, when he was eighty-one; however, one of the students in his Educational Mission, Lee Yan Phou (1861–1938?) published an autobiography in 1887, at the age of twenty-six. Thus, Lee Yan Phou's *When I Was a Boy in China* has the distinction of being the first text written in English and published by an Asian in the United States. The first Chinese American fiction writers were two Eurasian sisters—Edith Maude Eaton (1865–1914), who published under the pen name Sui Sin Far, and her younger sister Winnifred Eaton (1875–1954), who employed the pseudonym Onoto Watanna. Sui Sin Far's "A Chinese Feud" (*Land of Sunshine*, 1896) is, as far as is presently known, the first Chinese American short story, while Onoto Watanna's 1899 *Miss Nume of Japan* is the first Chinese American novel. In fact, these texts are the first Asian American fiction.

One may wonder why the first Chinese American novel is set in Japan and published by a woman with a Japanese-sounding pseudonym. For a more complete explanation, I refer the reader to my book *Between Worlds: Women Writers of Chinese Ancestry*,[8] but a brief summary may be useful here: the Japanese were highly regarded at the turn of the century, while the Chinese were much despised. Though their mother was Chinese and their father English, Winnifred assumed a Japanese persona in order, she later claimed, to avoid competition with her older sister. At the turn of the century in both Europe and the United States, the Japanese were in vogue for the aesthetic qualities of their culture and admired for their military victories against larger continental nations, namely China in 1895 and Russia in 1905. The Chinese, on the other hand, as noted above, were regarded as cheap coolie labor, a "yellow horde," stealing jobs from red-blooded American workers. If no one could differentiate between a Chinese and a Japanese anyway, and if one were Eurasian with facial features that didn't look particularly Asian, then one could choose one's identity and create one's self. This Winnifred Eaton did. Her Japanese-sounding pseudonym in conjunction with her storytelling powers stood her in good stead through a stream of novels (roughly one a year from 1899 to 1916), mostly best-sellers published by Harper's. Her second novel, *A Japanese Nightingale* (1901) was translated into several European languages and received a lavish stage production on Broadway, making Winnifred Eaton's work Asian America's first produced play. From 1916 to 1924, Winnifred Eaton wrote and adapted screenplays for Universal Studios and MGM. In her lifetime, she achieved the pinnacles of popular success: best-selling books, a Broadway play and Hollywood films. Though perhaps not a writer for all time, she was certainly a writer of her time. Her success was largely due to her exploitation of contemporary racial prejudices, and her current value to us is as a barometer of the taste of her day. Her assumption of an ethnic persona not hers by birth may be read in absolute terms as a morally reprehensible act, or in context, as the clever ruse of a trickster figure, a survival tactic, like camouflage in a time of war.

In the late nineteenth century, the Chinese in America were indeed embattled; however, sinophobia in the western portion of the United States was more fierce than in the East, where few Chinese were to be found. Yung Wing, by his own account, received a cordial reception in New England in 1846 (at age eighteen) upon his arrival in the train of the missionary, Reverend Samuel Robins Brown (Yale class of 1832). Yung Wing's ship's passage had been a gift of the ship owners, the Olyphant Brothers of New York. His expenses for two years as well as provision for his aging parents on Pedro Island, where he was born, near Macao, were provided by several generous patrons. Though Yung Wing never questioned, in print, the motives of his benefactors, attributing their generosity only to their goodness of character, we may speculate that the philanthropists and missionaries may have been interested in Yung Wing as an experiment: Can a Chinese, if taken young enough, be made into an American? Can a heathen be transformed into a Christian? The answer to both questions turned out to be yes.

For his part, Yung Wing, who had attended Miss Gutzlaff's boarding school in Macao from age seven onward, believed in the technical superiority of the West and longed to learn all he could. His command of the English language had to be excellent to enable him to attend Monson Academy in Monson, Massachusetts, where he did his college preparatory work, and then Yale, where he nearly flunked in mathematics but won prizes in English composition. Between 1847 and 1854, Yung Wing converted to Christianity, is recorded as a Congregationalist, and became a naturalized American citizen before the passage of the law prohibiting Asians from citizenship. He married an American woman and reared two sons in Hartford, Connecticut, while directing the Chinese Education Mission.

At the same time, however, he did not become so totally assimilated that he completely forgot his origins, for he was also a patriotic Chinese who spent his life shuttling back and forth between his two countries. While still an undergraduate at Yale, he noted that "the lamentable condition of China was before my mind constantly and weighed on my spirits."[9] Comparing his two countries, he recognized the technological superiority of the West, and longed to put his special education to the use of his native land. He thought to assist her by two methods: importing American technology into China and exporting Chinese youths to the United States for a Western education. As he put it:

> Before the close of my last year in college I had already sketched out what I should do. I was determined that the rising generation of China should enjoy the same educational advantages that I had enjoyed; that through Western education China might be regenerated, become enlightened and powerful. To accomplish that object became the guiding star of my ambition. (40–41)

After graduation from Yale, he pursued a variety of occupations in China. Finally, in 1863, he met and won the confidence of Tsang Kwoh Fan, the Viceroy of China and the general who had quelled the Taiping Rebellion, who was "literally and practically the supreme power of China at the time" (142). Tsang commissioned Yung Wing to buy arms-making machinery from the West. After visiting factories in France and England, Yung Wing decided to purchase the machinery from a manufacturer in Fitchburg, Massachusetts. The machinery was shipped to China, and was set up at a location northwest of Shanghai, in a machine shop that later became the Kiang Nan Arsenal. It was an impressive "establishment that cover[ed] several acres of ground and embrace[ed] under its roof all the leading branches of mechanical work" (153).

In 1871, with the support of Tsang Kwoh Fan, Yung Wing's vision of extending to other boys the educational advantages he had enjoyed became a reality. He persuaded the Manchu government to establish the Chinese Educational Mission, which was to sponsor 120 young Chinese boys between the ages of twelve and fifteen for fifteen years of study in the United States. They were to be sent to the United States in four yearly installments of thirty each, along with one teacher of Chinese so that the boys would not lose their facility in their native tongue. The Mission was in operation for ten years when conservative elements in China, fearing the Americanization of so many Chinese youths, combined with the increasing sinophobia in United States, brought it to an end. All one hundred students then in the program were recalled to China before any group had been able to complete the full fifteen-year program. Lee Yan Phou was one of these students in this Mission, but he managed to return to the U.S. and to graduate from Yale with the class of 1887. He also won a first prize in English composition and other prizes for oratory, honors in political science, history and law, and was elected to Phi Beta Kappa.[10]

All of the above facts concerning his career are to be found in Yung Wing's autobiography. Of his meetings with important officials of China and religious ministers and benefactors in the United States, Yung Wing is expansive and detailed, providing many names and dates. But the details of his personal life, apart from his voyages between his two nations, he reveals very little. Such information emerges only obliquely. For example, on 24 February 1875 Yung Wing married Mary Louise Kellogg, but this information cannot be found in his 246-page autobiography. His marriage is alluded to only in a nonrestrictive clause, referring to his wife by association when recounting his trip to Peru to investigate the living conditions of the Chinese coolies. He writes, "My friend, the Rev. J. H. Twichell, and Dr. E. W. Kellogg, who afterwards became my brother-in-law, accompanied me on my trip." His brother-in-law's name deserves mention, and later even his mother-in-law's, who assisted him with their two sons after his wife's untimely death, but his wife's name never appears in Yung Wing's text. Furthermore, that miscegnation was illegal in approximately one half of the states in the union is another topic on which he is completely silent. However, he devoted an entire chapter to his investigation of the inhumane treatment of the coolies in Peru and to his role in stopping the coolie traffic there. Undoubtedly, it was safe to write of racist exploitation in a far-off land, but much more difficult to treat such matters close to home.

Clearly, Yung Wing's intended audience is a white readership. His tone is polite and restrained. He is well aware of the privilege conferred on him, for as he put it, "Being the first Chinaman who had even been known to go through a first-class American college, I naturally attracted considerable attention" (39). As a Yale graduate and a Confucian gentleman, he bore the weighty responsibility of service to his country. Like an earlier American autobiographer, Ben Franklin, Yung Wing recognizes that he has played a singular role in history, and while he believes he should assume the cloak of modesty, at the same time he revels in all his public accomplishments.

Both Yung Wing's *My Life in China and America* and Sui Sin Far's "Leaves from the Mental Portfolio of an Eurasian" were published in 1909; both appeared close to the end of their authors' lives, though Sui Sin Far, dying at age forty-nine, lived slightly more than half of Yung Wing's eighty-four years. Her seven-page autobiographical essay is a mere fraction of the length of his 246-page book, but both are works of summing up, of looking backward over a lifetime of accomplishment, and both are written from a perspective between worlds. Sui Sin Far's between-world perspective is apparent in the essay's focus on her Eurasian identity while Yung Wing's position must be interpolated from his numerous oceanic crossings and his single overt disclosure. This disclosure centers on the occasion of his ship's landing in Hong Kong after his eight-year stay in the United States. Here is his description of that event:

> As we approached Hong Kong, a Chinese pilot boarded us. The captain wanted me to ask him whether there were any dangerous rocks and shoals nearby. I could not for the life of me recall my Chinese in order to interpret for him; the pilot himself understood English, and he was the first Chinese teacher to give me the terms in Chinese for dangerous rocks and shoals. So the skipper and Macy, and a few other persons who were present at the time, had the laugh on me, who, being a Chinese, yet was not able to speak the language. (48)

Though the scene is presented in a light, humorous fashion, it must have been traumatic to discover himself, a proud graduate of Yale University, no longer able to communicate with his compatriots. Yung does, however, describe an emotional reunion and a long conversation with his mother that took place a few days later, during which he mentions no difficulty with the language. Therefore, either his native dialect was not Cantonese or the required specific nautical vocabulary was not forthcoming at the moment of landing. Yet, he does explain that, having studied Chinese only four years, he had not had a firm grounding in his mother tongue. He needed six months to regain his verbal facility with Cantonese and, since Chinese is a nonalphabetic language, two years of intensive study to acquire a writing ability.

These few pages devoted to his efforts to regain his native tongue are one of the rare opportunities Yung Wing indulges in personal disclosure. Though Sui Sin Far is reluctant to reveal specific dates and names of persons and places, the very focus of her essay—what it was to be an Eurasian in the English-speaking world (Macclesfield, England; Hudson City, New York; Montreal, Quebec; and Kingston, Jamaica)—requires personal disclosure. After an extensive study of the autobiographical canon in Western literature, Jelinek concluded; "Neither women nor men are likely to explore or to reveal painful and intimate memories in their autobiographies" (10). However, "Leaves" centers on the uncomfortable subject of racism, specifically sinophobia and its ramifications in Sui Sin Far's life. Though she never names the disease, Sui Sin Far provides a catalogue of symptoms. The poignant anecdotes that structure her entire essay all pinpoint the alienation and awareness of difference imposed on her from age four through forty.

A few examples from "Leaves" will demonstrate my point. As a four-year old attending a child's birthday party in England, she is called from her play for inspection by an elderly man who had just been informed about her ancestry. "Ah yes, a curious little creature," he says examining her features through his eyeglasses. Made to feel like anthropological specimen, she no longer enjoys the party and hides behind a door until the party's end. As adolescents in Montreal, her sisters overhear a young man in their dancing class remark that "he'd rather marry a pig than a girl with Chinese blood in her veins." As a adult and a newcomer to a "little town away off on the north shore of a big lake," she attends a dinner party during which her new employer remarks, "Somehow or other . . . I cannot reconcile myself to the thought that the Chinese are humans like ourselves." The town clerk responds, "A Chinaman is, in my eyes, more repulsive than a nigger." To which her employer adds, "Now, the Japanese are different altogether. There is something bright and likable about those men."[11]

Though her younger sister's response to this last statement was to masquerade as the admired Japanese, Sui Sin Far's reaction was to fight the injustice of this sentiment. She shared Yung Wing's "patriotism," a feeling of pride in her mother's people as evident in the following disclosure:

> Whenever I have the opportunity I steal away to the library and read every book I can find on China and the Chinese. I learn that China is the oldest civilized nation on the face of the earth and a few other things. At eighteen years of age what troubles me is not that I am what I am, but that others are ignorant of my superiority. I am small, but my feelings are big—and great is my vanity. (128)

Later, as a journalist, she asserts her maternal ancestry by choosing a Chinese pseudonym and uses her pen as a weapon in the battle against the discrimination and abuse of the Chinese:

> I meet many Chinese persons, and when they get into trouble am often called upon to fight their battles in the papers. This I enjoy. My heart leaps for joy when I read one day an article signed by a New York Chinese in which he declares "The Chinese in America owe an everlasting debt of gratitude to Sui Sin Far for the bold stand she has taken in their defense." (128)

This is the only passage in "Leaves" that may be construed as focused on her work as a means of making a mark on the world, but the thrust of this episode is not so much to call attention to the recognition she received as to show what she has done with the heightened consciousness of her chosen ethnicity. The entire essay has been devoted to the gradual growth of this consciousness.

Sui Sin Far's sense of purpose and her desire to serve her mother's people was no less strong than Yung Wing's, yet her autobiographical essay is not filled with her public accomplishments, nor the names of the famous people she met. (She did meet famous people, including Dr. Sun Yat Sen, the first president of the Republic of China.) She does not tell the reader about the national magazines in which her stories were published nor the positive reviews she received from such influential publications as *The New York Times* and *The Independent*. Instead, she focuses on the development of her own Chinese identity and pride, forged in the furnaces of pain and humiliation.

Of the experience of being a Chinese in a white society, the entire focus of Sui Sin Far's essay, Yung Wing writes not a word. Nor does courtship and marriage enter into his narrative, though he lived with his wife nearly twenty years and she bore him two sons. Sui Sin Far, on the other hand, devotes a disproportionately large amount of space to a marriage that didn't take place in the story of one Chinese Eurasian she knows "who allowed herself to become engaged to a white man after refusing him nine times." This woman had finally agreed to the man's persistent proposals only "because the world is so cruel and sneering to a single woman" and "because the young woman had a married mother and married sisters, who were always picking at her and gossiping over her independent manner of living" (131). But when the fiancé hints one day that he would feel more comfortable if she would pretend to be Japanese, she returns his ring and writes in her diary: "Joy, oh, joy! I'm free once more. Never again shall I be untrue to my own heart. Never again will I allow any one to 'hound' or 'sneer' me into matrimony" (132). Though she claims that this is the story of an acquaintance by introducing it with the words, "I know of one who . . . ," it has the ring of a personal disclosure, for how often do acquaintances share journal entries?

The space devoted to this episode is clearly intended to be an explication of the author's own courageous spirit of independence. In a virulently sinophobic period, Sui Sin Far dares to claim her Chinese ancestry; during a period when unmarried women were regarded with opprobrium, Sui Sin Far calls herself "a very serious and sober-minded spinster indeed" (130).

At one juncture in his life, Yung Wing also chose independence to conforming to external pressures. After completing his studies at the Monson School, he was offered a college scholarship on the condition that he become a Christian missionary after graduation. He refused this scholarship despite the fact that he himself had converted and that he had no alternate means of support at the time. It is much easier to be swept along with a current than to stand firm against it; to hold fast to principles that seem to go against one's immediate best interests requires unusual courage and determination. This both Yung Wing and Sui Sin Far did.

It should be clear by now that though their texts reveal a shared love for China as well as a strong independence of spirit, the tone and content of both writings differ greatly. Yung Wing's autobiography is a public document, written, like Benjamin Franklin's *Autobiography*, with an eye to posterity. He reveals his attempts to bring China out of her feudal somnolence into a technologically advanced modernity. Sui Sin Far's essay by contrast is an intimate piece, more a personal musing directed to herself than a public statement directed to others. She is aware of an audience, of course, which is why she is not more forthcoming with names and dates, but she courageously probes the troubling intimate questions which plagued her as a child:

> Why are we what we are? I and my brothers and sisters? Why did God make us to be hooted and stared at? Papa is English, mamma is Chinese. Why couldn't we have been either one thing or the other? Why is my mother's race despised? I look into the faces of my father and mother. Is she not every bit as dear and good as he? Why? Why? (127–28)

She is engaged in introspection, in exploring her own complex identity. The plight of the Eurasian, not wholly accepted by either side of her parentage, engaged her sympathies, and several of the best stories in her collection *Mrs. Spring Fragrance*[12] are devoted to the Eurasian.

In contrast to the texts by Yung Wing and Sui Sin Far, Lee Yan Phou's *When I Was a Boy In China* and Onoto Watanna's *Me: A Book of Remembrance* are both rather strange texts when read in the light of their claims to be autobiographical. The former was the brainchild of the publisher, the first in a series of books solicited by the D. Lothrop Publishing company, as Elaine Kim revealed,[13] and the latter is structured and written like a novel, with rising action, complication and denouement—the seventeen-year-old protagonist, whom the author names Nora Ascough, leaves home to make her way in the world, becomes engaged to three men in one year while falling in love with a fourth, is disillusioned in her first love but writes and publishes her first novel. To write what purports to be an autobiography (subtitled "A Book of Remembrance") but to publish it anonymously and to give oneself a fictional name throughout is to produce a very odd text.

Lee's book is very consciously addressed to an audience that knows little or nothing about Chinese culture and customs, and the author takes up the role of tourist guide, or as Elaine Kim puts it of another Asian American author, a "transmitter of Chinese 'culture' to non-Chinese" and "ambassador of good will."[14] Lee's text clearly has an anthropological and didactic thrust; its purpose is to inform, as evidenced in the general topics which make up most of the chapter titles: "Chinese Cookery," "Games and Pastimes," "Girls of My

Acquaintance," "Schools and School Life," "Religions," "Chinese Holidays." Lee is most conscientious in his undertaking: for example, it takes him an entire paragraph to tell us his birthdate because such a seemingly simple fact entails a rather detailed explanation of the Chinese calendar. Though such an overwhelming task might lead a reader into the expectation of unrelieved dullness, occasionally Lee's personality comes though in the informal and even humorous quality of his tone. The first paragraph is a fitting example:

> On a certain day in the year 1861, I was born. I cannot give you the exact date, because the Chinese year is different from the English year, and our months being lunar, that is, reckoned by the revolution of the moon around the earth, are consequently shorter than yours. We reckon time from the accessions of Emperors, and also by cycles of sixty years each. The year of my birth, 1861, was the first year of the Emperor Tung-che. We have twelve months ordinarily; and we say, instead of "January, February," etc., "Regular Moon, Second Moon, Third Moon," etc. Each third year is a leap year, and has an extra month so as to make each of the lunar years equal to a solar year. Accordingly, taking the English calendar as a standard, our New Year's Day varies. Therefore, although I am sure that I was born on the twenty-first day of the Second Moon, in Chinese, I don't know my exact birthday in English; and consequently, living in America as I have for many years, I have been cheated of my birthday celebration.[15]

His explanation of the Chinese calendrical system, in its minute specificity and complexity, verges on the ludicrous, but it is offset by the direct address to his non-Chinese audience, his awareness of their lack of information, and, at the very end, by his personal humorous touch. In the very last clause, the passage is redeemed and raised from the level of an encyclopedia article. The book is the same. To counteract the deadening effect of a compendium of facts, Lee seeks to draw his audience in and to make the experience an immediate one. After telling us that the household servants are going to market, he writes, "Let us follow them" and then proceeds to describe in visual and auditory detail the sights on their way, in the fashion of a National Geographic film: "Here are incense-shops, butcher-shops and grocery-stores, fish-stalls and vegetable-stands. The stone pavement is slippery with mud. The din is deafening" (27). Lee Yan Phou seems a reasonable, urbane, well-read, Christian Chinese gentleman, equally comfortable with alluding to the witches in *Macbeth* and at the same time asserting that few books in English are the equal of the Chinese classic, "the unfailing delight of all classes; I mean the *History* [*Romance*] *of the Three Kingdoms*" (82).

The illustrations in the book, however, are very much at odds with the text. It would seem that the publisher made a random selection from a readily accessible photographic archive of Chinese people and life and inserted them throughout the book often in total disregard for the text. For example, while Lee is describing the layout of his upper-middle-class grandfather's fifteen-room home and its furnishings, we are given the photograph of a barefoot "Chinese beggar boy." What has this photo to do with the text? The discrepancy is jarring, and it seems odd that no one involved in putting together this volume noticed the disjuncture. Another jarring juxtaposition is the book's cover and the author's photograph. The cover drawing shows a highly-exoticized slant-eyed boy flying a bat-shaped kite; his queue flies tail-like in the wind while the kite string trails tail-like at his back. By contrast, the author's photograph, opposite the title page, reveals a wide-eyed young man with short cropped hair and a mustache in a double-breasted western jacket, looking bright and intense. The two images clash in their intent: the cover exoticized and estranging, the author's photograph familiar and engaging. It is very unlikely that Lee Yan Phou, who later married an American woman and became a journalist in the United States, would have selected these particular images and this cover to represent him. In fact, the topics of the chapters themselves may not even have been the ones he would have written had he been given his choice.

The text takes on greater interest in the last three chapters, which finally become a personal narrative. They are entitled "How I Went to Shanghai," "How I Prepared for America," and "First Experiences in America." The most amusing sentence in the entire book may be found in the last chapter in which Lee describes his railroad journey cross-country:

> Nothing occurred on our Eastward journey to mar the enjoyment of our first ride on the steam cars—excepting a train robbery, a consequent smash-up of the engine, and the murder of the engineer. (107)

The matter-of-fact tone of the bland assertion "nothing occurred" is counteracted by the series of catastrophic events "train robbery," "smash-up," "murder," leading clearly to the conclusion that the author is in jest. This intriguing introductory sentence is followed by a brief description of these mishaps in which the author's sense of adventure is readily apparent.

A final example of his bemused tone occurs in the last paragraph of the book. Lee knew little English on his arrival in Springfield, Massachusetts, at age thirteen, but he learned quickly, as he describes in his language lessons at the hands of his sober Puritan hosts:

> We learned English by object-lessons. At table we were always told the names of certain dishes, and then assured that if we could not remember the name we were not to partake of that article of food. Taught by this method, our progress was rapid and surprising. (111)

But since Lee, at this point, has begun to deal with life in the United States, he is falling outside the stated scope of the book—his boyhood in China—and the narrative is abruptly and unfortunately cut short just as it begins to become really interesting. Though I have focused on these few humorous and personable passages, they are, however, actually the exception in a book mainly given to rather dry explications of culture and customs.

Me, on the other hand, is an entirely personal book—so personal and revealing that the author published it anonymously for fear of dispelling the persona she had created for herself as a best-selling Japanese author. In *Me*, Winnifred Eaton clearly states that she was born in Montreal, the eighth in a family of sixteen children. She reveals the poverty of her childhood home, where her father set up his easel in the kitchen because that was the only warm room in the house and where the noise and confusion of so many siblings became her image of hell. Of her mother's ethnicity, she writes only vaguely, "She was a native of a far-distant land, and I do not think she ever got over the feeling of being a stranger in Canada."[16]

Like her sister Edith, in fact, like all women, Winnifred Eaton was conscious of the gaze of others, for as R. D. Laing has pointed out, "Self-identity ('I' looking at 'me') is constituted not only by our looking at ourselves, but also by our looking at us and our reconstitution of and alteration of these views of others about us."[17] Winnifred mentions others' curiosity about her ethnicity, noting that they looked at her "as if I interested them or they were puzzled to know my nationality. I would have given anything to look less foreign. My darkness marked and crushed me, I who loved blondness like the sun" (166).

Nothing in either Yung Wing's book or Lee Yan Phou's gives the slightest indication of their awareness of or concern about how others perceived them, despite the fact that a Chinese man in the Eastern United States in the late nineteenth century was undoubtedly a rarity and and must have provoked numerous and varied responses and despite the fact that this period was one of virulent sinophobia. For the men, this facet of life in the United States seemed to be beneath their notice. Yung was more concerned with relating how he had made his mark on the world; Lee with explaining the world from which he had come. Winnifred Eaton also explained her early world in order to show how far she had had to come to write her first book. Though she gives her protagonist a fictional name, her narrative is filled with personal revelations, with the inferiority complex of a dark-haired girl in a blond-loving society, with the emotions of unrequited first love, with the hopes and fears of a beginning writer, with the sexual harassment a young woman encounters making her way in the world without the insulation and support of a wealthy family:

> I have known what it is to be pitied, chafed, insulted, "jollied"; I have had coarse or delicate compliments paid me; I have been cursed at and ordered to "clear out"—Oh, all the crucifying experiences that only a girl who looks hard for work knows! I've had a fat broker tell me that a girl like me didn't need to work; I've had a pious-looking hypocrite chuck me under the chin out of sight of the clerks in the outer offices. I've had a man make me a cold business proposition of $10 a week for my services as a stenographer and typewriter, and $10 a week for my services as something else. I've had men brutally touch me, and when I have resented it, I have seen them spit across the room in my direction. (124)

In conclusion, I realize that the smallness of my sample makes any generalizations drawn from them of limited value. Other factors may also need to be taken into account, such as the age of the authors when they arrived in America; Sui Sin Far was six and Onoto Watanna was born in Montreal while the men were in their late or mid-teens, with their sense of identity already formed in a land where they were the dominant people. However, the four texts themselves clearly substantiate certain gender differences noted by other scholars of women's autobiographies. Men are more concerned with conveying information, with solving problems, with their selves as actors upon the world. Women are more concerned with weaving relationships and interacting with others and with their own subjectivity, their inner, emotional, and psychological lives. Our ways are different, but gender roles are by definition learned ways. As Bell and Yalom put it their introduction to *Revealing Lives:*

> Gender, as we understand and use it, is that deep imprinting of cultural beliefs, values and expectations on one's biological sex, forming a fundamental component in a person's sense of identity. When viewed collectively, it is a system of difference between men and women, and a system of relations between the two groups, with males almost universally in a position of dominance.[18]

Despite the Chinese ethnicity of these four turn-of-the-century writers, an ethnicity that would put them at a disadvantage in the dominant American society, the males clearly wrote from a position of strength and confidence while the women wrote with an awareness of weakness stemming both from their ethnicity and their sex. This would seem to corroborate Bell and Yalom's assertion that "males [are] almost universally in a position of dominance." However, in the genre of autobiography, greater awareness of the interior self and greater revelation of this interiority result undoubtedly in more interesting and better autobiographies. Thus, the hierarchy is inverted.

Notes

1. From *Journals and Miscellaneous Notebooks of Ralph Waldo Emerson*, ed. William H. Gilman, et al. (Cambridge: Belknap Press of Harvard University, 1960-82), 2: 224. Quoted in Stuart Creighton Miller, *The Unwelcome Immigrant: The American Image of the Chinese, 1785-1882* (Berkeley and Los Angeles: University of California Press, 1969), 16.
2. See Judy Yung, *Chinese Women of America: A Pictorial History* (San Francisco: Chinese Culture Foundation of San Francisco, 1986), 16-17.
3. According to historian Ronald Takaki, "The *New York Globe* had to publish Harte's poem twice in order to satisfy the demands of its readership." See *Strangers from a Different Shore* (New York: Penguin Books, 1989), 104.
4. See Diane Mark and Ginger Chih, *A Place Called Chinese America* (Dubuque: Kendall/Hunt Publishing Company, 1982), 35.
5. *Mountanian*, 27 March 1873. Quoted in Stanford Lyman, "Strangers in the City: the Chinese in the Urban Frontier" in *Roots: An Asian American Reader*, ed. Amy Tachiki, Eddie Wong, and Franklin Odo, with Buck Wong (Los Angeles: UCLA Asian American Studies Center, 1971), 165.
6. For more complete accounts of the anti-Chinese violence, see Sucheng Chan, *Asian Americans: An Interpretative History* (Boston: Twayne, 1991); Ronald Takaki, *Strangers from a Different Shore* (New York: Penguin, 1989); Jack Chen, *The*

Chinese of America (San Francisco: Harper & Row, 1980); and Stanford Lyman, "Strangers in the City: the Chinese in the Urban Frontier" in *Roots: An Asian American Reader.*

7. Estelle C. Jelinek, "Introduction: Women's Autobiography and the Male Tradition" in *Women's Autobiography* (Bloomington: Indiana University Press, 1980), 7-8.

8. Amy Ling, *Between Worlds: Women Writers of Chinese Ancestry* (New York: Pergamon Press, now Teacher's Press of Columbia University, 1990).

9. Yung Wing, *My Life in China and America* (New York: Henry Holt and Company, 1909), 40.

10. Information provided in the Quarter Century Record Class of 1887 by Yale University. I am indebted to my graduate student, Anne Nahn, for her unflagging effort in tracking down this information.

11. Sui Sin Far, "Leaves from the Mental Portfolio of an Eurasian," *The Independent* (21 January 1909): 125-32.

12. Sui Sin Far, *Mrs. Spring Fragrance* (Chicago: A. C. McClurg, 1912).

13. Indeed, I note after writing this sentence that Elaine Kim has stated that the publisher initiated this series: "At the turn of the century, a series of books by young men from various lands was solicited by the D. Lothrop Publishing Company. Lee Yan Phou's *When I Was a Boy in China* (1887) was one of the first of these, and New Il-Han's *When I Was a Boy in Korea* (1928) was one of the last." See *Asian American Literature: An Introduction to the Writings and Their Social Context* (Philadelphia: Temple University Press, 1982), 25.

14. Kim, *Asian American Literature*, 72, 24.

15. Lee Yan Phou, *When I was a Boy in China* (Boston, Mass.: D. Lothrop, 1887), 7-8. (Subsequent references will be in parentheses in the text.)

16. Anonymous, *Me: A Book of Rememberance* (New York: Century, 1915).

17. H. Phillipson Laing and A. R. Lee, *Interpersonal Perception* (London: Tavistock Publications, 1966), 5-6, quoted in Elizabeth W. Bruss, *Autobiographical Acts: The Changing Situation of a Literary Genre* (Baltimore: Johns Hopkins University Press, 1976), 13.

18. Susan Groag Bell and Marilyn Yalom, eds., *Revealing Lives: Autobiography, Biography, and Gender* (Albany: State University of New York Press, 1990), 5.

Native American Literatures and the Canon: The Case of Zitkala-Ša

PATRICIA OKKER

CANON formation is, among other things, a process of transplantation. When the editors of an American literature anthology decide to include, say, Stephen Crane's "The Blue Hotel," they remove it from its original place of publication (in this case *Collier's Weekly*) and place it amidst other American "masterpieces." Such changes in context pose considerable challenges for any canon revision that seeks to include Native American literatures. While the new readership of Crane's story shares roughly the same cultural backgrounds and assumptions as its original audience, Native American texts are often placed within a completely alien context. In the case of oral narratives, for instance, Kenneth M. Roemer has explained how readers unfamiliar with their cultural contexts may dismiss them as "'quaint' or 'primitive' fairy tales, folklore, or superstitions."[1] Finding space in an American literature anthology for Native American texts, then, may ensure that some Euroamerican students read these texts, but it is no guarantee they will understand or appreciate them.

That writers, when canonized, are placed not simply within American literature but rather within a particular literary period heightens the difficulties of canonizing Native American literatures. Such texts are often excluded from discussions of mid-nineteenth-century literature in part because, with their typical emphasis on tribal identity and community, they are not likely to celebrate individualism, as do canonical romantic writers. The very dating of literary periods, moreover, can decrease the likelihood of canonization. However questionable it may be within the American Canon to mark literary periods, as we so typically do, with reference to major wars, it is even more dubious in regard to Native American and other minority literatures. Might not the removal policies of the 1830s or the Dawes Severalty Act of 1887, which divided Native

American tribal lands into individually owned sections, more accurately reflect changes within Native American cultures than would the traditional dating of American literature? Even if one were to accept wars as viable frames for literary periods, surely one could find more appropriate starting and ending points than the Civil War and World War I, a frame that significantly overlooks the series of wars undertaken during the same period by the United States government against Native Americans. Perhaps the Black Hawk or Seminole Wars or the battles at Sand Creek, Little Bighorn, or Wounded Knee ought to be used to frame Native American texts and be identified as more appropriate cultural and literary turning points.

Despite the problems of periodization and the dangers of removing texts from their tribal contexts, nevertheless Native American writers have been increasingly included within the canon of American literature. Virtually all American literature anthologies now include some Native American texts, and conference programs and job lists demonstrate the belated but sincere academic recognition of Native American literature.

One Native American writer included in the process of canon revision and who will serve as a case study of the problems I have specified is Zitkala-Ša (Red Bird) or Gertrude Simmons Bonnin (1876–1938).[2] She was a Dakota Sioux woman who lived on the Yankton reservation until she was eight, when she left to attend and later to teach at Indian schools for children. Zitkala-Ša's writing career began with the publication of three autobiographical essays in *The Atlantic Monthly* in 1900. Although she became increasingly active in politics rather than writing, Zitkala-Ša's literary productions include short stories, poetry, essays, and a book titled *Old Indian Legends* (1901). A collected volume of some of her work appeared in 1921 as *American Indian Stories*.[3]

Zitkala-Ša presents an important opportunity to study the addition of Native American literatures to the canon during the realistic period. While several other Native American writers are included in current literary anthologies during this period (Sarah Winnemucca Hopkins, Standing Bear, and Charles Alexander Eastman, for instance), no other appears as often as does Zitkala-Ša. Her writings now appear in *The Heath Anthology of American Literature* and both the two-volume and short editions of *The Norton Anthology of American Literature*, and she has recently been included in anthologies of American women writers, including Judith Fetterley and

Marjorie Pryse's *American Women Regionalists*, 1850–1910 and Eileen Barrett and Mary Cullinan's *American Women Writers*. Moreover, Zitkala-Ša's two books are both currently in print.[4]

Despite her presence in these anthologies, however, few scholars have studied Zitkala-Ša's works in much detail. Several biographical essays have appeared, most notably Dexter Fisher's study of her career,[5] but literary analysis of her work remains scanty and partial. I have found only three entries on Zitkala-Ša in the bibliography of the Modern Language Association, and she is absent even from literary studies of Native American autobiography.[6] Like the woman herself, who moved between Dakota and Euroamerican cultures, Zitkala-Ša's place within literary culture is at best tentative and perhaps precarious. Neither fully admitted to the canon nor completely excluded from it, Zitkala-Ša's work demonstrates that, for most Native American texts, entrance into the canon of literary anthologies is a difficult and problematic process. The same qualities that justify a text's inclusion into one canon, say the canon of American women writers, may eliminate it from another, and the canons themselves often function not only as sets of "great" texts, but as frames with which to interpret—and even misinterpret—texts.

Although we now too often simplistically associate canon revision with antiracism, the process of canonization for Zitkala-Ša ironically began with the popular fascination with the "exotic Indian" at the beginning of the twentieth century. Much of her periodical pieces published between 1900 and 1902, in fact, appeared alongside literature by whites about Native Americans. Her stories "The Soft-Hearted Sioux" and "The Trial Path," for instance, appeared in the same volumes of *Harper's Monthly Magazine* as George Bird Grinnell's ethnographic work, a story by Frederic Remington (best known for his sculptures and paintings depicting Indians as hostile and inferior to whites), and even an essay by James Mooney titled "Our Last Cannibal Tribe." Even more jarring is the context of Zitkala-Ša's series of three autobiographical essays, which first appeared in *The Atlantic Monthly* in 1900 while the magazine was publishing Mary Johnston's historical novel, *To Have and To Hold*. In the issue in which Zitkala-Ša's first essay appeared, Johnston's protagonist, the gentleman Captain Ralph Percy, is being held captive by the Indians, repeatedly described in the novel as violent "heathens" and deceitful "savages," capable of "hellish" torture. By the third installment of her autobiography, the contrast between Zitkala-Ša's portrait of Native Americans and Johnston's was even greater.

As one reviewer admiringly put it, Johnston's characterization of Indians is "the picture of the wily Opechancanough, his body sleek with oil, glistening all over in the sunshine with powdered antimony, speaking fair words with a smiling face, while the inner devil looks through his cold snake eyes,—this is very fine."[7] The ironies of this context are heightened even further when one considers that Johnston's *To Have and To Hold* almost doubled *The Atlantic Monthly's* circulation.[8] The popularity of this highly stereotypical and racist image of Native Americans, then, ironically contributed to the canonization of Zitkala-Ša.

While the condescending fascination with Native Americans suggests at least one of the reasons that Zitkala-Ša's work found its way into popular periodicals, the importance of *The Atlantic Monthly* and *Harper's Monthly Magazine* in the historical formation of American literary realism no doubt contributed to her subsequent inclusion in late twentieth-century literary anthologies. Although not appearing during William Dean Howells's editorship, Zitkala-Ša's *Atlantic* essays were published amidst such established writers as Edith Wharton, Henry James, Howells, and Jack London; and her pieces in *Harper's* in 1901 appeared alongside work by Thomas Hardy, Mark Twain, Bret Harte, Edith Wharton, Grace King, and Mary Wilkins Freeman. Had these same texts appeared in Native American periodicals such as *Twin Territories* or *Iapi oaye*, anthology editors would likely have never found them.[9] Indeed, none of the current anthologies include or even mention her story published in the *Indian Leader* or her poetry in *American Indian Magazine*, which she edited from 1918 until 1919.[10]

The status of *Harper's* and *The Atlantic Monthly*, however, cannot fully account for the canonization of Zitkala-Ša's work, for only some of her publications in these magazines have been included in current anthologies. Canon formation has always involved the selection not merely of writers, but also of particular texts,[11] and to a great extent editors of anthologies have elected to canonize Zitkala-Ša's essays instead of her fiction or poetry, especially the autobiographical series that traces her life from her tribal home with her mother on the reservation to her "education" at the Indian school away from home and, finally, to her work as a teacher at an eastern school for Indian children. The fourth essay currently included in some anthologies is titled "Why I Am a Pagan." With the exception of Fetterley and Pryse's inclusion of "The Trial Path," the two short stories published in *Harper's* do not appear in American literature anthologies. Nor do any current American literature anthologies include any of the traditional legends Zitkala-Ša published in 1901 as *Old Indian Legends*.

As is the case with many Native American writers, the preference for Zitkala-Ša's essays within the canon is best understood in terms of the extent to which her writings fit within the Euroamerican literary tradition. Her *Old Indian Legends*, for example, does not fulfill the conventions either of realism or, more generally, of the Euroamerican literary tradition. Although Zitkala-Ša explains in her introduction that the legends "belong quite as much to the blue-eyed little patriot as to the black-haired aborigine," the legends themselves never refer to the world of blue-eyed people. Furthermore, with muskrats that speak, a man that transforms into a peacock, a red eagle that terrorizes an entire village, and an evil spirit disguised as a baby, these legends cannot be characterized as conventionally realistic. Rather than seek to represent actual contemporary American life and common people, these legends tell of the mythic past in which the currently probable or ordinary is of no particular concern. As written versions of oral stories, moreover, these tales represent a very different idea of authorship from that in Euroamerican literature. Rejecting the idea of an individual author producing an original written text, Zitkala-Ša highlights her role as one of many storytellers. The title page lists the tales as "Retold by Zitkala-Ša," and in the preface she discussed the oral origins of these texts: "Under an open sky, nestling close to the earth, the old Dakota story-tellers have told me these legends. In both Dakotas, North and South, I have often listened to the same story told over again by a new storyteller."[12] By emphasizing the oral traditions of these tales, Zitkala-Ša distances herself from the Euroamerican notion that written texts—rather than oral performances—are the primary means of cultural memory.

Although Zitkala-Ša's short stories are presented as original written texts and, thus, much closer to Euroamerican understandings of literature, they, too, have been neglected in American literature anthologies.[13] In order to explore why that might be, consider "The Soft-Hearted Sioux," first published in *Harper's* in March 1901. The story, told in first-person narration by a man in his twenties, begins as he remembers his family's instructions, years earlier, for him to become a great warrior, husband, and hunter. The narrator rejected these instructions, however, spending nine years at a mission school: "I did not grow up the warrior, huntsman, and husband I was to have been. At the mission school I learned it was wrong to kill. Nine winters I hunted for the soft heart of Christ."[14] Returning home as a Christian missionary, the narrator finds his father ill and the villagers distrustful of his own "soft heart" that cannot even feed his father. When the village moves on and leaves him alone with his mother and father, now starving, the father instructs his son to kill one of the white man's cattle. The son obeys, but on his way home, he kills a white man who, presumably, pursued him for the "crime" of stealing the animal. In the final section of the story, the narrator writes from a jail cell, awaiting his hanging scheduled for the following day.

The absence of "The Soft-Hearted Sioux" in current anthologies may well arise from its departure from the conventions of American literary realism. Although the story does portray a contemporary part of American life and focuses, as do many realistic novels, on the moral tensions between a character and his or her society, it does so with none of the detailed observation found within realism. Quite the contrary, "The Soft-Hearted Sioux" focuses on the protagonist's emotional trauma, which cannot be detected through observation. Rather than document the details of daily life, the narrator repeatedly describes how his "heart was too much stirred," how with "every heart-throb [he] grew more impatient," and how a "tremor played about [his] heart and a chill cooled the fire in [his] veins" (505–7). Similarly, the narrator describes in melodramatic terms the image of his father's starvation:

> There I grew dizzy and numb. My eyes swam in tears. Before me lay my old gray-haired father sobbing like a child. In his horny hands he clutched the buffalo-robe, and with his teeth he was gnawing off the edges. Chewing the dry stiff hair and buffalo-skin, my father's eyes sought my hands. (507–8)

American realistic fiction is not, of course, without its moments of emotional intensity, but the degree to which this story immerses its readers in such moments at the expense of verisimilitude of detail suggests its departure from the conventions of literary realism.

While eliminating "The Soft-Hearted Sioux" from a truly realistic canon, the melodramatic elements within "The Soft-Hearted Sioux" suggest its affinity with late nineteenth-century American naturalism. Like the conventional naturalistic text, the story portrays a violent act that emerges from a common person's struggle for existence. Moreover, like many naturalistic novels, "The Soft-Hearted

Sioux" portrays both the powerful determinism of the environment and what Donald Pizer has described as a character's "compensating humanistic value."[15] Here, the protagonist's violent act is simultaneously a heroic insistence on ethical principles and a virtually unavoidable response to a controlling environment.

Ironically, however, these naturalistic elements within "The Soft-Hearted Sioux" may have contributed to the story's critical neglect because its melodrama and active, violent protagonist strongly contrast with the romanticized stereotype, popular throughout the nineteenth and twentieth centuries, of the dying and generally stoic Indian. Naturalism's melodrama and heroic violence, in other words, may be canonical only when depicted in terms of Euroamerican characters. Indeed, the best known depiction of a Native American character in naturalistic fiction—in Jack London's "The Law of Life"—depends entirely on the stereotype of the dying and stoic Indian. However sympathetic the portrait of Old Koskoosh may be and despite its insistence on the importance of the race rather than the individual, "The Law of Life" can be read as one of the many stories of the time that portray the death of a single, noble Native American. Like the texts published earlier in the century that, as Robert F. Berkhofer, Jr., has described, "romanticize the safely dead Indian,"[16] this story presents Old Koskoosh's death as natural and inevitable, and it does so while glorifying his—and our—limited emotional response to his dying.

While London's portrayal of the stoic Old Koskoosh has found a place within the canon (and immediately precedes the selection of Zitkala-Ša's writings in *The Norton Anthology*), Zitkala-Ša's emotional rendering of death has not. Unlike "The Law of the Life," which encourages our detachment from Old Koskoosh by portraying his death as inevitable, the deaths of the narrator and his father in "The Soft-Hearted Sioux" are neither natural nor inevitable. With the Sioux starving while the whites use the traditional hunting ground for cattle grazing, Zitkala-Ša explains these deaths as a result of white greed and imperialism. Moreover, in contrast to London's celebration of Old Koskoosh's stoicism, Zitkala-Ša depicts the narrator's ultimate stoicism as a mark of his cultural dislocation. Initially seen by the narrator himself as a sign of Christian strength, the narrator's "soft heart" is redefined by both the village's medicine man and his own father as a sign of weakness. As his father declares shortly before he dies, "My son, your soft heart will let me starve before you bring me meat."[17] Ironically, Zitkala-Ša uses the language of Christianity to demonstrate the narrator's ultimate rejection of Christianity and its "soft heart." When he goes to kill the cattle, the narrator chooses the "best-fattened creature" and then returns to his father—as the prodigal son returning home. But he finds no welcome, and the sacrifice of both animal and man is in vain. The father is dead, and the narrator, now a murderer, soon faces his own death. Suggesting how Christianity has failed him, Zitkala-Ša ends the story by describing the narrator's heart as "strong," his face "calm," and his eyes "dry" (508). Unlike the respect London shows for Old Koskoosh's stoic resignation, then, Zitkala-Ša portrays the narrator's emotional detachment from his own fate as a sign of cultural displacement, and she does so while demanding the reader's own emotional involvement.

The complexities of canonization are further emphasized when one considers that the same qualities that keep "The Soft-Hearted Sioux" outside the canons of American realism and naturalism suggest its connections with another canon—namely that of American women's writings. Judith Fetterley and Marjorie Pryse have recently placed Zitkala-Ša, though not this story, in the tradition of American women regionalists, whom they distinguish from local color writers: "[I]n practice the regionalists did differentiate themselves from the 'local colorists,' primarily in their desire not to hold up regional characters to potential ridicule by eastern urban readers but to present regional experience from within, so as to engage the reader's sympathy and identification." Because regionalists work from within the culture they describe, they often demand the kind of emotional connection between reader and subject found in Zitkala-Ša's "The Soft-Hearted Sioux." As Fetterley and Pryse explain, "regionalist texts allow the reader to view the regional speaker as subject and not as object and to include empathic feeling as an aspect of critical response."[18]

Fetterley and Pryse's association of local color with writing by white men but regionalism with that by women and some minority writers suggests that race—in addition to gender—influences a writer's decision to write from within a culture. Such is certainly the case with Zitkala-Ša's "The Soft-Hearted Sioux." Told from the perspective of the dying Sioux rather than a detached observer, this is a story of considerable melodrama. Zitkala-Ša's similarities with her narrator—they are both caught between two cultures—heighten the writer's and reader's empathy with the narrator. Significantly, the kind of detached, outside observation notable in realistic fiction parallels the perspective of the early twentieth-century ethnographers. Given the racial biases of early twentieth-century ethnography, Zitkala-Ša may well have intentionally chosen a more personal perspective for her fiction.

It is precisely this perspective of writing from within Sioux culture that establishes Zitkala-Ša's place within the tradition of Native American literatures. Although Zitkala-Ša is hardly considered a major figure within that tradition, as it is presently being defined, her story "A Warrior's Daughter" has been included in Paula Gunn Allen's recent collection, *Spider Woman's Granddaughters.*[19] This story differs significantly from "The Soft-Hearted Sioux," yet again, the same features that exclude it from canonical realism place it well within Native American literatures. Its grand and dramatic portrayal of a young girl killing one of her lover's enemies and then rescuing the captured lover makes it an unlikely candidate for either realism or naturalism. At the same time, however, these same characteristics connect the story, as Allen suggests, with traditional tales of women warriors.

The personal perspective noted within much of Zitkala-Ša's fiction is accepted and even expected within canonical realism when written as autobiography. It is therefore understandable why, in contrast to "The Soft-Hearted Sioux" or "A Warrior's Daughter," Zitkala-Ša's autobiographical essays seem more familiar to readers of American realism.[20] Stylistically, these three essays employ many fictional techniques associated with realism. Rather than summarize her life story, she uses dialogue and dramatizes specific scenes, often of common events such as carrying water from the river or learning the art of beadwork. Also noteworthy is her avoidance of authorial interpretation. Although she clearly relies on Biblical images throughout these three essays to demonstrate her "fall" from Dakota culture into the white world, she does not instruct the reader regarding their interpretation. The "big red apples" offered her by the missionaries become the tempting, dangerous apple of the Garden of Eden only by ironic implication.

Thematically, Zitkala-Ša's essays compare with canonical realistic literature as well. Like *Sister Carrie* or *Daisy Miller*, which trace a young woman's development and thus become studies of the "American girl," Zitkala-Ša's three essays—"Impressions of an Indian Childhood," "The School Days of an Indian Girl," and "An Indian Teacher Among Indians"—focus on her individual trials and tribulations as she matures. Similarly, like the canonical autobiographer

Henry Adams (or the earlier Henry David Thoreau), Zitkala-Ša combines the telling of her life story with social criticism. In describing this quality of her essays, Gretchen M. Bataille and Kathleen Mullen Sands have described her narrative as "only secondarily [a] personal life stor[y]."[21]

The most significant comparison, thematically, between these three essays and their canonical counterparts is their depiction of Zitkala-Ša's cultural dislocation. Because they portray her never fully in either Dakota or white culture, she has been compared in her alienation to modernist writers. *The Norton Anthology of American Literature*, for example, describes her autobiography as a

> peculiarly modern story of a multiple outsider who has made the painful passage from one culture to another and who is left angry and indignant but without self-pity. Bonnin has abandoned both her mother and the Great White Father, and she must make her way alone.[22]

In regard to these three autobiographical essays, such an assessment is clearly appropriate. Near the end of "An Indian Teacher Among Indians," Zitkala-Ša compares herself to a "cold bare pole... planted in a strange earth":

> For the white man's papers I had given up my faith in the Great Spirit. For these same papers I had forgotten the healing in trees and brooks. On account of my mother's simple view of life, and my lack of any, I gave her up, also. I made no friends among the race of people I loathed. Like a slender tree, I had been uprooted from my mother, nature, and God. I was shorn of my branches, which had waved in sympathy and love for home and friends. The natural coat of bark which had protected my oversensitive nature was scraped off to the very quick.[23]

Zitkala-Ša's language here is more sentimental than later canonical writers, but the sense of alienation here explains why some readers have described the text as anticipating modernism.

Ironically, while this modern theme has likely contributed to the canonization of Zitkala-Ša, it is itself a construct of that same process. Read in the context of her essay "Why I Am a Pagan," the three autobiographical essays do not at all present the modernist theme of alienation. Although the first three essays were published in consecutive issues of *The Atlantic Monthly* almost two years before the publication of "Why I Am a Pagan," good reasons exist for placing these four works together. The fourth essay continues the story of

Zitkala-Ša's life. Moreover, Zitkala-Ša herself places these four essays together in her 1921 volume, *American Indian Stories*. Even more importantly, Zitkala-Ša uses many of the same images and settings in "Why I Am a Pagan" as she had in the earlier series. This fourth essay begins, as did "Impressions of an Indian Childhood," along the edge of the Missouri River, and the author's admiration of the prairie flowers "nodding in the breeze" recalls the association of wind with Dakota identity in the first three essays. Furthermore, like the earlier series that relied on episodic impressions, this essay explains the author's rejection of Christianity not through careful enumeration of her reasons but by dramatizing two scenes—one with the author on the Missouri River, the other a visit from a "'native preacher'" who urges her to attend church.

In this fourth autobiographical essay, however, Zitkala-Ša reverses the sense of alienation and cultural dislocation she described in the "An Indian Teacher Among Indians." In contrast to the earlier image of herself as a transplanted tree surrounded by "strange earth," in "Why I Am a Pagan" Zitkala-Ša portrays her reunification with the natural world. No longer at the Eastern school, Zitkala-Ša describes wandering along the Missouri:

> When the spirit swells my breast I love to roam leisurely among the green hills; or sometimes, sitting on the brink of the murmuring Missouri, I marvel at the great blue overhead. With half closed eyes I watch the huge cloud shadows in their noiseless play upon the high bluffs opposite me, while into my ear ripple the sweet, soft cadences of the river's song. Folded hands lie in my lap, for the time forgot. My heart and I lie small upon the earth like a grain of throbbing sand.[24]

Gone, too, is the sense of having given up her belief in the Great Spirit. Repeatedly insisting on her faith in "Why I Am a Pagan," Zitkala-Ša describes the wild prairie flowers as "living symbols of omnipotent thought" and marvels at the "spiritual essence they embody." Similarly, she describes herself as feeling "buoyant," knowing that "both great and small are so surely enfolded in His magnitude" (802). Rejecting the Christianity previously forced upon her, Zitkala-Ša declares:

> I prefer to their dogma my excursions into the natural gardens where the voice of the Great Spirit is heard in the twittering of birds, the rippling of mighty waters, and the sweet breathing of flowers. If this is Paganism, then at present, at least, I am a Pagan. (803)

Thus, although "Why I Am a Pagan" does not suggest a complete return to tribal life, it does reverse the earlier emphasis on alienation by portraying Zitkala-Ša's celebration of tribal identity.

The contrast between this image of Zitkala-Ša within her own texts and that of her as alienated and "modern" within the canon is well worth pondering. Does canonization necessarily involve imposing Euroamerican "isms"? If so, can we transform that process so as to avoid the dangers of "imposing" interpretive frameworks and create instead a productive interaction between the American Canon and Native American texts?

While I recognize the potential—even likelihood—of "misreading" a Native American text when read solely in the context of the larger canon of American literature, an absolute segregation of Native American texts from Euroamerican frameworks raises even more serious problems. Many Native American authors, after all, including Zitkala-Ša, have been educated within and influenced by the Euroamerican literary culture. To discount those influences entirely would seriously limit our analysis. In addition, if we are ever to create interpretive frames that do not exclude on the basis of race or gender or class, we must allow previously "marginal" texts to help us reshape the interpretive frames themselves. In this case, then, we need Native American texts like Zitkala-Ša's "The Soft-Hearted Sioux" in order to reconfigure our definitions of realism and naturalism.[25]

One strategy of transforming the process of canonization so that it does not simply impose the "isms" of the American Canon is to consider both parts of the canonization process as it is now being practiced; that is, both the making of an anthology and the writing of scholarship. Traditionally, scholarship was a prerequisite to canonization. Authors were included in anthologies only after critics began debating their relative worth. Now, however, as anthology editors increasingly strive for diversity, authors, like Zitkala-Ša, are anthologized long before they have been studied by critics and scholars. Once given the sole task of determining consensus, anthology editors now are in a position to introduce texts not only to students but also to teachers and scholars.

But the process of canon formation cannot end with an anthology editor's decisions. However much editors try to provide adequate frames for "new" writers or to escape the limitations of conventional understandings of literary history, including a text within an anthology does mean reading (and even misreading) that text in terms of traditional interpretive frameworks. As long as American literature anthologies are used in survey courses that move from Puritanism and early nationalism to romanticism and realism, writers like Zitkala-Ša will be read in the context of such traditions, if they are to be read at all.

It is in the current second stage of canonization that we can escape the limitations of such understandings of literary history. By considering, as I have tried to do here, how certain texts become canonized, we can begin to explore and to question the frame with which we have worked so long and within which many anthologies still operate. My point here is not to diminish the work of editors. Quite the contrary. They have begun to take seriously the task of representing the diversity of American literature. But finding a space in an anthology is not the same as establishing an author's place in literary history, and that more difficult project can be accomplished not in anthologies but within critical debate and scholarship. But, as in the case of Zitkala-Ša, this second part of canonization has been sorely neglected, and with considerable risks. Without the support of published criticism and scholarship, teachers may be less likely to teach the "new" writers, and without teaching these writers, we will continue to reassert traditional understandings of literary history. By teaching *and* writing about these "new" texts, however, we can move along the process of canonization, so as to fully realize a new and always changing conception of American literature.

Notes

1. "Native American Oral Narratives: Context and Continuity," in *Smoothing the Ground: Essays on Native American Oral Literature*, ed. Brian Swann (Berkeley: University of California Press, 1983), 39.

2. Because she published her literary texts as Zitkala-Ša, I have decided to use that name. She published as Gertrude Bonnin in some of her political writings.

3. She also collaborated on *Sun Dance*, an opera performed in Utah and New York.

4. See *The Heath Anthology of American Literature*, ed. Paul Lauter et al. (Lexington, MA: Heath, 1990); *The Norton Anthology of American Literature*, ed. Nina Baym et al., 3rd ed. (New York: Norton, 1989); *American Women Regionalists, 1850–1910: A Norton Anthology*, ed. Judith Fetterley and Marjorie Pryse (New York: Norton, 1992); *American Women Writers: Diverse Voices in Prose Since 1845*, ed. Eileen Barrett and Mary Cullinan (New York: St. Martin's Press, 1992); Zitkala-Ša, *Old Indian Legends* (1901; rpt. Lincoln: University of Nebraska Press, 1985); Zitkala-Ša, *American Indian Stories* (1921; rpt. Lincoln: University of Nebraska Press, 1985).

5. Scholarship on Zitkala-Ša includes Dexter Fisher, "Zitkala-Ša: The Evolution of a Writer," *American Indian Quarterly* 5 (1979): 229–38; and David L. Johnson and Raymond Wilson, "Gertrude Simmons Bonnin, 1876–1938: 'Americanize the First American,'" *American Indian Quarterly* 12 (1988): 27–40. See also Alice Poindexter Fisher, "The Transformation of Tradition: A Study of Zitkala-Ša and Mourning Dove, Two Transitional American Indian Writers," Diss. City University of New York, 1979. For a brief biographical sketch, see Mary E. Young, "Gertrude Simmons Bonnin," in *Notable American Women 1607–1950*, ed. Edward T. James, Janet Wilson James, and Paul S. Boyer (Cambridge: Belknap Press of Harvard University, 1971).

6. Although she is probably the first Native American woman to write her life story without the mediation of a white editor or translator, Zitkala-Ša is not mentioned in either H. David Brumble III's *American Indian Autobiography* (Berkeley: University of California Press, 1988) nor in Arnold Krupat's *For Those Who Come After: A Study of Native American Autobiography* (Berkeley: University of California Press, 1985), though Krupat's distinction between "Indian" autobiographies and "autobiographies by 'civilized' or christianized Indians" explains her absence there.

7. William E. Simonds, "Three American Historical Romances," *The Atlantic Monthly* (March 1900): 414. For an analysis of images of Native Americans, see Robert F. Berkhofer, Jr., *The White Man's Indian: Images of the American Indian from Columbus to the Present* (New York: Knopf, 1978).

8. Ellery Sedgwick, "Horace Scudder and Sarah Orne Jewett: Market Forces in Publishing in the 1890s," *American Periodicals: A Journal of History, Criticism, and Bibliography* 2 (1992): 86.

9. For information on Native American periodicals, see *American Indian and Alaska Native Newspapers and Periodicals, 1826–1924*, comp. Daniel F. Littlefield, Jr., and James W. Parins (Westport, CT: Greenwood, 1984); and *Native American Periodicals and Newspapers, 1828–1982*, ed. James P. Danky, comp. Maureen E. Hady (Westport, CT: Greenwood, 1984).

10. See "Shooting of the Red Eagle," *Indian Leader,* 12 August 1904; "The Indian's Awakening," *American Indian Magazine,* January-March 1916, 57–59; "The Red Man's America," *American Indian Magazine,* January-March 1917, 64; "A Sioux Woman's Love for Her Grandchild," *American Indian Magazine*, October-December 1917, 230–31. For a bibliography of Zitkala-Ša's works that includes her publications in Native American periodicals, see *A Biobibliography of Native American Writers, 1772–1924*, comp. Daniel F. Littlefield, Jr., and James W. Parins, Native American Bibliography Series, no. 2 (Metuchen, NJ: Scarecrow, 1981); and *A Biobibliography of Native American Writers, 1772–1924: A Supplement*, comp. Daniel F. Littlefield, Jr., and James W. Parins, Native American Bibliography Series, no. 5 (Metuchen, NJ: Scarecrow, 1985).

11. For a study of the issue of text selection and canonicity with Henry James, see Richard A. Hock's "The Several Canons of Henry James," included elsewhere in this collection.

12. Zitkala-Ša, *Old Indian Legends*, vi, v.

13. Neither *The Heath Anthology of American Literature* nor *The Norton Anthology of American Literature* includes any of Zitkala-Ša's fiction. However, "The Trial Path" is included in Fetterley and Pryse's *American Women Regionalists*, and "A Dream of Her Grandfather" appears in Barrett and Cullinan's *American Women Writers.*

14. "The Soft-Hearted Sioux," *Harper's Monthly Magazine,* March 1901, 505.

15. Donald Pizer, *Realism and Naturalism in Nineteenth-Century American Lit-*

erature, rev. ed. (Carbondale: Southern Illinois University Press, 1984), 11. Throughout my discussion of the relation of "The Soft-Hearted Sioux" to canonical realism and naturalism, I am indebted to Pizer's careful analysis.

16. Simonds, *The White Man's Indian*, 90.

17. Zitkala-Ša, "Soft-Hearted Sioux," 508.

18. Fetterley and Pryse, xii, xvii.

19. *Spider Woman's Granddaughters: Traditional Tales and Contemporary Writing by Native American Women*, ed. Paula Gunn Allen (Boston: Beacon, 1989).

20. Another explanation for the familiarity is that Euroamerican readers are more comfortable with Native American writers when they are presented as "Native Americans" rather than primarily as writers. Autobiography, after all, is not considered a primary genre.

21. *American Indian Women: Telling Their Lives* (Lincoln: University of Nebraska Press, 1984), 12–13.

22. *The Norton Anthology of American Literature*, 2: 864.

23. "An Indian Teacher among Indians," *The Atlantic Monthly,* March 1900, 386.

24. "Why I Am a Pagan," *The Atlantic Monthly,* December 1902, 801–802.

25. I am grateful to Stacy Alaimo for her comments regarding the necessity of creating a dialogue between Euroamerican interpretive frames and Native American texts.

Romance and Realism: Children of the New Colossus and the Jewish Struggle Within

SANFORD E. MAROVITZ

Introduction

JEWISH American literary realism may best be understood by considering the authors and their work from both external and internal perspectives. An external viewpoint will expose the attitudes of Gentile American writers toward an unfamiliar and alien but rapidly expanding Jewish minority in their midst. Examining the cultural milieu of this minority and analyzing a cross-section of the writing that emerged from it provides access to an inner perspective. Jointly, these multiple viewpoints lead one to recognize that Jewish American realism is more than another facet of the broader American realism with its Howellsian center. Unlike the Gentile writer traditionally associated with that movement, Jewish authors were responding not only to harsh economic, social, and other environmental forces, including anti-Semitism, all set in motion by mass Eastern European immigration, but also to their own internal emotional and psychological pressures emanating from the same awesome phenomenon. Far more than simply the merging of ethnicity with local color and Howellsian "truthful treatment," Jewish American realism has features and qualities that make it unique, however closely related it may be to the critical dicta which Howells set forth in *Criticism and Fiction.*

i

After nearly two weeks in steerage aboard the *British Queen* from Liverpool, Abraham Cahan docked in Philadelphia on 6 June 1882. Before long he was on an overnight train to New York, where a ferryboat carried him and scores of other immigrants to Castle Garden, on the Battery. There a providential meeting occurred, though neither he nor anyone else present at the time could have been aware of its significance. As Cahan recalled many years later in his autobiography: "When I arrived the immigration committee included one wealthy young Jewish lady who belonged to the cream of the moneyed aristocracy. She was Emma Lazarus . . . of the Portuguese Jews, the oldest Jewish families in America."[1] Emma Lazarus was also the foremost Jewish American author to date. Later in 1882 she published *Songs of a Semite,* the first collection of Jewish poems by an American Jew, and in November 1883 she wrote "The New Colossus," one of the most popular and evocative poems every written by an American. A topical sonnet penned to help finance the base for the new Statue of Liberty, "The New Colossus" was eventually inscribed in the pedestal of that figure, where it "has become part of the living voice of America."[2] What of Cahan himself? Though his English was limited at the time of his arrival, this Russian immigrant rapidly gained fluency and become a predominant force in the literature and lives of American Jews for well over a half a century.

Although neither knew the other when the Sephardic aristocrat met the Ashkenazic immigrant, they had more in common then either one could have realized. Both were to become prominent authors on behalf of Jewish causes, both would establish reputations based chiefly on writings that pertained to the rapidly increasing flow of immigrants into America, and both would be celebrants of literary realism. Lazarus did not turn from her earlier secular themes and classicism to matters related to Judaism until late in her writing career. Soon after reading George Eliot's *Daniel Deronda* (1876), she became an outspoken advocate of Zionism, the return of European Jews to Palestine (Zion) both to escape the persecution they were suffering under the czars and to fulfill a destined role. Simultaneously she expressed her outrage over the viciousness of the pogroms in Eastern Europe and the broader historical phenomenon of anti-Semitism, which she addressed in numerous journalistic articles during the early 1880s as well as in her poetry.

Cahan was no poet, but he, too, helped awaken America to the truth about contemporary Russia through both journalism and literary art, though at the time he was far more concerned with the ideals of socialism than with Jewish causes. As one telling example of this advocacy, in supporting his views only two months after his arrival in America, he became the first spokesman to deliver a socialist speech in Yiddish, the common tongue of European Jews from countries north of the Mediterranean.[3] Only a year later he fired his opening volley in English, an article published in the New York *World,* in which he denied the Russian dispatches that described the love of the Russian people for their new czar, Alexander III, whose father had been assassinated in 1881 (250–251).

Such outspoken truth-telling was no less characteristic of Cahan's fiction than his early journalism. As a major contribution to American realism, his fiction will be discussed in context later, though it may be noted here that one of Emma Lazarus's most pertinent comments on realism was published within days of his scornful anti-Romanov article in the *World.* Of special interest is her seemingly paradoxical association of *realistic* with *romantic,* though immediately after juxtaposing the two words in a theater review of June 1883 for the *Century,* she explains her usage with reference to Ludwig Barnay's art.

> [It] belongs to the romantic, realistic school, as opposed to the classic and antique. I use, advisedly, the apparently contradictory terms "romantic" and "realistic," for the great romantic revival initiated in literature by Rousseau and his followers, and developed by Goethe, Byron, Scott, and all the poets of the eighteenth [nineteenth?] century, was but the protest of truth, nature, and realism, against cant in morals and the artificial in art. By the singular effect of a violent reaction, romanticism to-day in its turn has come to signify the very antithesis of truth and reality. But this interpretation is only a passing accident resulting from the extreme point to which the movement was carried, and does not alter the fact that the best art may be at the same time very romantic and very real.[4]

For this reason, it is not ill-advised to consider the romance that often glimmers both in the optimistic, idealistic core and on the sentimental surface of Jewish American realistic fiction even while focusing upon the dark, hard details of the commonplace in a ghetto world of pushcarts and tenements. In fact, application of the distinguishing terms themselves—*romance* and *realism*— is not at all clear. Not only ambiguous, they are at times interchangeable according to the individual usage.

Therefore, before discussing selected Jewish American realism, it may be useful to define the genre by relating it briefly both to antebellum American romanticism and to Howells's characterization of realism, especially as derived from his *Criticism and Fiction* (1891).

With respect to romanticism, I refer not to the fiction intended to provide readers with "a romantic escape," as James D. Hart and Jules Chametzky use the term in discussing popular novels of the late nineteenth and early twentieth centuries.[5] Nor do I mean to suggest that Cahan and his contemporary immigrant writers were directly influenced by the work of Emerson, Hawthorne, and others. Such direct influence is doubtful. Yet correspondences exist between them in two ways: first, the idealism and optimism expressed by Emerson in his essays and published lectures had a parallel in the vision and hope that the immigrants associated with the New Colossus; and second, the sense of alienation and the poignancy of suffering common in Hawthorne's fiction are no less evident in much of the writing done by the Jewish American realists.

One should not overlook, also, in making the comparison, how consistently Emerson, Hawthorne, and many of their most highly regarded contemporaries emphasized the importance of representing commonplace reality in their work. Emerson wrote in *Nature* (1836), for example, "The invariable mark of wisdom is to see the miraculous in the common,"[6] and a year later in "The American Scholar," he told the Phi Beta Kappa graduates, "I ask not for the great, the remote, the romantic; . . . I embrace the common, I explore and sit at the feet of the familiar, the low" (78), a passage which Howells quotes at length in chapter 16 of *Criticism and Fiction*. Of what are such statements indicative if not realism as Howells advocated it? Similarly, Hawthorne consistently based his fiction on the theme of alienation and drew heavily from his notebooks in describing the fictive settings and the quasi-autobiographical sketches interpolated among the tales of his collections. Echoes from Emerson and Hawthorne, to both of whom Howells acknowledged a great debt, resonate in the pronounced moralism of his realist doctrine and in such phrases as "the comedy and tragedy of everyday life." In fact, these basic carryovers from romanticism pervade Howells's own realistic fiction, which exemplifies the criteria he set forth in *Criticism and Fiction,* considered by many as a gospel for American literary realism.

Basically, Howells advanced only a few principal ideals. Like Emerson, he insisted on the value of breaking from a rigorous adherence to literary tradition; contemporary writers are limited, he said, because "they have been rather imitators of one another than of nature."[7] He also called for "fidelity to experience" and "probability of motive" as essential, and said that nothing is insignificant to "the true realist." Again like Emerson, Howells believed that whatever is beautiful "is perforce moral" and therefore will illustrate poetic justice (61, 93). In representing the commonplace, realism is fundamentally democratic; the characters in realistic fiction speak in the vernacular of their regions rather than in what traditionalists would consider proper English. In short, for Howells, "realism is nothing more and nothing less than the truthful treatment of material" (73), physically and morally.

Jewish American realism largely conforms with the criteria posited in *Criticism and Fiction,* but the two overriding concerns embedded in the work of early Jewish fiction writers—anti-Semitic hostility and the ramifications of mass immigration—appear either marginally or not at all in the fiction by most Gentile realists. Surely, the Jewish authors are realists in the Howellsian sense, but the two major themes that are all but universal in their work distinguish their fiction within the broader American school of realism. Therefore, this distinction should be recognized in any comprehensive account of the fiction published in the United States between the Civil War and the passage of the anti-immigration laws in the early 1920s.

ii

Although Jewish authors advocated the realistic presentation of immigrant life, because American romanticism and realism should be understood as complementary rather than conflictive, both modes proved essential for the full representation of literary "truth" in their fiction. The urban ghettos that provided the setting for much Jewish American fiction of the late nineteenth and early twentieth centuries expanded and darkened with the increasing tens of thousands of immigrants, mostly impoverished, who were entering the country during those years. If life was bleak for most, the golden dream nevertheless remained alive, and it was not long before enough of the new Jewish citizens and their children began to transform hopes into possibilities and then into realities. They worked, struggled, and saved until eventually they bought themselves a new life, economically and socially. Although the tribulations of ghetto existence constitute the primary substance of this fiction, then, because they were often imbued with sentiment and hope for the future, they were depicted most effectively through a combination of romantic and realistic elements.

Once in America, visionary or not, the immigrants soon learned that Jews were subject to discrimination in the New World as they had been in the Old—however cordially the torch of welcome beckoned over New York Harbor. Anti-Semitism had existed in America long before the decades of mass immigration, but it was relatively inconsequential as a social barrier until after the Civil War. By that time a significant number of the Jews who had emigrated from Germany earlier in the century and become entrepreneurs had established themselves well enough commercially in the United States to compete successfully with Gentile-owned firms. "By 1870," Louis Harap points out, "Jews had become much more visible than before. A number had enriched themselves by manufacturing and trade during the Civil War. The erstwhile peddlers of the 1830s, 1840s, and 1850s had by now become leading retail merchants, manufacturers, and even bankers."[8] As a consequence of this expanded and intensified competition from Jews, doors that might have been open to them socially in earlier decades were rapidly closing. Of course, the anti-Semitic discrimination that evolved during the Gilded Age and hardened later was not universal in American society. When the prominent banker Joseph Seligman was prohibited in 1877 from registering at an elite hotel in Saratoga Springs, many non-Jews protested, including such distinguished authors as Oliver Wendell Holmes and Bret Harte, but the social mold was set, and Jews often found themselves excluded.

Unlike the earlier—and later—European ghettos, however, the burgeoning Jewish communities on the Lower East Side and other urban areas cannot be attributed to anti-Semitism. The immigrants were not forced by governmental decree to live in the squalor of overcrowded tenements but were drawn there by a combination of poverty, "the desire for *kehillah* [community],"[9] and the availability of mutual support. Nonetheless, the expansion of the Lower East Side ghetto and its rapidly thickening density, the result of ever-greater numbers of Jewish immigrants entering the country annually from the early 1880s and settling in New York, eventually led to hostile feelings toward the newcomers and to calls for the influx to be either limited or cut off altogether, an action finally taken in 1924. During the intervening years nearly two and a half million Jews had entered the United States through the gates of Castle Garden and Ellis Island, and most of them remained in New York.

Depending upon the observer, the Lower East Side was either an area of degrading squalor or romantic poverty. In *How the Other*

Half Lives (1890), for example, Jacob Riis creates a hypothetical map of New York City using various shades to represent nationalities and identifies dull gray with the Jew—"his favorite color."[10] Like the Italians, Riis says, the Jews "carry their slums with them wherever they go." He describes "Jewtown" (36) as a pandemonium of the poor with its confusion of alien smells and sounds among overcrowded, darkened, and airless tenements. For Riis the Jews were but one of the immigrant peoples that made it a vain gesture to seek "in this chief city of America . . . a distinctively American community" amid "this queer conglomerate mass of heterogeneous elements" (18–19). As Lewis Fried has pointed out, however, Riis was ambivalent about the Jews in his desire for what Fried calls his quest for "the city as Christian community."[11]

Whereas Riis observed "the other half" among the tenements with the eye of an analytical reformer, pencil and camera at hand, Henry James was utterly amazed as he toured the Lower East Side a few years later. His excursion was made during his last visit to the United States early in the century, though he was less condemnatory than speculative about "the Hebrew conquest of New York," as he phrased it in *The American Scene* (1907). In an oft-quoted passage, James compared the "swarming" ghetto, where "multiplication of everything was the dominant note," with "the bottom of some vast sallow aquarium in which innumerable fish, of over-developed proboscis, were to bump together, for ever, amid heaped spoils of the sea."[12] The stereotypical nose reference in James's grotesque representation of "a Jewry that had burst all bounds" would seem to connote blatant anti-Semitism, yet the author was clearly ambivalent over the world of the ghetto as he reconsidered the impressions he had received during his visit to the Lower East Side. "For what did it all really come to," he rhetorically asks, "but that one had seen with one's eyes the new Jerusalem on earth?" The short passage that follows, remarkable as a measure of James's open-mindedness despite the earlier stereotyping, warrants being quoted in full:

> What less than that could it all have been, in its far-spreading light and its celestial serenity of multiplication? There it was, and there it is, and when I think of the dark, foul, stifling Ghettos of other remembered cities [notably Rome and Venice, I suspect], I shall think by the same stroke of the city of redemption, and evoke in particular the rich Rutgers Street perspective. (133)

The crowds, the bustle, the altogether foreign sounds of Yiddish in the New York streets, all lead James to ponder over what the future holds for America and Americans, yet, though astonished by the changes that had occurred in the city since he had last seen it, he does not moralize on the differences or treat them as literary fare. In contrast, William Dean Howells occasionally visited the streets of the lower classes in New York during the 1890s and exposed his ambivalence toward the poor, including the Lower East Side Jews, in a number of magazine articles, many of which were later included in two collections, *Impressions and Experiences* (1896) and *Literature and Life* (1902). Though genuinely sympathetic, Howells seems to have lacked the empathy that would have made it possible for him to gain a true sense of the suffering that poverty brings. In one of his uncollected commentaries for *Harper's Weekly,* he remarks on the dullness of the lives of the poor and adds in the detached voice of the litterateur, "wherever poverty, virtuous or vicious, abides there is the charm of a more dramatized being; . . . nothing save enterprise or fire can change the picturesque shabbiness of the houses."[13] His observations on the Jews specifically appeared in "An East Side Ramble," published in *Impressions and Experiences.* Here he describes their cheerfulness and orderliness relative to the inhabitants of the "American" quarter. Yet their lives are hopeless, Howells believes, and he wonders whether the low death rate among the ghetto Jews might not "for their final advantage . . . better be the highest."[14] In describing Lower East Side life, he employs animal imagery, speaking of the inhabitants as "inmates of the dens and lairs about me" (139), yet Howells admits that despite the poverty—or perhaps because of it—he finds parts of ghetto life "attractive," and he "was loath" to leave it (147).

No such ambivalence as that of James and Howells affected Henry Adams, who seems to have "exceeded the rest [of his Brahmin caste] in the intensity of his hatred of the Jews," Louis Harap observes; "Whatever or whomever he wished to denigrate, he associated with the Jews."[15] Correspondingly, in the fiction of this period one of the most vitriolic examples of anti-Semitism appears in Frank Norris's obscene portrait of Zerkow the junkman in *McTeague* (1899), a red-haired Polish Jew described an embodiment of rapacious greed. Ironically, Norris's repulsive characterization of Zerkow in San Francisco reflects obversely from his glowing vision of romance personified as a maiden on the Lower East Side only a few years later in *The Responsibilities of the Novelist* (1903). In the original essay,

"A Plea for Romantic Fiction," Norris contrasts the detailed, superficial representation of the commonplace that he calls *realism* with the penetrating mystery and morality that he identifies with *romance*. Romance is not limited to medieval castles and Renaissance chateaux, he says; "this very day, in this very hour, she is sitting among the rags and wretchedness, the dirt and despair of the tenements of the East Side of New York."[16] Perhaps Norris had Crane's Maggie in mind as he wrote these words, thinking more of a young Irish woman on the Bowery than a Jewish one such as Cahan's Gitl (in *Yekl*) from the ghetto. In either case, however, his portrait of Zerkow in the slums of San Francisco is ironically tied more closely to romance, as Norris himself defines it, than to his perception of Howellsian realism. Undoubtedly, Norris was taking too narrow a view of realism as characterized a decade earlier in *Criticism and Fiction* (1891), but romantic or realistic, his anti-Semitism in *McTeague* is beyond question.

Like Norris, Owen Wister, the celebrated author of *The Virginian* (1902), was passionately hostile to the shifting balance of population in the United States; he perceived this transformation as the corruption of the Anglo-Saxon legacy that underlies and charges American civilization. In *Lady Baltimore* (1906), for example, the narrator, who serves as the author's persona, takes no issue with an aristocratic southern lady who complains to him disgustedly about the "pest of Hebrew and other low immigrants" in the North.[17] Later the narrator himself carries the idea farther when he refers to the many social problems that America faces, while "into this mess the immigrant sewage of Europe is steadily pouring" (331). "Give me your tired, your poor, / Your huddled masses yearning to breathe free, / The wretched refuse of your teeming shore," Wister's fellow American, Emma Lazarus, had written in "The New Colossus," and *Lady Baltimore* constituted his reply.

Some viewpoints regarding the Jews were incomprehensible, whereas others were simply perverse. For example, in his late years James Russell Lowell is alleged to have seen Jews in positions of wealth and authority wherever he turned,[18] and at about the same time Ignatius Donnelly represented them in *Caesar's Column* (1890) as malicious figures in control of both the national economy and the revolutionary activity that aims to undermine it. Moderate anti-Semitism became conventional among the upper classes after the Civil War, but jaundiced opinions such as those held by Adams, Norris, and Wister were extreme.

For a more balanced perspective from which to gauge the attitudes of American intellectuals and literati toward the immigrants, especially the Jews, one might turn to Hutchins Hapgood's *The Spirit of the Ghetto* (1902). "This first book-length profile of Yiddish New York," as Moses Rischin identifies it in his introduction to a later edition, probably represents better than any other single work a sympathetic outsider's depiction of Lower East Side Jewry around the turn of the century. He characterizes it as "devoid of sentimentality, sympathetic yet sober and realistic, intimate yet judicious and restrained."[19] Originally published as a series of sketches in the *Atlantic Monthly* between 1898 and 1902, the same years during which Hapgood and Cahan worked together as reporters for the New York *Commercial Advertiser* under the editorship of Lincoln Steffens, *The Spirit of the Ghetto* comprises portraits of representative Ghetto dwellers and individual writers, in addition to descriptions of the local newspapers and the stage. Interpolated among the pages are numerous expressive "drawings from life" by Jacob Epstein.

In his brief preface to the volume, Hapgood quickly acknowledges the "unpleasant aspect" of the ghetto, its dirt and immorality, but he says that his interest is not philanthropic or sociological; instead, he is motivated by "the charm [he] felt in men and things there."[20] The most distinctive quality he recognizes in "the intellectual and artistic life" of the Jewish East Side is "the spirit of realism" on the stage as well as in the printed word (135). As David M. Fine has noted, Hapgood saw "realism as an inborn quality of the Jewish mind."[21] "Love of truth," Hapgood says, "pleasant or unpleasant," is what "the best" of the Lower East Side novelists desire.[22] Clearly, Hapgood perceives as *realistic* what Norris concurrently identifies as *romantic;* taken together, they seem to confirm Emma Lazarus's view two decades earlier: "the best art may be at the same time very romantic and very real."[23]

Mark Twain, too, sometimes visited the Lower East Side, and the Jews there appreciated the lack of prejudice he expressed towards them in his writings.[24] Although he referred to Jews only occasionally in his major publications, in an article for *Harper's* in 1899—"Concerning the Jews"—he elucidated his favorable attitude toward them and denied any disposition toward anti-Semitism. Referring to anti-Semites as "crippled," he praised the Jewish people for their achievements through history. Because Twain showed evidence of stereotyping in this article, it was criticized by some Jews and praised by others, though as Louis Harap observes, his error was not attributable to malice but to his limitations as a historian or social analyst.[25] Similarly, Everett Emerson notes that although Twain himself was proud of the article and considered it a "gem," in it he "parades his good will but shows no real insight into anti-Semitism."[26] Whatever its limitations, "Concerning the Jews" was written by Mark Twain at the height of his popularity, and it represents, with the best of his fiction and other imaginative prose, the strong bias in favor of equality and democracy for which he—"the Lincoln of our literature," as Howells eulogized him—has long been praised.

The foregoing allusions to prominent authors of the period confirm that in the American consciousness a de facto isolation of Jews existed historically as an ethnic group that was decidedly different from the rest of the populace and in most cases less desirable. Nevertheless, during the half century after the Civil War the Jews as an immigrant population attracted considerable attention from Gentile American writers. Some of this attention was simply a matter of curiosity about an unfamiliar alien culture, but much of it was negative if not overtly hostile.

iii

Negative, positive, or merely curious, however, this attention to which the Jews were subject as an alien people had a major effect on the way that Jewish authors thought and wrote about themselves as a community. The immigrants had been moving in mass from a religious, largely homogeneous, and restrictive culture into a secular, heterogeneous country that welcomed them with no governmental restrictions imposed. If this drastic change in their lives brought new possibilities for them economically and socially, it also severed or at least seriously weakened the traditional ties that had bound them to generations of custom in the Old Country as well as to religious ritual and law as traceable through their biblical and talmudic heritage. For many of the immigrants, especially the older family members, the transformation of circumstances was not a happy one, and for most, regardless of age, it evoked a sense of loss even with the recognition that life in America could bring opportunities that were no more than dreams in the hostile world they had left behind.

This change of homeland with all of its ramifications—social, economic, emotional, and psychological—constitutes the principal thematic concern of most Jewish American literature published during the period of American literary realism and naturalism. Although like Howells and most of his contemporaries, Cahan was seeking "the *thrill of truth,*" as he stated his literary aim, the circumstances that engaged these two authors were so decidedly different that the Jewish American fiction of the period should be considered as a category or variety of realism unique to the specific culture from which it emerged.

Yet the importance of Howells's influence on Jewish American realism cannot be overstated. One of the chief beneficiaries of it among the new Jewish immigrants, Abraham Cahan, was to become the most prominent writer to arise from the Yiddish culture of the Lower East Side. As the author of three novels in English, a collection of short fiction, dozens of uncollected stories and sketches, as well as a massive amount of journalism in English and Yiddish written during a period of nearly seventy years in the United States, Cahan is surely the most appropriate author to focus upon in a general discussion of Jewish American realism. As Jules Chametzky has suggested, "no other immigrant or American . . . saw the problems in as full a dimension as Cahan did or addressed them with as much integrity and art."[27] Clearly the most prolific and highly regarded author among the Jewish immigrants, Cahan remains known best for his *chef d'oeuvre, The Rise of David Levinsky* (1917). Many literary historians and critics still identify this work as the most revealing and aesthetically satisfying novel of the period to deal holistically with mass immigration and its ramifications both for Jewish American life and more broadly for the rapidly developing garment industry. With the proliferation of the Singer sewing machine late in the nineteenth century, the ready-to-wear garment manufactory gained supremacy over traditional individualized tailoring, and the Jews from Eastern Europe were central in its growth.

The themes and conflicts in Cahan's *The Rise of David Levinsky* are already evident in his first novel, *Yekl: A Tale of the New York Ghetto* (1896), and in some of his earliest English stories, published during the 1890s. In a statement Cahan wrote for the *Atlantic* near the end of the century, he contrasted the goal of a realist like himself with that of a "romanticist" (i.e., the popular romantic writer who aimed to achieve escapism and sentimentality); and in so doing, he advocated the kind of literary "truth" for which both Emerson and Howells had called:

> Would that the public would gain a deeper insight into these [sweatshop] struggles than is afforded by [scornful] newspaper reports! Hidden under an uncouth surface would be found a great deal of what constitutes the true poetry of modern life,—a tragedy more heart-rending, examples of a heroism more touching, more noble, and more thrilling, than anything that the richest imagination of the romanticist can invent. While to the outside observer the struggles may appear a fruitless repetition of meaningless conflicts, they are, like the great labor movement of which they are a part, ever marching onward, ever advancing.[28]

To achieve a truly vital American literature Cahan recognized the need for "strong, new American writers . . . who will give us life—real life, with its comedy and its tragedy mingled—give us what in my Russian day we called the *thrill of truth*."[29] For Cahan, this *truth* had to include not only the struggle to survive in the ghetto but also the immigrant Jew's estrangement in the New World. Cahan noted the essential role of Judaism in the lives of the Eastern European immigrants, especially the older generation for whom the *Yidishkayt* of the *shtetl* provided a pattern of cultural existence that had guided their daily behavior as it did that of their families and neighbors. In America, many of them retained of it what they could; even under vastly different circumstances, the strong ties of their Hebraic traditions helped them sustain their faith. Cahan emphasized the relation of historical piety to the daily pressures of ghetto poverty when he wrote: "Their religion is to many of them the only thing which makes life worth living. In the fervor of prayer or the abandon of religious study they forget the grinding poverty of their homes."[30]

Ironically, however, in his fiction it is not the pious Jew who suffers the pangs of longing and loneliness, but the secularized individual who becomes, as Yekl becomes Jake in *Yekl,* "an American feller, a Yankee."[31] Soon after Yekl immigrates, he becomes infatuated with secular American life. A handsome young workman with a wife and child in Russia, Yekl habituates the local dance hall and rapidly gains favor with the ladies there. By the time his wife, Gitl, arrives with their child, Yekl has transformed into Jake, the Yankee, and he finds Gitl repulsive, a dowdy "greenhorn" (new immigrant characterized by Old Country mannerisms). Before long he insists upon a divorce, which Gitl tearfully grants in exchange for a cash settlement, but Gitl, too—magnificently played by a sloe-eyed Carol Kane in the film *Hester Street,* based on Cahan's novel—has gained a sense of independence during her short time in New York. Her future looks promising with a more favorable second marriage soon to come, but

Jake appears destined for a life of grief with the overbearing woman who gave him divorce money in exchange for his hand. He has traded a loving, dutiful wife for a brazen, domineering one, and his Jewish faith, no more than part of "a charming tale" from the past, seems permanently out of reach.

Whereas the religious Jews of the ghetto suffered and celebrated together, the secularized aliens in Cahan's fiction, from the early stories to Levinsky himself, cannot satisfy the loneliness to which their detachment from *Yidishkayt* has led; they are the ones who in moments of solitude suffer the persistent twinges of their stretching hearts. For example, Asriel and his daughter, Flora, in the title story of Cahan's *The Imported Bridegroom and Other Tales of the New York Ghetto* (1898), may be taken to represent the plight of most of his Americanized immigrant Jews. The wealthy, retired Asriel returns to Russia briefly in order to lure, with the offer of an immense dowry, a devout young rabbinical scholar to become the husband of his secular daughter. Unattracted to the youth until he has become Americanized himself, Flora weds her imported bridegroom, but both she and her father are soon left in despair as the brilliant Russian lad forgoes his Judaism and his bride in favor of secular philosophizing among a group of Lower East Side intellectuals with whom he associates. A comparable situation occurs in "A Providential Match," Cahan's first story published in English and the one that elicited Howells's initial encouragement when the "Dean of American Letters" read it in a small literary magazine. After many years of living as a lonely bachelor in America, Rouvke Arbel hires a *shadchen* (marriage broker) to find his "predestined one" because his heart is stretching for someone to love. The *shadchen* arranges for a young woman to come from Europe and become Arbel's bride, but when she is attracted on the ship to a scholar closer to her own age, Arbel is left desolate again. Perhaps the most poignant of his short stories is "The Apostate of Chego-Chegg," in which a young Jewish immigrant from Poland has surrendered her faith to wed a Catholic. Scorned by Gentiles as a Jew and by the Jews for her conversion, Michalina yearns to return to Judaism, but thoroughly devoted to her Catholic husband in America, she refuses to leave him and consequently lives under the curse of an insatiable spiritual desire that cannot be assuaged.

In fact, the leading figures in nearly all of Cahan's short fiction undergo a continual cycle of desire and disappointment comparable with that of Asriel, Flora, Rouvke Arbel, and Machalina. More free in America than they could ever have been in the European *shtetlach,* they cannot gain satisfaction because, as they inevitably discover too late, they have nothing to be free *for* in a culture shaped by materialism, expedience, and self-indulgence rather than the traditional community of faith. When Judaism and piety no longer provide them with guidance for their behavior and existence, no equivalent replaces it, and they have nowhere to turn for solace.

This theme is most fully developed in *The Rise of David Levinsky.* Having fled the poverty and persecution he was forced to suffer in Russia, the orphaned David Levinsky immigrates to America where he becomes a millionaire within a few decades in the ready-made clothing industry. While it is a naturalistic account of American industrialization of the garment trade, the novel is also a psychological portrait of the central character, a conflictive, often self-contradictory figure. Levinsky remains nominally Jewish but forsakes his piety and Hebrew scholarship. As a large-scale employer he is drawn by Spencerian Social Darwinism, yet stays sympathetic with socialism and organized labor. He is attracted to prostitutes, to the wives of other men, and to vague idealizations of the poetic and maternal feminine, but he never marries or goes beyond the stages of lust and infatuation. Finally, he yearns for a college education but makes no effort to achieve one. Levinsky is simultaneously a romantic and a systematic, hard-headed realist—as to a large extent was Cahan himself. But whereas Cahan worked chiefly for others, Levinsky is entirely self-serving. In his case, it is a confusion of his own drives and motives, not American anti-Semitism, that underlies his moral failure and personal insatiability.

iv

The Rise of David Levinsky, like much of Cahan's other fiction, illustrates that if anti-Semitism was a limiting factor in the lives of the new immigrants, it was not necessarily determinative; many of the ghetto dwellers were not affected by it directly because they existed entirely within their own Yiddish-speaking communities. In creating stress for the others, however, it also provided an incentive to slough off their Old Country ways and Americanize as quickly as possible. The rapid transformation from a "greenhorn" to an American enabled immigrants to assimilate more readily with the host culture than would have been possible otherwise, and it led to a greater likelihood of economic success. Cahan illustrates this process time and again in his fiction from *Yekl* to *The Rise of David Levinsky*. For example, like Cahan, Levinsky quickly gains fluency in English and conscientiously emulates the behavioral patterns and manners of the more sophisticated Americans he meets. In this respect, Levinsky exemplifies the effect of America as a great melting pot, as Israel Zangwill referred to the dynamic process of acculturation in 1908, an idea readily traceable in American writing all the way back to Crevecoeur's third Letter from an American Farmer (1782): "Here individuals of all nations are melted into a new race."

One of Cahan's principal aims during the early decades of *The Forward* was to help immigrants assimilate by teaching them to Americanize their manners, and he was not alone in this advocacy. In one off the most popular autobiographies of the period, Mary Antin's *The Promised Land* (1912), the author relates the story of her immigration from Russia to Boston, taking immense pride in secularizing her Jewish faith into a nationalistic religion of America. Similarly, Anzia Yezierska, whose first story was published in 1915, believed in the American dream, which Alice Kessler Harris says "was essential to sustaining her faith in this land of immigrants."[32] In her autobiographical story "America and I," Yezierska recalls romantically yearning for America from her original home in the Pale near Warsaw: "American was a land of living hope, woven of dreams, aflame with loving and desire . . . the Promised Land."[33] Deceived into working like a drudge for no wages after she first arrived, Anzia becomes embittered over the lack of opportunity for self-fulfillment that she faces as an immigrant in the ghetto. Then a sudden illumination reveals to her that America is still unfinished and that she can share in its making. How? "Fired up by this revealing light," she says, "I began to build a bridge of understanding, between the American-born and myself" (33). Her novels, too, illustrate this attempt to acculturate and become a part of the American dream. In the best of them, *Bread Givers* (1925) Sara Smolinsky flees from her tyrannical father on Hester Street; she becomes a working girl and at last a college graduate. Ultimately, however, she discovers that she is not happy because she cannot leave Hester Street behind. "Even in college," she tearfully laments, "I had not escaped from the ghetto." In a contrived ending, she eventually gains happiness by marrying the principal of the school in which she teaches and restoring relations with her father. Although Yezierska describes the poverty and struggles of her young heroines realistically, stereotyped characters and melodramatic twists in the plot often undermine her verisimilitude.

Both Yezierska and Antin found early success in "the Promised Land," but neither achieved lifelong happiness. Steven J. Rubin characterizes Yezierska's fictionalized autobiography, *Red Ribbon on a White Horse* (1950), as "a chronicle of failure" despite the optimism of a few brief concluding paragraphs "that seem forced and unauthentic," so glaringly does their tone contrast with the work as a whole.[34] Nor for Antin was the promise realized for long. As Sol Lipzin points out, "her later years belied her earlier optimism," and ultimately, on the edge of poverty, she turned back to Judaism.[35]

Cahan and Yezierska were but two of the many Jewish American authors of the realistic period who described New York Jewish life in their fiction. However, the first significant novel written by an American Jew was set partially in New York and published only two years after the Civil War ended. *Differences* (1867), by Nathan Mayer, is somewhat comparable with John William De Forest's *Miss Ravenel's Conversion from Secession to Loyalty,* published the same year, in that both novels include a love theme complicated by the North-South conflict and a related moral transformation. Unlike De Forest, however, Mayer satirizes the German-Jewish nouveaux riches in New York who have gained their wealth through recent commercial success. In this respect, Mayer anticipated by exactly half a century Cahan's derisive portrait of vulgar Jewish merchant families on vacation in *The Rise of David Levinsky.*

Mayer himself did not reside in New York as did most other authors who employed that city as a principal setting for Jewish fiction. Henry Harland was the best-known of them though ironically he was not Jewish. Writing under the pseudonym Sidney Luska, Harland wrote three novels in the mid-1880s about Jewish life in New York: *As It Was Written: A Jewish Musician's Story* (1885), *Mrs. Peixada* (1886), and the *Yoke of the Thorah* (*sic*: 1887). The last of these titles generated a strong adverse reaction because of the implication that the Hebrew Torah is a *yoke,* a confinement by which Jews are held back unwillingly from full assimilation, especially through intermarriage. Harland also sharply satirizes the German-Jewish nouveaux riches, which led some reviewers to criticize him as prejudiced. Such perceptions were on the mark. Within a few years Harland immigrated to England, converted to Catholicism, became literary editor of *The Yellow Book,* and manifested the anti-Semitism displayed by numerous characters in his later fiction.[36]

Harland was for a time the most popular Gentile author writing about Jewish New York, but he was by no means the only one. Edward King's *Joseph Zalmonah* (1893) is a reform novel based on the life of Joseph Barondess, "King of the Cloakmakers," whom David M. Fine calls "one of the most interesting, enigmatic, and controversial of the labor leaders the Jews were to produce."[37] A decade later, Myra Kelly began publishing her poignant if sentimental series of stories about Jewish children on the Lower East Side. She and King were teachers in the ghetto, so they knew from experience what life was like among the East Side Jews. Kelly published three collections of stories before 1910, the year of her death, but the first, *Little Citizens* (1904), is considered her best.

Apart from Cahan, one of the earliest Jewish authors to use the Lower East Side as a setting for his fiction was Herman Bernstein, whose stories were collected in 1902 under the title *In the Gates of Israel.* Thematically similar to Cahan's stories, they are more sentimental and contrived, but they bring out the alienation suffered by the Yiddish-speaking immigrants upon finding themselves no longer in their Old World nor yet truly part of the New. What Stanley F. Chyet calls "the wrench of change" is manifest in many of Bernstein's stories.[38] A year later another collection of stories set in the Lower East Side was published; *Children of Men* (1903), written by Rudolph Block under the pseudonym Bruno Lessing, is more varied in tone than one might expect of such material. Whereas one story is highly sentimental, another is comic, a third hinges dramatically upon sheer coincidence, and another points compellingly to the value of traditional faith. What realism they present comes largely through their diversity; as a whole, *Children of Men* offers telling glimpses into the mundane conflicts of ghetto life.

In 1909 James Oppenheim brought out a different kind of collection, *Doctor Rast,* a novelistic series of stories based on episodes in the life of the title figure. Oppenheim's realism corresponds largely with Howellsian views in that it conjoins social issues and idealistic philanthropy with graphically realistic description. Added to it, however, is the Jewish theme, for Dr. Rast practices medicine on the Lower East Side, where he vacillates for a time over his faith, but ultimately remains firm in his association with Judaism. Two years later Oppenheim directed his attention to labor problems in the garment district when drafting his novel *The Nine-Tenths* (1911); he based it largely on a recent strike among the Lower East Side sweatshop workers and the disastrous Triangle Shirtwaist Company fire that killed 143 young working women in March of that year. As Harap points out, *The Nine-Tenths* is one of the earliest novels to focus upon the Jewish working woman no longer bound by traditional responsibilities to home and family. Other novelists from the second decade of the century whom he discusses in this respect are Florence Converse, Zoe Beckley, and Arthur Bullard; ironically, none of them is Jewish.[39]

At about the same time as these novels appeared, the garment industry became the central concern of an altogether different type of fiction, a series of stories, developed chiefly through humorous dialogue with assorted stylistic threads drawn from Lower East Side life and heightened by exaggeration. Begun serially in 1910, these stories about two partners in the garment trade were written by Montague Glass and collected the next year as *Potash and Perlmutter: Their Copartnership Ventures and Adventures.* Glass himself was an attorney with strong professional and social ties to New York's Jewish community; his experiences on the Lower East Side made it possible for him to be authentic as well as entertaining in his fiction.

Although *Potash and Perlmutter* includes the satirical portrait of a lawyer, Glass is amusing rather than caustic in his characterization of Henry D. Feldman with his polysyllabic Latinate diction. In stark contrast is an anonymous novel published about a decade later, *Haunch Paunch and Jowl* (1923), written by Samuel Ornitz. Narrated in the first person, Meyer Hirsch tells his own story of growing up among boyhood gangs in the ghetto and grasping power as a lawyer and judge; "money works and money talks in America," Hirsch says, and "idealism is the refuge of the incompetent."[40] By the end of his narrative Ornitz has presented a repulsive picture of exploitive, materialistic values in the sociopolitical infrastructure of America early in the century.

V

Of course, New York held the largest Jewish community in America between the end of the Civil War and the immigration laws of 1924, as it does still, but the largest is not the only one. Nor is it the only community that included authors eager to represent Jewish American life in fiction. Although occasional examples of such writing emerged from a number of cities in different parts of the country, I shall focus here only on a representative few, a selection based partly on regional diversity and partly on literary merit. Readers seeking additional titles can find them in historical surveys of this period by Harap and Fine.

Already mentioned is Nathan Mayer's early novel, *Differences,* set predominantly in Tennessee as well as New York. German by birth, Mayer himself studied medicine in Cincinnati before the Civil War, and after completing his service in the Union army, he settled in Hartford. *Differences* is his principal contribution to Jewish American letters; in fact, Harap praises it as "the first American novel by a Jew about Jews in which literary talent is exhibited,"[41] as opposed to those published earlier that were melodramatic and blatantly didactic.

Although the Jewish poetry and journalism of Emma Lazarus appeared in the early 1880s, little Jewish American fiction of consequence was published before 1890. In 1893 Emma Wolf brought out the first of her San Francisco novels dealing realistically with middle-class Jewish life on the west coast; her major theme in *Other Things Being Equal* (1893) and *Heirs of Yesterday* (1900) is intermarriage, including the commitment to Jewish identity, the familial implications of such marriages, and the anti-Semitism present among the couple's circle of acquaintances. Some of the same intra-Jewish and interreligious concerns are explored in *Doctor Cavallo* (1895), a midwestern novel written by Maurice Eisenberg in collaboration with Eugene F. Baldwin, a journalist from Peoria, Illinois. Aesthetically limited, the chief value of *Doctor Cavallo* lies in its comprehensiveness, in the diversity of attitudes represented among and toward Jews in the midwest at the turn of the century. Two decades later Elias Tobenkin also described midwestern Jewish life during the same period, though in *Witte Arrives* (1916) he centers on the theme of assimilation. Like Tobenkin himself, Aaron Witkowski and his family emigrated from Russia to settle in Wisconsin. By the time his wife and children arrive in the rural community of Spring Water, Aaron has been in the Promised Land for four years, during which time he has shortened his name and become a peddler. The center of interest in the novel is his youngest son Emil, who graduates from the University of Wisconsin and establishes himself as a journalist, first in a nameless Wisconsin city ("N______"), then in Chicago, and finally in New York. In the process of gaining an education and developing his career, Emil becomes assimilated to the extent of shedding his Jewish faith and identity in favor of socialism. Idealistic himself with respect to the process of secularizing into true Americanism, Tobenkin nonetheless depicts a plausible view of Witte's struggle for success amid an array of forces both contrary and supportive.

In complete contrast to Tobenkin's fiction is the work of Sidney L. Nyburg, a contemporary whose best-known novel, *The Chosen People* (1917), offers a panoramic view of the diverse Jewish community in Baltimore. This provocative novel compares with Cahan's *The Rise of David Levinsky* it its comprehensiveness, though it is more polemical. At times, advocates for various causes, including Zionism, gain the ear of Philip Graetz, a young man who assumes his first rabbinical post in a large, well-to-do, and complacent Reform temple of Baltimore. Rabbi Graetz struggles, as if with a hydra, in a sea of conflicting forces and desires, religious and economic, communal and personal, spiritual and erotic. *The Chosen People* constitutes a useful southern complement to Cahan's major New York novel. Many of the issues involved are similar, though one distinguishing feature between them is the civic consciousness that links the Jewish community of Baltimore with the socioeconomic infrastructure of the city, in contrast to the relative detachment of the garment district and the Lower East Side from the "American" parts of metropolitan New York.

Because this chapter on Jewish American realism opened with a glimpse of Abraham Cahan's docking in Philadelphia in 1882, perhaps it is most appropriate to conclude this brief survey with reference to Henry Berman's *The Worshippers* (1906), which has that city as its setting. David M. Fine points out that it is one of the few novels of the period to center on "The Americanized middle-class Russian-Jewish community."[42] According to Harap, Berman "probably intended to compose a satire on the pseudointellectual, pretentious radicals whose socialism is only talk."[43] Apart from the satire, *The Worshippers* is a novel of disillusionment in which the aspiring wife of a Philadelphia pharmacist flees with a Yiddish poet whom she accepts as a lover. She fails as an actress, however, and he is not the romantic paramour she imagined, so she returns to her husband. The novel is of interest chiefly because of its Philadelphia setting, though it may be worthwhile to compare the circumstances and character of Berman's heroine with those of Kate Chopin's Edna Pontellier in *The Awakening*, published a few years earlier (1899).

vi

What conclusions may be drawn from this exploration of Jewish American realistic fiction? First, because of generic confusion over the term *realism* itself, Jewish American realism—with its sentimental nostalgia, its emotionally laden pictures of suffering in poverty, its emphasis on hope and dream, and its more-than-occasional celebration of social ideology—often corresponds with romantic aims no less than realistic ones. Next, Jewish American realism has been presented in a double milieu, that of the broader American culture as well as the inner circle of its own diverse Jewish community. Through this dualistic approach, one can immediately recognize the difference between work written by the Gentile American realists and that of their Jewish contemporaries. Most significantly among the Jewish authors (usually first-generation Americans in the late nineteenth-century and early twentieth, occasionally second-generation in the next decade) three principal and nearly ubiquitous topics of concern are prominent. First is the effect of the increasing mass immigration on the development of an expanding Jewish community and on the lives of the individual Yiddish-speaking immigrants it comprises. This broad theme includes the transferal of *Yidishkayt* to the Promised Land, the "streets-of-gold" motif and the accompanying struggle for wealth, the Old Country nostalgia often sentimentalized in the fiction, the quest for education and freedom, the strong democratic impulse that had been squelched by European restrictions, and the concept of America as the great Melting Pot. Second is the constant presence of anti-Semitism outside of this community and the tensions it necessarily generated among the Jews forced to confront it. Third, and equally important, is the matter of assimilation and the controversies it provoked among the Jewish populace, controversies with many complex ramifications, the most crucial of which was the diminishing role of Judaic law and tradition in everyday life. All three of these issues and the plethora of complications they created distinguish Jewish American writing from the generally accepted canon of American realism. Moreover, although other ethnic literatures of the period similarly represent both the problems that evolved from immigration and the question of assimilation, the enduring struggle against anti-Semitism as Jewish American authors depicted it made their work unique.

Many subsidiary themes help to characterize this writing as well, and by recognizing them as part of a pattern, one can gain both a better understanding of the culture from which it emerged and a better appreciation of the novels and stories themselves. Among the more important of these themes is, first, the conflict that evolved with the earlier Sephardic and German immigrants on the one side and the Eastern European Orthodox Jews on the other. Whereas the earlier generations were mostly settled and far less pious in their faith—they were the emerging Jewish nouveaux riches—the Poles, Russians, Slavs, and others were mostly impoverished, and their lives were governed by religious law and customs. Second, public American education in English fostered intrafamilial dissension and the dilution of traditional family bonds. A third prominent theme was labor organization, including the stages of recognition from unrepresented single workers in the sweatshops to full unions, steps that occurred among the chaotic polemics of various socialist, communist, and anarchist radicals, many with their own daily and weekly newspapers. Finally, Zionism is a theme less often represented in the fiction than those already cited, but as a central concern in the minds of many Jewish authors of the period it is occasionally developed with considerable vigor, as in Nyburg's *The Chosen People.*

By the mid-1920s the struggle of Jewish American immigrants to achieve social stability and economic security beneath the torch of the New Colossus was far from resolved. Consequently, broad social and economic issues continued to dominate Jewish American literature through the next two decades, and realism prevailed in their exposition, as may be seen in the novels of Michael Gold, Henry Roth, and Meyer Levin. Moreover, although psychological themes and postmodern methods have inevitably found a place in more recent Jewish American letters, such leading contemporaries as Saul Bellow, Grace Paley, and Chaim Potok provide unmistakable evidence that "the truthful treatment of material" graphically and realistically presented is no less important a consideration for Jewish American fiction writers today than it was in the era of Howells and Cahan.

Notes

1. Abraham Cahan, "The Education of Abraham Cahan" *[Bleter Fun Mein Leben]*, trans. Leon Stein, et al. (Philadelphia: Jewish Publication Society of America, 1969), 217–219.
2. Dan Vogel, *Emma Lazarus* (Boston: Twayne, 1980), 159.
3. Cahan, *Education*, 237.
4. Emma Lazarus, "Barnay as 'Mark Antony,'" *Century*, 26, N.S. 4 (June 1883): 312.
5. James D. Hart, *The Popular Book: A History of America's Literary Taste* (1950; rpt. Berkeley: University of California Press, 1963), 185–86; Jules Chametzky, *From the Ghetto: The Fiction of Abraham Cahan* (Amherst: University of Massachusetts Press, 1977), 32–33.
6. *Selections from Ralph Waldo Emerson*, ed. Stephen E. Whicher (Boston: Houghton Mifflin, 1957), 55.
7. W. D. Howells, *Criticism and Fiction* (1891; rpt. Cambridge: Walker-de-Berry, 1962), 7.
8. Louis Harap, *The Image of the Jew in American Literature from Early Republic to Mass Immigration* (Philadelphia: Jewish Publication Society of America, 1974), 304.
9. Lewis Fried, "Jacob Riis and the Jews: The Ambivalent Quest for Community," *American Studies* 20, no. 1 (Spring 1979): 16.
10. *Jacob Riis Revisited: Poverty and the Slum in Another Era*, ed. Francisco Cordasco (Garden City, NY: Doubleday, 1968), 23.
11. Lewis Fried, "Jacob Riis"; and *Makers of the City* (Amherst: University of Massachusetts Press, 1990), 10–63.
12. Henry James, *The American Scene* (London: Chapman & Hall, 1907), 131–33.
13. W. D. Howells, "Life in Letters," *Harper's Weekly* (25 July 1898): 726.
14. W. D. Howells, *Impression and Experiences* (New York: Harper & Bros., 1896), 143.
15. Harap, *Image*, 363.
16. Frank Norris, *The Responsibilities of the Novelist* (1903; rpt. Cambridge: Walker-de-Berry, 1962), 281.
17. Owen Wister, *Lady Baltimore* (New York: Macmillan, 1906), 140.
18. Harap, *Image*, 97–98.
19. Moses Rischin, "Introduction" to *The Spirit of the Ghetto* by Hutchins Hapgood (1901; rpt. Cambridge: Harvard University Press, 1967), vii.
20. Hutchins Hapgood, *The Spirit of the Ghetto* (1901; rpt. Cambridge: Harvard University Press, 1967), 5.
21. David M. Fine, *The City, The Immigrant and American Fiction, 1880-1920* (Metuchen, NJ: Scarecrow, 1977), 31.
22. Hapgood, *Spirit*, 235.
23. Lazarus, "Barnay," p. 312.
24. Harap, *Image*, 353, 357.
25. Harap, *Image*, 356.
26. Everett Emerson, *The Authentic Mark Twain: A Literary Biography of Samuel L. Clemens* (Philadelphia: University of Pennsylvania Press, 1984), 217.
27. Chametzky, *Ghetto*, xi.
28. Abraham Cahan, "The Russian Jew in America," *Atlantic Monthly* 82 (July 1898): 135.

29. Ernest Poole, "Abraham Cahan: Socialist—Journalist—Friend of the Ghetto," *Outlook* (28 October 1911): 478.
30. Cahan, "The Russian Jew in America," 138.
31. Abraham Cahan, *Yekl, A Tale of the New York Ghetto* (New York: D. Appleton, 1896), 149.
32. Alice Kessler Harris, "Introduction" to *The Open Cage: An Anzia Yezierska Collection* (New York: Persea, 1979), viii–ix.
33. *The Open Cage: An Anzia Yesierska Collection,* ed. Alice Kessler Harris (New York: Persea, 1979), 21.
34. Steven J. Rubin, "American-Jewish Autobiography," in *Handbook of American-Jewish Literature,* ed. Lewis Fried (Westport, CT: Greenwood, 1988), 296.
35. Sol Liptzin, *The Jew in American Literature* (New York: Bloch, 1966), 125. In contrast, see Allen Guttmann, *The Jewish Writer in America: Assimilation and the Crisis of Identity* (New York: Oxford University Press, 1971), 28, who says that she "never repudiated the witness borne in *The Promised Land.*"
36. See Harap, *Image,* 455–71.
37. Fine, *City,* 77.
38. Stanley F. Chyet, "Forgotten Fiction: American-Jewish Life, 1890–1920," *American Jewish Archives* 37, no. 1 (April 1985): 6.
39. Louis Harap, *Creative Awakening: The Jewish Presence in Twentieth-Century American Literature, 1900–1940s* (Westport, CT: Greenwood, 1987), 40.
40. Samuel Ornitz, *Haunch Paunch and Jowl: An Anonymous Autobiography* (New York: Boni and Liveright, 1923), 85, 122.
41. Harap, *Image,* 2–79.
42. Fine, *City,* 67.
43. Harap, *Creative Awakening,* p. 36.

Problems of Representation in Turn-of-the-Century Immigrant Fiction

SUSAN K. HARRIS

IN Abraham Cahan's "The Imported Bridegroom" (1898), the portrait of Asriel, the first generation immigrant, is disturbing throughout, but perhaps nowhere so much so as in the scene set in the synagogue in his hometown in Poland, where he destroys the peace. Though a boorish peasant there, Asriel also knows that in America he is a self-made man, and in his anxiety to prove his success to his "landsmen," he loses all sense of decorum, bidding loudly, rancorously, and lavishly for a chance to lead the Torah reading and then voicing his resentment when a long-standing member of the community is chosen in his stead. This could be a psychologically compelling scene, yet Cahan's narrator deflects serious consideration of the cultural issues in his generally pejorative portrayal not only of Asriel, but of the entire congregation. At prayer, for instance, the men are described in minute, even obsessive, physical detail:

> Here and there a sigh made itself heard amid the monotony of speechless, gesticulating ardor; a pair of fingers snapped in an outburst of ecstasy, a sob broke from some corner, or a lugubrious murmur from the women's room. The prodigy, his eyes shut, and his countenance stern with unfeigned rapture, was violently working his lips. . . . Asriel was shaking and tossing about. His face was distorted with the piteous, reproachful mien of a neglected child about to burst into tears, his twin imperials dancing plaintively to his whispered intonations.[1]

Not unlike descriptions of American revivals, this portrait suggests that Asriel, far from being odd, is actually typical of the people among whom he was born. His raptures, gesticulations, plaintiveness—all foreign to the American ideal of male self-control—mark him, with them, as Other, an Other presented as irretrievably alien and, from the mainstream American point of view, not one whom it is desirable to try to see as Self.[2] Throughout "The Imported Bridegroom," Cahan employs verbs, adjectives, and nouns in reference to Jewish males that, in mainstream America, have pejorative implications: the men "gesticulate," they act out "dumb shows," they "wail," "murmur," "boast," "burst out." They are, in short, physical, emotional, self-absorbed, unreserved; they act out private emotions upon a public—or at least a communal—stage; they are the antithesis of approved (i.e., reserved) American manhood. Positioned by Cahan's narrative as voyeurs, mainstream readers of this text are not encouraged to see his characters sympathetically, that is, in the archaic sense of the word, to feel with them, to share, at least imaginatively, their sense of self and world, and to welcome them into the American family.

Using "The Imported Bridegroom" as a representative text, this essay will suggest a complex of factors useful for contextually examining turn-of-the-century immigrant stories. Though sociologically compelling, these stories are often problematic in their aesthetic and ideological constructions of their ethnic characters, often recreating stereotypes prevalent in mainstream culture rather than representing ethnic characters' own subjectivity. I suggest that a confluence of formal and political factors created this problem for the immigrant writers themselves, and that it was not until the advent of modernism that they were able to break through the strictures of American narrative forms and create immigrant characters who spoke for themselves rather than for the dominant community.

June Howard discusses a related problem in her study of American naturalism, where she notes that the narrator and reader (or spectator) of naturalistic novels is somehow assumed to stand outside the determined worlds within the novels; both watch, as through a window, the predetermined story work its way out. The binary relationship between narrator and reader on the one hand, and story, on the other, further enhances the objectification of the characters into the Other (in naturalistic novels, often the Brute). This objectification also characterizes the discourses of *progressivism* and *scientific management,* which, as sociopolitical and industrial movements, sought to control as well as "improve" the way the society and its workers functioned.[3] In her study of American realism, on the other hand, Amy Kaplan claims that the realists differed from the naturalists in that "realistic strategies tend less to regulate conflict by formalizing otherness than to negotiate conflict in the narrative construction of common ground among classes both to efface and reinscribe social hierarchies."[4]

I think examination of the turn-of-the-century immigrant story needs to be conducted somewhere between these claims, in an arena reflecting a variety of cultural discourses. The first set of discourses is political: it concerns the relationship of the immigrant group to the dominant community. Immigrant writers faced the specter of American nativism, the reflex response, closely related to American racism, that rejected outright the presence of non–Western European immigrants onto American ground. In its literary manifestation, late nineteenth-century nativism is clearly articulated by Thomas Bailey Aldrich, William Dean Howells's successor at the *Atlantic Monthly,* in his well-known poem "Unguarded Gates," the second stanza of which runs:

> Wide open and unguarded stand our gates,
> And through them presses a wild motley throng—
> Men from the Volga and the Tartar steppes,
> Featureless figures of the Hoang-Ho,
> Malayan, Scythian, Teuton, Kelt, and Slav,
> Flying the Old World's poverty and scorn,
> These bringing with them unknown gods and rites,—
> Those, tiger passions, here to stretch their claws.
> In street and alley what strange tongues are loud,
> Accents of menace alien to our air,
> Voices that once the Tower of Babel knew![5]

Even those sympathetic to the new arrivals divided into camps, however, and this subcategory of the political discourses is more directly relevant to immigrant writers' struggles to articulate their communities than was the nativist manifesto. By definition not nativists, immigrant writers were committed to providing "features" to the figures they represented. With many of the native-born, however, they were divided over the extent to which recent arrivals were to be acculturated. Hence they were embroiled in the debate over assimilation or multiculturalism, which frames, even when distant, the presentation of ethnic voices in both native-born and immigrant writers. In *Beyond Ethnicity: Consent and Descent in American Culture,* Werner Sollars has traced the philosophical origins of the American concept of ethnicity, noting the tensions between assimilationist and multiculturalist views.[6] As he notes, participants in the debate were able to theorize their own positions. The assimilationist view—familiarly known as the melting pot theory—held that "fusion is a law of progress" and that "racial amalgamation is the heroic problem of the present, with all it implies in purification and revision of old social, religious, and political ideals, with all it demands in new sympathy outside of blood and race, and in a willingness to forego old-time privileges."[7] Such an ethos finds its reflection in works such as Israel Zangwill's play "The Melting Pot" (1909), where the protagonists, the son of Russian Jews slain in a pogrom, and the daughter of the Russian baron who directed it, vow that "The sins of the fathers shall not be visited on the children" and hail the New World as "the great melting pot," the "crucible" where "the great Alchemist melts and fuses . . . Celt and Latin, Slav and Teuton, Greek and Syrian, black and yellow."[8]

The multiculturalist view, on the other hand, held that America's destiny was to become a federation of many cultures, English-speaking and politically democratic but culturally diverse, a commonwealth whose goal is "self-realization through the perfection of men according to their kind." Writing in 1915, Horace Kallen suggested that "what is inalienable in the life of mankind is its intrinsic positive quality—its psychophysical inheritance. Men may change their clothes, their politics, their wives, their religions, their philosophies . . . they cannot change their grandfathers."[9] Resting on a benign essentialism, such a view encourages the kinds of activities undertaken by agencies such as Jane Addams's Hull House, which recognized the difficulty of forming "genuine relations with the Italian Women"[10] but sought to ease the familial and personal stresses of immigration by encouraging immigrants and their children to preserve, practice, and value the Old World cultures they brought with them.

Turn-of-the-century writers who sought to represent immigrant characters were ipso facto implicated in this political debate, and it is reflected in their narrative points of view much as it is reflected in mainstream writers' narrative judgments. Those siding with the assimilationists accepted the implicit superiority assumed by mainstream narrators because, the unspoken argument ran, the ethnic characters were eventually going to lose their unsavory Old World characteristics anyway. This future orientation had its own pros and cons; as Allen Guttman observes, Cahan's own reservations about the materialism of second generation Jews did not yield a particularly optimistic vision.[11] For the multiculturalists the problem was more acute, because the hegemonic drive of traditional narrative forms precluded the central item on the multiculturalist agenda: voicing a given ethnic reality that was both different from and equal to the reality of the native-born population.

A related example here is *Adventures of Huckleberry Finn*. Long established as *the* masterpiece of American dialect writing, *Huckleberry Finn* nevertheless exhibits several of the problems listed above. Certainly as a character, a fictional construct, Huck has a voice, but what voice? From what community of values does he speak? Certainly not from his own class, "Pap's kind of people"; in fact Huck mediates between "those people" and the reader much as earlier framing narrators mediated between all dialect characters and readers. Although Twain removed the narrative frame from around Huck himself, in fact his vernacular narrator is so close to mainstream values that little interpretation needs to be done. When we applaud the outcome of Huck's crisis of conscience, we are celebrating his turning traitor both to his class and to his region. The values *Adventures of Huckleberry Finn* presents and celebrates are liberal white northern values, the values of Clemens's social group and primary audience. The voice that is omitted from *Adventures of Huckleberry Finn* is the voice of Huck's own social class.

This brings us to the second set of cultural discourses affecting the representation of subjectivity in turn-of-the-century immigrant fiction: the formal features and literary history of the American dialect tale. American-born writers entered the assimilationist/multiculturalist debate freighted with two kinds of specifically literary baggage: the tradition of the vernacular short story, which had been developing its American forms since early in the century, and the recent theoretical ruminations on realism by William Dean Howells. By the 1890s, these traditions had developed into an ideological framework for representing the Other in mainstream writing that further limited immigrant writers' choices of narrative strategies that were useful in creating fiction about themselves in a borrowed tongue.

It may seem odd phrasing to call narrative frames *ideological*. But as Kenneth Lynn makes clear, nineteenth-century American dialect stories, especially those emerging from the Southwest and South, are introduced by a narrator who functions to mediate between the characters of his or her tale and the putative readership of the story.[12] I want to distinguish here between the American dialect story as developed in the vein of "Southwest humor," and the regionalist story, which, as Judith Fetterley and Marge Pryse have noted, is a primarily female genre that focuses far more intently and sympathetically on its characters' lives and aspirations than does the predominantly male genre of dialect stories.[13] For the purposes of this essay, the major difference between the regionalist story and the dialect story, in addition to its sympathetic stance toward its characters, is that the regionalist story explores a territory that is accepted as a part of American life; it is *recognized* in a way that the characters of dialect stories are not. Characters in regionalist stories may be viewed as pathetic, lamentable, odd, but they are nonetheless sympathetic, characters of whom mainstream readers can, at worst, say "There but for the grace of God go I."

In contrast, characters in dialect stories are the Other, at best Neanderthalian ancestors of present-day Americans, relics of the past to be disavowed, poked fun at, encouraged only in so far as they provide the kind of comic relief that assures readers that they are not, themselves, anything like "those people." In dialect stories the narrator, generally male, points to "those people," distancing them from his readers at the same time that he introduces them. When A. B. Longstreet's narrator in "Georgia Theatrics" avows that "what I am about to relate" is *not* "characteristic of the county in which it occurred"[14]—or at least not any more—he is at once separating his subject from contemporary American life and also titillating readers' appetites for the bizarre, which he promptly furnishes. Similarly, the framing narrators of George Washington Harris's "Sut Lovingood" stories, or Johnson J. Hooper's "Simon Suggs," prepare their readers to expect that their dialect characters will articulate alien values and undergo bizarre adventures. The ideological component of narrative framing came increasingly in the strengthening of the preexisting implication of superiority—intellectual, social, and moral—of the narrator, that is, his signals of class solidarity with his readers, who would meet *his* voice before those of his characters, and so begin with unspoken agreement about their common values as against those of "those people" whom he is about to introduce.

William Dean Howells liked these stories; he was particularly enthusiastic about dialect tales because, as he says in *Criticism and Fiction,* "I hope that our inherited English may be constantly freshened and revived from the native sources which our literary decentralization will help to keep open."[15] For him, dialect indicated the youthfulness of a language—and realism, for him, was admirable in part because it had room for this linguistic freshness.[16] With Daudet and the other continental writers he quotes, Howells seems to equate linguistic "youth" and "freshness" with lack of a national literary history. That is, Shakespeare and Turgenev had "barbaric" languages—i.e., artistically unused—to wade into, whereas Daudet and Henry James had only "the language of an old civilization."[17] Dialect "freshening," then, revived and revised languages that were in danger of becoming too refined.

But for Howells as the theoretician of realism, this began and ended with transcribed language. Unable to see or hear beyond his own white, male, middle-class construction of "Reality," he was not aware of the potential for dialect sounds to become voices, that is, to speak and be heard as expressing a subjectivity that was legitimate as well as different. A putative multiculturalist, Howells acknowledged a "universal" human nature while remaining convinced that each ethnic group had unique characteristics that could be introduced to mainstream white culture. But "introducing" is not the same as "knowing"; the very fact of the introduction influences readers' perceptions of the works. Like narrative frames, introductions preserve the alienness of "those people" even as they purport to present them to mainstream readers. And, depending on the particular biases of the one doing the Introducing, portrayals of the Other can be celebratory, denigrating, or distorting.

Howells himself, for instance, in a critique of Charles Dudley Warner's manuscript "From Jaffa to Jerusalem," suggests that "you don't give enough personality to your narrative: I would rather have one good Turk or dirty Jew got by heart than a whole generalized population. Your Yankee woman at Jaffa, for example, was excellent."[18] Here Howells is insisting that Warner paint his characters according to "type," but as the remarks about the "dirty Jew" or the "Yankee woman" suggest, he had definite ideas as to what constituted a particular type. Similarly, a letter to his father suggests Howells's image of African Americans: "I have been at the colored Methodist Church this morning, in a bath of primitive Christianity. Boston gives its stamp of decorum to most things, but it doesn't get through the black skin. On the whole I felt softened and humbled among these lowly and kindly people."[19]

In a critique of Howells's influence, his contemporary Gertrude Atherton attacks his insistence on the ordinary, the "real," complaining that "he has produced, and his followers maintain, a literary style that is all *l*'s and *n*'s and *r*'s. It is the cultivation of a perfectly flat, even surface. It is afraid of rough surfaces, of mountain peaks and deep valleys. It exalts the miniature and condemns the broad sweep of impressionism in art."[20] The faults with Howells's celebration of the American "average" that Atherton and other critics of Howells's influence detect also pertains to his strictures on the presentation of the Other: Howells insisted that the "best" kind of ethnic writing portrays its given subject within the confines of preexisting molds. In his introduction to Paul Laurence Dunbar's poetry, he remarks that

> there is a precious difference of temperament between the races . . . and this is most charmingly suggested by Mr. Dunbar in those pieces of his where he studies the moods and traits of his race in its own accent of our English. We call such pieces dialect pieces for want of some closer phrase, but they are really not dialect so much as delightful personal attempts and failures for the written spoken language. In nothing is his essentially refined and delicate art so well shown as in these pieces, which, as I ventured to say, described the range between appetite and emotion, with certain lifts far beyond and above it, which is the range of the race. He reveals in these a finely ironical perception of the negro's limitations, with a tenderness for them which I think so very rare as to be almost quite new.[21]

As these remarks (which become more pernicious the more one reads them, especially, perhaps, the phrase "our English") reveal, Howells not only felt that dialect represented difference, he also conformed to—perhaps inherited—the notion that dialect writing was an essentially comic mode, further distancing readers and characters by posing the latter as objects to be laughed at. While he was content to see the "primitive" nature of contemporary African Americans represented in Dunbar's poems, his remarks about Edward Eggleston's dialect characters suggest that he thought that dialect writing about whites should indicate the distance whites had traveled from the primitive stage. In his 1872 review of Eggleston's *Hoosier Schoolmaster,* he remarks that the portrait of the West "before the days of civilization" is set in "a locality which we hope the traveller would now have some difficulty in finding."[22] For Howells as the theoretician of realism, then, writings about American ethnicity had to explore a priori concepts of the given ethnic group. The virtues of realism lay in the close delineation of ethnic stereotypes, not in the attempt to reassess the nature of human beings or to reconfigure white Americans' notions of what constitutes "civilization," the "Like Me"—a task that would entail exploration of the "rough surfaces" Atherton wished to see.

In addition to their political choices, then, the confluence of a tradition of narrative framing for dialect stories and the definition of Reality promulgated by Howells posed ideological problems for turn-of-the-century immigrant writers who sought to join the literary mainstream. The problem became one of voice, of creating literary voices that spoke out of the immigrant communities' sensibilities rather than out of the mainstream values, of presenting immigrant characters who spoke for themselves, and ultimately of producing, in both Poulet and Iser's formulations of the reading process, an alien subject within the reader's consciousness that would ultimately serve to alter her or his values.[23] If a minority language is, as Deleuze and Guattari suggest, inherently revolutionary, the problem faced by turn-of-the-century immigrant writers was they had not yet developed the kind of revolutionary consciousness that would enable them to create a minority language within the major tongue.[24] That they felt their deterritorialization—the dislocation consequent on changing cultures—is manifest. But they spoke neither with a sense of the collectivity—either of their own group or of some possible future community—or of the political dimensions of their materials. Even Cahan, himself a socialist, does not realize the potential socialist community in his work: it exists either as a dark window onto an unspecified, unexplored territory, as at the end of "The Imported Bridegroom," or, at its best, in the evocation of family solidarity in the socialist Tevkin home in *The Rise of David Levinsky*. Unlike contemporary African American writers such as Charles Chesnutt, whose African American double-consciousness empowered him to both use and subvert traditional narrative frames and dominant tones, turn-of-the-century immigrant writers adopted rather than adapted the majority language. The "double-consciousness" articulated by American-born W. E. B. Du Bois, practised by Charles Chesnutt and other African American writers, and assumed as an ethnic universal by Sollars[25] was not, in other words, yet realized in the work of these newly-arrived writers. Rather, in writing about immigrants within an American context, they had at first only available to them the forms already developed in that culture, and these were inherently biased against sympathetic representations of the Other.

On a technical level, this impasse is evident in the strains and contradictions in the immigrant stories themselves. Unlike contemporary immigrant autobiographies, fiction writers had only limited success in creating narrators flexible enough to project the tale from both inside and outside the community at the same time. Autobiography, with its retrospective nature, its assumption that the teller has "arrived," may be a technically more congenial genre for immigrant writers than fiction. For example, both Mary Antin, a Polish Jew who structured her autobiography, *The Promised Land* (serialized 1911–12; published 1912) around the biblical story of Exodus, and Gertrude Bonnin (Zitkala-Ša), a Dakota-Sioux who structured the history of her move from the reservation to mainstream white culture around the Biblical story of the Fall, consciously build their tales on myths deeply embedded in the consciousness of the mainstream readers they address. In doing so, they also manipulate mainstream readers' sympathies, both in terms of Americans' early (i.e., Puritan) identification with the ancient Jews, and their later romantic identification with prelapsarian nature. Similarly, when Edith Maud Eaton (Sui Sin Far), writes her autobiographical essays, *Leaves from the Mental Portfolio of an Eurasian,* she creates, through prose rhythms, geographical references, and short sketches of Chinese and American characters, material that supports her thematic preoccupation with the placelessness of growing up Eurasian.

When fiction writers sought to use similarly preset forms to represent not the personal Self, but the as-yet-voiceless members of the immigrant community, however, they encountered the barriers that the forms themselves imposed. Sui Sin Far's stories in the volume *Mrs. Spring Fragrance* use dialect and scenery that project Chinese characters as Other and plots that figure the reader as voyeur. In her desire to write "serious" fiction abut the Chinese immigrant community (which she herself came to know in adulthood) she overdetermines the differences between immigrant characters and mainstream readers. "In the Land of the Free," a story recently reprinted for the Heath Anthology, Chinese language is represented by way of the antiquated English second person familiar and the rigidly hierarchical nature of Chinese society is highlighted by the obedience to authority, however reluctant, of the protagonists. This is especially so in her portrayal of Lae Choo, a woman whose child is taken away by the immigration authorities. At the bottom of the social hierarchy, Lae Choo is obedient to a husband who is in turn frustrated by immigration authorities and cheated by a white lawyer. When her son, after ten months' residence in a mission school, rejects her, the finality of her position as oppressed female Other is manifest. An object of pity for mainstream readers, she is not, however, a subject for sympathy; such readers may be stimulated to work for reform of unjust immigration laws, but they will not reconfigure their understanding of Chinese women. Unlike her autobiographical essays, Sui Sin Far's fiction highlights differences rather than similarities between immigrant and native-born customs.[26]

Since I began with Cahan's "Imported Bridegroom," I want to devote the last section of this essay to explicating it in light of the above concerns, using it as an example of the kinds of problems turn-of-the-century immigrant writers faced.

"The Imported Bridegroom" is the story of three Jews: Asriel Stroon, a Polish immigrant who has done well in New York but has never ceased feeling the inferiority of his childhood poverty and lack of a Talmudic education; his Americanized daughter, Flora; and Shaya, the "prodigy," a young Talmudic scholar whom Asriel buys as a husband for Flora while on a nostalgic visit back to Poland.

The story is told by a third person omniscient narrator, who positions himself as the mediator between the ethnicity of the characters and his readers. The latter may or may not be knowledgeable about cultural specifics; Cahan has his mediator explain just enough to outline customs. For instance, Asriel "led the way downstairs. There they paused to kiss the divine name on the *Mezuzah* of the doorpost."[27] Here adepts in the culture are given a little more than they need—a story written for practicing Jews need only mention that Asriel kissed the *Mezuzah* to communicate the fact that he is devout; nonadepts need at least a hint ("the divine name") that orthodox Jews protect their homes with some tangible object containing a reference to their God. Narrative passages such as this educate the uninitiated; they also clue us in to the author's implied readership and to the narratee.

Given a projected readership of the relatively uninitiated, the narrator's job, then, is to translate the culture as well as to tell a tale. The question, however, is how his intercession will shape the reader's perception of the culture. "The Imported Bridegroom" is problematic in a way that many of Cahan's stories are, knowing where the final intentions lie—authorial intention, if you will. Cahan's stories often tend to deconstruct all the possible values, so that no position is finally presented as preferable, although almost all are viable. As Pole, immigrant, and Jew to an American, native-born, Christian readership, Asriel and his associates are Other, and in the hands of a nativist writer, they would be caricatured as grotesques: ill-shapen, unassimilable, coarse, and irredeemable. Cahan, however, is an assimilationist, not a nativist. But he is also a committed socialist who questioned the social values promulgated by American capitalism.

Cahan's ambivalence toward his characters rests in part on this ambivalence about social values. But the question of narrative form and realistic technique complicates the issue. As technique, realism is, here, intensely problematic because the close focus on physicality highlights aspects of the immigrant culture that are inimical to American sensibilities. In reproducing language, for instance, Cahan, like Sui Sin Far, either writes dialect—i.e., represents broken English—or "translates" Yiddish, that is, purports to have his characters speak in Yiddish, but gives their dialogue to his readers in English. Here, the difference between the fictional Yiddish and English is often rendered with a high degree of ornamentation in the Yiddish dialogue passages. "'I beg you, my daughter, do not shorten my days, and come down-stairs,' [Asriel] entreated with heartfelt ardor. 'I have so little to live, and the Uppermost has sent me a piece of comfort so that I may die a righteous Jew,—will you take it away from me? Will you put me to shame before God and man?'" (64). This passage, rendered in "Yiddish," projects Asriel as the self-pitying man who is trying to buy, for nostalgia's sake, the security that the exigencies of his working life prevented him from acquiring through genuine piety. In Yiddish, then, Asriel is a confused hypocrite. In English, he is an ignoramus: "Dis a choych?" he asks a passerby in front of the Astor library, and hearing the building identified, says to himself, in "Yiddish," "Ah, a lot of Gentile books!" (104).

Neither language, as represented, gives the space for Cahan to develop Asriel's situation. Here, individual psychology is glossed and mocked, rather than explored for its representative status. Asriel may be typical of the first generation immigrant, but Cahan's projection rarely even hints at the relationship between Asriel and the social, economic, or political situation of the immigrant community as a whole. Like Stephen Crane, he attacks Asriel's nostalgia and hypocrisy; unlike Crane, he does not project them as functions of Asriel's situation. Similarly, he undermines Flora, whose Americanized values he sees as pretentious. In fact, the only character he does not completely undermine is Tamara, the genuinely pious and unworldly housekeeper.

In addition to typing and denigrating his characters, in "The Imported Bridegroom" Cahan is also ambivalent about the ends to which they are being acculturated. Shaya, the "prodigy," whom the narrator likens physically to Byron, may be the only viably Americanizable character in the story and, like a Dreiser character, he is viable because he is the least rooted in the culture from which he has come. In telling us that Shaya looks like Byron, Cahan is telling us that the young man looks like a mainstream white person—he can pass. Shaya is also not only bright but, despite his fame as a brilliant young adept at Talmudic Law, an intellectual chameleon: his own values are so little grounded in Eastern European Jewish culture that he doesn't care what he studies, as long as it is worthy of his intelligence. All he really cares about are mental gymnastics, so, for instance, geometry, when he discovers it, is as much fun for him as Talmudic argumentation, and Comte's Positivist Philosophy is more attractive than his new wife.

At the end of "The Imported Bridegroom," Shaya is studying medicine, Asriel and Tamara are about to emigrate to Palestine, yoking their fortunes and opting out of the American experiment, and Flora and Shaya are married. This apparently happy ending, however, is shadowed by the fact that Shaya has clearly already outgrown Flora's values—and she knows it—and that the intellectual community of assorted shabby socialists that so draws Shaya is itself an implicit critique of the American system that has begun reshaping the immigrants' lives. Cahan leaves his characters—and his readers—in limbo at the end of "The Imported Bridegroom," looking at the room of disputants from Flora's point of view and thus seeing them "more like some of the grotesque and uncouth characters in Dickens's novels than an assemblage of educated people" (119), including Shaya, whose anxieties are manifested in "a St. Vitus's dance of impotent pugnacity" (120). "Excluded," from Shaya's "entire future" (121), Flora sees no communal march into the future, and neither does Cahan. Rather, the grasping for money and status that has destroyed Asriel will destroy Flora; the Dickensian group of socialists provide the critique without the answer.

The answer could not begin to come, I suggest, until there were forms in which it could be expressed. The advent of modernism, itself an import onto the American scene, freed immigrant writers, as it freed the American-born, to develop new ways to give voice to the voiceless. By breaking through the conventions of narrative and temporal frames, developing techniques of stream-of-consciousness that could project individual sensibility without dialect stereotypes, and celebrating the Self stripped of its historical or cultural baggage, the modernists paved the way for immigrant writers, as it did for native-born writers such as Faulkner and Ellison, to reterritorialize their communities, first representing individual voices, then, under the additional influence of political writing in the 1930s, the communal and political ramifications that reshaped immigrant writing into an American minority tongue. Michael Gold's *Jews Without Money* (1930), which positions the first person narrator inside the community, then freights short, declarative sentences with an overtly political consciousness, may be the first well-known novel to emerge from this transformative process, but it is evident soon after in the work of Henry Roth, William Saroyan, Carlos Bulosan, and, more recently, Leslie Silko and Maxine Hong Kingston.

In the continual jostling for economic and political power that characterizes the process through which immigrant groups become Americans, the evolution of fictional voices marks watersheds in American consciousness, first for the group itself, then for the surrounding communities that begin to "hear" these voices for the first time. From the literary standpoint, over the last century the multicultural side of the political debate has emerged victorious, and the voices for which it makes room are impacting on the political sphere. Hence a shift in the values that dictate the canon. Able to hear Other voices for the first time, we are beginning to reshape our conception of the hyphenated American Self. Here literary technique, social values, and political agendas begin to work in tandem. Retrospectively, we can see how literary history helps pave a way for social change; specifically, how the loss of the hegemonic narrative frame has in part been responsible for our broadened understanding of the varieties and possibilities of the human.

Notes

1. Abraham Cahan, *The Imported Bridegroom and Other Stories of the New York Ghetto* (New York: Garrett Press, Inc., 1968), 31.

2. Anti-Jewish writing of the period was prevalent and popular, and partook of the same vocabulary to emphasize the same traits as in Cahan's descriptions. "What are the particular objectionable qualities in the Jew guest?" runs one study of the Jew in America. "In the first place, the Jew is loud, vulgar, and intrusive. He is loud in his speech and in his dress; he is vulgar in his deportment . . . his table manners are execrable . . . he is intrusive in forcing his company . . . upon people." From Anon., *The American Jew* (New York, 1888). Quoted in Michael Selzer, ed.,

"Kike!": A Documentary History of Anti-Semitism in America, (New York: World Publishing Co., 1972), 59.

There is a general consensus that turn-of-the-century immigrant writers had difficulty creating sympathetic portraits of their own groups. In *The City, The Immigrant and American Fiction, 1880–1920* (Metuchen, NJ: The Scarecrow Press, Inc., 1977), David M. Fine sums up the consensus as follows: "If, as Leslie Fiedler has said, the task for the American-Jewish writer is to create Jewish character out of experience and against the grain of the popular image of the Jew in the American imagination, then these early explorers of Jewish life in America were not prepared for the task. The experience they wrote about was not their own, and they relied, far too much, on popular conceptions and conventions" (62). The same problem, I shall argue, skews the fiction of immigrant writers from other ethnic groups.

3. June Howard, *Form and History in American Literary Naturalism* (Chapel Hill: University of North Carolina Press, 1985). See esp. ch. 4, "The Naturalist and the Spectator."

4. Amy Kaplan, *The Social Construction of American Realism* (Chicago: University of Chicago Press, 1988), 11.

5. Thomas Bailey Aldrich, "Unguarded Gates." Reprinted in Edward Ifkovic, ed., *American Letter: Immigrant and Ethnic Writing* (Englewood Cliffs, NJ: Prentice-Hall, 1975), 136.

6. See Werner Sollors, *Beyond Ethnicity: Consent and Descent in American Culture* (New York: Oxford University Press, 1986).

7. Percy S. Grant, "American Ideals and Race Mixture," originally published in *North American Review,* 1912; reprinted in Oscar Handlin, ed., *Immigration as a Factor in American History* (Englewood Cliffs, NJ: Prentice-Hall, 1959), 150–53.

8. Ifkovic, ed., *American Letter,* 133–34.

9. Handlin, ed., *Immigration as a Factor in American History,* 154.

10. Ifkovic, ed., *American Letter,* 138.

11. Robert J. DiPietro and Edward Ifkovic, eds., *Ethnic Perspectives in American Literature: Selected Essays on the European Contribution* (New York: Modern Language Association, 1983), 137.

12. See Kenneth S. Lynn, *Mark Twain and Southwest Humor* (Boston: Little, Brown, 1959). For related analysis of the forms of American dialect stories see also Carolyn S. Brown, *The Tall Tale in American Folklore and Literature* (Knoxville: University of Tennessee Press, 1987), James M. Cox, *Mark Twain: The Fate of Humor* (Princeton: Princeton University Press, 1966) and Kenneth S. Lynn, ed., *The Comic Tradition in America: An Anthology of American Humor* (New York: W. W. Norton & Co., 1958).

13. Marjorie Pryse, "Distilling Essences: Regionalism and 'Female Culture'," American Literature Association Conference, Washington, DC, May 24–26, 1991.

14. Lynn, ed., *The Comic Tradition in America,* 59.

15. William Dean Howells, *Criticism and Fiction and Other Essays* (New York: New York University Press, 1959), 64.

16. Howells, *Criticism,* 65.

17. Howells, *Criticism,* 64.

18. George Arms and Christoph K. Lohmann, eds., *Selected Letters of W. D. Howells* (Boston: Twayne Publishers, 1979), 2:117.

19. Arms and Lohmann, *Letters,* 264.

20. Arms and Lohmann, *Letters,* 4:306n2.

21. W. D. Howells, Introduction to *The Complete Poems of Paul Laurence Dunbar* (New York: Dodd, Mead & Co., 1896), ix.

22. Howells, *Criticism and Fiction,* 224.

23. See Wolfgang Iser, *The Implied Reader: Patterns of Communication in Prose Fiction from Bunyan to Beckett* (Baltimore: The Johns Hopkins University Press, 1974), 292–93.

24. See Gilles Deleuze and Felix Guattari, "What is a Minor Literature?" in *Kafka: Toward a Minor Literature,* trans. by Dana Polan (Minneapolis: University of Minnesota Press, 1975), 16–27.

25. Sollars, *Beyond Ethnicity,* 249.

26. Interestingly, Sui Sin Far's sister, Winifred Eaton (Onoto Watanna), was far more successful at representing the Other, perhaps precisely because she did not attempt serious fiction. Unlike her sibling, Onoto Watanna adopted various ethnic guises as she produced "ethnic" stories for a popular mainstream audience. As Amy Ling has noted, (*Melus,* 2, no. 3 [Fall, 1984]: 5–15), because Watanna took her ethnicity lightly (she passed for Japanese because they were more fashionable than Chinese among whites) she managed to produce novels that mixed Asian and white characters, good and evil, on a fairly even basis and that were relaxed even about such explosive subjects as interracial (Japanese-white) marriages, as she did in *Miss Nume of Japan* (1899).

27. Cahan, *Imported Bridegroom,* 50.

Three Black Writers and the Anthologized Canon

KENETH KINNAMON

An empirical definition of the American literary canon might be those writers recurrently included in general anthologies of American literature and discussed in general literary histories.[1] For the most part, especially in recent years, such works are compiled or written by academicians in English departments who specialize in American literature.[2] Occasionally a literary journalist such as John Macy or a novelist such as Ludwig Lewisohn undertakes a literary history of the country, but they are exceptional. The contributors to *Literary History of the United States* (1948) included several historians (e.g., Brand Blandshard, Henry Steele Commager, Eric Goldman, Allan Nevins), a couple of literary journalists (Malcolm Cowley and Maxwell Geismar), and even a poet (Carl Sandburg), but forty years later all seventy-four contributors to the *Columbia Literary History of the United States,* from Daniel Aaron to Ruth Bernard Yeazell, were professors of English, American literature, or American Studies. (Elaine H. Kim is affiliated with an Asian American Studies program). Today, more than ever, the canon is what professors say it is.

As we all know, professors are not exempt from social and political influences on their literary judgments, if indeed one can speak at all of literary judgments divorced from nonliterary considerations. It follows that what the professors say the canon is changes over time as the social and political climate changes. Historically, one of the most powerful nonliterary considerations affecting American literary taste has been race. Its effect can be clearly illustrated by reviewing the literary reputations of three black writers whose work emerged between 1887 and 1912: Charles Waddell Chesnutt, Paul Laurence Dunbar, and James Weldon Johnson. One is forced to say that the work, rather than the authors, emerged, for when "The

Goophered Grapevine" appeared in the *Atlantic Monthly* in August 1887, Chesnutt's name but not his race was revealed. In addition, *The Autobiography of an Ex-Coloured Man* was published anonymously in 1912, Johnson waiting fifteen years until it was reissued before acknowledging the novel as his own. Of the three writers considered, only Dunbar's race was clearly evident early on in his career, but, as Peter Revell has pointed out, even Dunbar's very first publications, two poems in his hometown newspaper, were nonracial.[3] That period from the failure of the Reconstruction to the advent of the World War, called by the historian Rayford W. Logan "the nadir" of postbellum racial experience, was not a propitious time for the coming of age of a black writer.[4]

In speaking of the racism of the anthologists of American literature, however, one is seldom referring to a virulent or even explicit assertion of the racial and literary inferiority of black people. Instead, until the past two decades, we find a pattern of exclusion by omission, an absence of Chesnutt, Dunbar, and Johnson attributable perhaps to ignorance as well as prejudice. The canonical status conferred by anthologies is self-perpetuating, for an anthology is seldom compiled without close attention to its predecessors. If Chesnutt, Dunbar, and Johnson are omitted from Anthology A and if there is not a wide public demand for them, the compiler of Anthology B, who may not have read the three writers in depth if at all, is not likely to undertake intensive study to decide whether they merit inclusion. The absence of such writers from anthologies becomes the excuse for not reading them, for if they were any good they would be anthologized. The result was the ubiquitous expression of surprise by specialists in (white) American literature in the sixties and seventies when they were made aware of the substantial tradition of African American literature from the eighteenth century on and of the individual writers within that tradition, including Chesnutt, Dunbar, and Johnson, deserving of consideration for canonical status. Underlying the whole process, of course, was the assumption, conscious or unconscious, on the part of many if not most white scholars that the voice from behind the veil, the invisible because subterranean writer, could not achieve the requisite eloquence, profundity, beauty, and imaginative power of great literature because that voice was black.

The story might have been quite otherwise if the college and high-school market for anthologies of American literature had developed a couple of decades earlier, when the abolitionist spirit was not yet utterly quenched. One can speculate plausibly that Higginson or Sanborn or Howells would have included samples of Chesnutt's short fiction and Dunbar's poetry in a compilation put together at the turn of the century. After all, Edmund Clarence Stedman and Ellen MacKay Hutchinson's massive *Library of American Literature* (1891), too early for Chesnutt and Dunbar, did contain selections from Phillis Wheatley, Frederick Douglass, and the historian George Washington Williams. As it turned out, however, of the nine anthologies I have examined published from 1915 to 1927—Sarah E. Simons's *American Literature Through Illustrative Readings* (1915), Mary Edwards Calhoun and Emma Leonore MacAlarney's *Readings from American Literature* (1915), Leonidas Warren Payne's *American Literary Readings* (1917), Alphonso G. Newcomer, Alice E. Adams, and Howard Judson Hall's *Three Centuries of American Poetry and Prose* (1917), Fred L. Pattee's influential *Century Readings in American Literature* (1919), Percy H. Boynton's *Milestones in American Literature* (1923), Norman Foerster's durable *American Poetry and Prose* (1925), Robert Shafer's *American Literature* (1926), and Franklin B. and Edward D. Snyder's *A Book of American Literature* (1927)—the first-named, a text for high-school use, reprinted Dunbar's "A Corn Song," but otherwise not a single selection by Chesnutt, Dunbar, or Johnson (whose *Fifty Years and Other Poems* appeared in 1917) was included. Instead, room was found in these collections for such writers as James Whitcomb Riley, Eugene Field, Joel Chandler Harris, Frank Stockton, John Burroughs, Henry Van Dyke, "Bill Arp," Celia Leighton Thaxter, "Charles Egbert Craddock," Richard Hovey, Edward Rowland Sill, John Banister Tabb, Richard Watson Gilder, Alan Seeger, William Ellery Leonard, Clyde Fitch, William Crary Brownell, and the like.

The socially conscious thirties showed only slight improvement over this dismal record. Arthur Hobson Quinn, Albert C. Baugh, and Will David Howe's *The Literature of America* (1929) included three of Dunbar's poems—a tribute to Harriet Beecher Stowe and a meditation on mortality, both in standard English, and the black dialect poem "Angelina." Harry R. Warfel, Ralph H. Gabriel, and Stanley T. Williams followed the same pattern in *The American Mind* (1937): "We Wear the Mask" and "Sympathy," both destined to become standard anthology pieces, in standard English, followed by "The Turning of the Babies in the Bed" in dialect. Oscar Cargill reprinted four Dunbar poems, two in standard English and two in dialect, in the fourth volume of *American Literature: A Period An-*

thology (1933), but added a note quoting approvingly Alfred Kreymborg's comment that Dunbar's "poems are smoother than [Irwin] Russell's, but the white man saw deeper into the darkies." These anthologies omitted Chesnutt and Johnson while including Dunbar. In *Our Land and Its Literature* (1936), Orton Lowe anthologized Johnson for the first time with one of his best poems, "Go Down Death" from *God's Trombones,* but omitted Dunbar and Chesnutt. Four other anthologies of the period ignored all three writers: H. S. Schwieckert, Remy Belle Inglis, and John Gehlmann's *Adventures in American Literature* (1930), a text used extensively in high schools for more than a quarter century thereafter; Ludwig Lewisohn's *Creative America: An Anthology* (1933); Jay B. Hubbell's widely adopted *American Life in Literature* (1936), used not only in colleges but in the military as well in the two editions issued during World War II by the U.S. Armed Forces Institute; and William Rose Benét and Norman Holmes Pearson's *The Oxford Anthology of American Literature* (1938). To the earlier list of some white writers included while Chesnutt, Dunbar, and Johnson were largely excluded may be added the names of Thomas Bailey Aldrich, David Graham Phillips, Lizette Woodworth Reese, Paul Hamilton Hayne, Louise Imogene Guiney, George Sterling, and Charles Erskine Scott Wood.

The forties were no better. Bernard Smith's *The Democratic Spirit* (1941) contained two poems by Johnson, but was not democratic—or informed—enough to include Chesnutt or Dunbar. A high-school anthology, Pearle Ethel Knight and Harry G. Paul's *In America* (1942), offered one dialect poem by Dunbar but nothing by Chesnutt or Johnson. W. Tasker Witham's *Living American Literature* (1947) presented a couple of Dunbar dialect poems while likewise omitting Chesnutt and Johnson. Five college texts rejected each of the three writers: Milton Ellis, Louise Pound, and George Weida Spohn's *A College Book of American Literature* (1940); Willard Thorp, Carlos Baker, James K. Folsom, and Merle Curti's *American Issues: The Literary Record* and *American Issues: The Social Record,* both published in 1941; Walter Blair, Theodore Hornberger, and Randall Stewart's *The Literature of the United States* (1947); and Joe Lee Davis, John T. Frederick, and Frank Luther Mott's *American Literature: An Anthology and Critical Survey* (1949). Deprived of Chesnutt, Dunbar, and Johnson, users of these anthologies could console themselves with selections by Richard Henry Stoddard, Edmund Clarence Stedman, Constance Fenimore Woolson, Ring Lardner,

Charles Heber Clark, Finley Peter Dunne, Thomas Nelson Page, and O. Henry. Similarly, the high-school student learning about American literature from Dudley Miles and Robert C. Pooley's popular *Literature and Life in America* (1943) would not encounter mention of any black writers at all, but could read Joaquin Miller and Sarah N. Cleghorn. Surely the worst example, though, was the Texas high-school text *High Lights in American Literature and Other Selections* (1940), edited by Ola Pauline Srygley, Otsie Verona Betts, Mattie W. Allison, and Benjamin Ford Fornaberger. Black writers did not appear therein either as highlights or other selections, but the student could peruse such worthies as Frances Alexander, Pernett Patterson, Lucy Furman, Estella Kelley, and Dallas Lore Sharp. During the war against fascism black Texas adolescents reading this book's section entitled "Americans All" would find selections by or about Jews, Italians, Swedes, Poles, and Portuguese, but not a word about their own race, then the largest minority group in the state, or Mexican Americans, the second largest.

By the fifties even Dunbar had faded from the memory of anthologists. Neither Chesnutt nor Dunbar nor Johnson is to be found in the five collections I have seen: Raymond W. Short and Wilbur S. Scott's *The Main Lines of American Literature* (1954), which by design includes "only background reading" and less than major authors; Leon Howard, Louis B. Wright, and Carl Bode's *American Heritage: An Anthology and Interpretive Survey of Our Literature* (1955), which includes Rebecca Harding Davis and Thomas Bangs Thorpe; James D. Hart and Clarence Gohdes's *America's Literature* (1955); Clifton Fadiman's *The American Treasury* (1955); and Sculley Bradley, Richmond Croom Beatty, and E. Hudson Long's highly successful *The American Tradition in Literature* (1956).

Bunched as they were in the middle fifties, already published or in advanced preparation as Martin Luther King, Jr., was first coming into prominence as the leader of the Montgomery bus boycott, these anthologies were not affected by the developing racial climate of the civil rights movement. In the sixties and early seventies, though, things began to change. Traditional exclusionary anthologies continued to appear, of course. Chesnutt, Dunbar, and Johnson are absent from R. W. Stallman and Arthur Waldhorn's *American Literature: Readings and Critiques* (1961), Thomas M. Davis and Willoughby Johnson's *An Anthology of American Literature* (1966), Richard Poirier and William L. Vance's *American Literature* (1970), and Irving Howe, Mark Schorer, and Larzer Ziff's *The Literature of*

America (1971). But other anthologies published during this period were less resistant to the canonical implications of social change. In 1960 the veteran Louis Untermeyer, who had included Dunbar and Johnson much earlier in his anthology *Modern American Poetry* (1925), printed the latter's "The Creation" in *The Britannia Library of Great American Writing. The Odyssey Surveys of American Writing* (1965, 1966) was a four-volume anthology with C. Hugh Holman as general editor and separate editors for each volume. In the third, *The Realistic Movement in American Writing,* Bruce R. McElderry, Jr., omitted Chesnutt and represented Dunbar wearing his mask in two dialect poems catering to fans of the Plantation School, "When de Co'n Pone's Hot" and, even worse, "The Coquette Conquered." Johnson does not appear in the fourth volume, *Twentieth Century American Writing,* edited by William T. Stafford. At the end of the decade Harrison T. Meserole, Walter Sutton, and Brom Weber included a Chesnutt story, "A Matter of Principle," in their *American Literature: Tradition and Innovation* (1969), probably the first appearance of this writer in a general anthology. Neither Dunbar nor Chesnutt appears in this book, but Langston Hughes, Richard Wright, Ralph Ellison, James Baldwin, and LeRoi Jones are represented. Other new anthologies also included one or two of the trio, Don Hausdorf and Charles Kaplan presenting a Chesnutt story and six Dunbar poems in *Literature in America* (1971) and George McMichael and associates offering Chesnutt's "The Goophered Grapevine" in *Anthology of American Literature* (1974).

Another indicator of the academic response to the increasing demand for black writers was their sudden appearance in previously lily-white collections. The first four editions of Norman Foerster's venerable *American Poetry and Prose* excluded black writers altogether, but when Norman S. Grabo, Russel B. Nye, E. Fred Carlisle, and Robert Falk joined Foerster as editors of the fifth edition (1970), Houghton Mifflin's "Publisher's Foreword" states that in subtle ways "this edition has taken the measure of the day and reflects the many and profound changes of the last decade." In fact, the ways the fifth edition differs from the fourth are not at all subtle. Not only did it add Wheatley, Jupiter Hammon, Douglass, Chesnutt ("The Goophered Grapevine"), Jean Toomer, Wright, Ellison, Baldwin, and LeRoi Jones to the table of contents, but it also used cover art to fulfill its obligation to help "to shape and inform the changing canon of our literature . . . for the critical generation of students coming of age in the 1970's." The blue, black, and silver design of the fourth edition (1957) presents five images—an open book, a doric column, a cherub with a lyre, a steamboat, and Brooklyn Bridge—inviting the reader to open the anthology and read in the colonial and revolutionary, the romantic, the realistic, and the modern periods of American literature. The red, white, and black front cover of the fifth edition displays from left to right across the bottom the images of Edwards, Franklin, Emerson, Twain, Whitman, Dickinson, Frost, Hemingway, Wright, Cummings, and—the largest figure—Baldwin, with the same images in reverse order on the back cover. Just as Houghton Mifflin canonized New England writers on its own list in the nineteenth century and canonized white writers only in the first four editions of *American Poetry and Prose,* it was now willing to expand the canon to include selected black writers, but not any of brown, red, or yellow hues. A similar pattern obtains in *The American Tradition in Literature* (1956, 1962, 1967, 1974, 1981, 1985, 1990), edited by Bradley, Beatty, Long, and, beginning in 1974, George Perkins. Predictably, the first two editions lack black content except for five "Negro Songs," but the third edition nervously includes two poems by LeRoi Jones. The fourth edition, prepared mostly by Perkins, adds Wheatley, Douglass, Chesnutt ("The Sheriff's Children"), Dunbar (four poems), Hughes, Wright, Ellison, Baldwin, and Baraka, but not Johnson. Dunbar was deleted from the sixth edition but restored in the seventh with an additional poem ("Sympathy"). The seventh edition also wisely substituted "The Passing of Grandison" for "The Sheriff's Children." The most satisfying revision was accomplished by Milton R. Stern and Seymour L. Gross in their four-volume *American Literature Survey* (1962, 1968, 1975). The first two editions do not contain Chesnutt, Dunbar, or Johnson, but the third edition includes good selections by all three: "The Passing of Grandison"; five Dunbar poems, more than any previous general anthology; and Johnson's "O Black and Unknown Bards" and the excellent but seldom anthologized "The White Witch." The headnotes by Stern are well-informed and perceptive, and the bibliographical notes are full.

Even better is *American Literature: The Makers and the Making* (1973), edited by Cleanth Brooks, R. W. B. Lewis, and Robert Penn Warren. The Chesnutt story is "The Wife of His Youth," the best of the color-line stories. The Dunbar choices are especially good. "We Wear the Mask" is predictable, almost inevitable, but the other two poems are excellent but usually overlooked. "The Haunted

Oak" is a grim lynching poem anticipating Countee Cullen's "The Black Christ" and Richard Wright's "Between the World and Me." "An Ante-Bellum Sermon" is perhaps the poet's most successful effort to use his black dialect mode to subvert the racist mentality conditioned by the Plantation School, just as the preacher in the poem uses white Christianity to subvert slavery and anticipate freedom. Johnson is amply represented by "O Black and Unknown Bards," "The Crucifixion" from *God's Trombones,* and the fifteen concluding pages of *The Autobiography of an Ex-Coloured Man.* The headnote to Chesnutt is brief and perfunctory, and that to Dunbar, treating him as a transitional figure, underestimates his achievement. But the very full headnote to Johnson demonstrates a close knowledge of his life and career, even quoting from two of his unpublished operas.[5] Today's fashionable and often doctrinaire repudiation of New Critics as elitist formalists incapable of concern for the political and social dimensions of literature does not take into account the fact that *American Literature: The Makers and the Making* was the first general anthology to include Chesnutt, Dunbar, and Johnson, in addition to Wheatley, Douglass, Washington, Du Bois, Hughes, Toomer, Cullen, McKay, Hurston, Bontemps, Wright, Ellison, Baldwin, and a liberal selection of black folk songs, including an eighteen-page section on the blues. As James A. Grimshaw has shown, Robert Penn Warren was responsible for the black material in this anthology.[6] From the overt racism of "The Briar Patch," his contribution to the Agrarian manifesto *I'll Take My Stand* (1930), Warren had indeed come a long way.

During the last dozen years or so African American literature has taken a secure, one hopes permanent, place in general anthologies of American literature. David Levin, Theodore L. Gross, Alan Trachtenberg, and Benjamin DeMott included "The Wife of His Youth," three Dunbar poems, and Johnson's "O Black and Unknown Bards" and "The Creation" in their *American Literature* (1978). In the following year Norton attempted to duplicate the immense success of its anthology of English literature with *The Norton Anthology of American Literature,* edited by Ronald Gottesman, Laurence B. Holland, David Kalstone, Francis Murphy, Hershel Parker, and William H. Pritchard, joined by Nina Baym and Patricia B. Wallace after the deaths of Holland and Kalstone. Chesnutt's "The Goophered Grapevine" appears in the three editions to date, but nothing by Dunbar or Johnson, even in the third edition (1989), which includes selections by Equiano, Wheatley, Douglass, Washington, Du Bois,

Hurston, Hughes, Cullen, Wright, Ellison, Baldwin, Alice Walker, Robert Hayden, Gwendolyn Brooks, Audre Lorde, Amiri Baraka, Michael Harper, and Rita Dove. Francis Hodgins and Kenneth Silverman's high-school anthology *Adventures in American Literature* (1980) is superior to its predecessor of the same title published half a century earlier, but it neglects Chesnutt and Johnson while reprinting Dunbar's "Douglass" and "Life's Tragedy." Donald McQuade, Robert Atwan, Martha Banta, Justin Kaplan, David Minter, Cecilia Tichi, and Helen Vendler's *The Harper American Literature* (1987), like its competitor *The Norton Anthology of American Literature,* includes a Chesnutt story but nothing by Dunbar or Johnson while representing reasonably other black authors of the twentieth century. The fullest representation of our three authors as well as black and other minority and women writers generally is in the much-heralded revisionary collection edited by Paul Lauter and associates, *The Heath Anthology of American Literature* (1990), a conscious effort on the part of its many contributing scholars to alter the canon permanently by expansion in some directions and contraction in others. Here we find *three* stories by Chesnutt ("The Goophered Grapevine," "Po' Sandy," and "The Passing of Grandison"), five poems by Dunbar *and* his short story "Mr. Cornelius Johnson, Office-Seeker," and two poems by Johnson. One could fairly quibble only with the Johnson selection for not including one of the verse sermons from *God's Trombones*. Certainly no one could claim that Chesnutt is underrepresented, his three stories exceeding the two each allocated to Sarah Orne Jewett, Henry James, and William Faulkner. A single story is the lot of William Dean Howells, Ambrose Bierce, Willa Cather, Sherwood Anderson, F. Scott Fitzgerald, Ernest Hemingway, John Steinbeck, Richard Wright, James Baldwin, and Flannery O'Connor. Balance would seem to be the issue here, not underrepresentation.

The two most recent anthologies are James E. Miller, Jr.'s *Heritage of American Literature* (1991), the first general collection edited by a single individual in decades, and *American Literature: A Prentice Hall Anthology* (1991), edited by Emory Elliott, Linda K. Kerber, A. Walton Litz, and Terence Martin. The first includes Chesnutt's "The Sheriff's Children," four poems by Dunbar, and Johnson's "We to America" (not elsewhere anthologized) and "The Creation." The second presents two stories by Chesnutt ("The Passing of Grandison" and "Sis' Becky's Pickaninny") and six well-chosen poems by Dunbar (including poetic tributes to Stowe, Douglass, and

Washington), but nothing—strange to say at this late date—by Johnson.

From this survey of the representation of Chesnutt, Dunbar, and Johnson in fifty general anthologies of American literature,[7] certain patterns emerge. Twenty-nine of the fifty omit all three writers, though three of these (Foerster et al., Bradley et al., and Stern and Gross) add one, two, or three of them in later editions. Fifteen of the fifty include one writer only, two include two, and four (five if one counts the third edition of Stern and Gross), include all three. The relation of racial attitudes to the anthologized canon is especially clear if one graphs these patterns against the racial history of our century. Of the twenty-nine anthologies that excluded all three writers, twenty-seven appeared before 1968, the year Dr. King was assassinated, and ten of the fifteen including only of the three were published before that year. Of these, seven include only Dunbar, mainly his dialect poems that invite the white reader's condescension. During the last two decades, when racist feeling in the academy and the publishing houses has subsided, only one of the eleven new anthologies appearing has omitted all three of our writers, four have included one, two have included two, and four have included all three.

It is also noteworthy that in the last eleven anthologies Chesnutt is more frequently represented than Dunbar (nine to seven), with Johnson a distant third (four appearances), whereas earlier Dunbar appeared in seven anthologies, Johnson in three, and Chesnutt in only one. The reason for Johnson's relative neglect may be as much literary as racial. In his brief but productive career at the turn of the century, Dunbar was writing at a low point in American poetry, but the poetry of Johnson, who was a year older than Dunbar, appeared much later in volumes published in 1917, 1927, and 1935. Thus he has to compete for anthology space with Pound, Eliot, Williams, Stevens, Crane, and the other great modernists as well as with such contemporaries as Robinson, Frost, and Sandburg. Nevertheless, all future anthologies should find room for one of the verse sermons and a couple of the shorter poems of Johnson.

Despite improving representation of these three poets in recent anthologies, one should guard against excessive optimism. African American history has been characterized by cycles of hope and despair, high expectations and grim disappointments, as the tide of white racism ebbed and flowed. The revolutionary euphoria aroused by the Declaration of Independence was dispelled by the constitutional provision designating slaves as three–fifths of a person for purposes of taxation and representation. The abolition movement, the Civil War, and Reconstruction destroyed slavery as an institution, but by 1877 white supremacy had been restored and black people in the South were being disfranchised and often reduced to peonage. The New Deal and the triumph over fascism in World War II were followed by the complacency and reaction of the fifties. Despite this pattern, one can at least hope that the best black writers are now achieving the permanent canonical status in anthologies of American literature so long denied in the past for racial reasons. Among these writers Charles Waddell Chesnutt, Paul Laurence Dunbar, and James Weldon Johnson—important for literary, historical, and social reasons—should take the prominent place they deserve.

Notes

1. For an excellent introduction to the complexity of the concept of *canon*, see Wendell V. Harris, "Canonicity," *PMLA* 106 (1991): 110–21.

2. As Kermit Vanderbilt has demonstrated, however, academic Americanists were in short supply early in the present century, when only a few pioneering institutions offered courses in American literature. Of the four editors of the *Cambridge History of American Literature,* not one was trained as a specialist in the field, though Carl Van Doren became one autodidactically after writing his doctoral dissertation at Columbia on Thomas Love Peacock. See *American Literature and the Academy* (Philadelphia: University of Pennsylvania Press, 1986), 6–14.

3. See Peter Revell *Paul Laurence Dunbar* (Boston: Twayne Publishers, 1979), 41.

4. See Logan's *The Negro in American Life and Thought: The Nadir, 1877–1901* (New York: Dial Press, 1954) and the enlarged edition entitled *The Betrayal of the Negro from Rutherford B. Hayes to Woodrow Wilson* (New York: Collier Books, 1965). For some literary implications see Dickson D. Bruce, *Black Writing from the Nadir: The Evolution of a Literary Tradition, 1877–1915* (Baton Rouge: Louisiana State University Press, 1989).

5. As professors at Yale, the editors had easy access to the great James Weldon Johnson Collection in the Beinecke Library.

6. See James A. Grimshaw *Robert Penn Warren: A Descriptive Bibliography, 1917–1978* (Charlottesville: University of Virginia Press, 1981), 438.

7. Some anthologies have probably escaped my attention, for I have examined only those in my own possession and in the libraries of the University of Arkansas, the University of Oklahoma, the University of Kansas, the University of Texas, and the University of Illinois. For obvious reasons I have excluded such "major-author" collections as Randall Stewart and Dorothy Bethurum's *Living Masterpieces of American Literature* (1954), Leon Edel, Thomas H. Johnson, Sherman Paul, and Claude Simpson's *Masters of American Literature* (1959), Perry Miller's *Major Writers of America* (1962), and Charles R. Anderson's *American Literary Masters* (1965).

Recanonizing the Multiple Canons of Henry James

RICHARD A. HOCKS

As the figure who until quite recently was apt to be denominated "the Master" of American prose fiction, Henry James is most unlikely to be much of a hero within the current debate about the recanonization of American literature; if anything, his credentials as a prime target are all too rank. Indeed, his status among the "top ten"—by analogy with collegiate athletics—has long been in place (and thus ripe for condemnation or removal) by virtue of his inclusion among the venerable "Eight American Authors," all of whom are white and male.[1] Hence, Henry James may well have the double-damned onus right now of *both* being a charter member of the "Eight American Authors" *and* carrying the appellation "the Master." Even within the more presumably friendly confines of James scholarship itself, Alfred Habegger recently sought to discredit James's authenticity, accusing him of "making [his own] literary history" by simultaneously appropriating and rewriting popular women's domestic fiction while he himself critically set about to "silence" it as a "covert act of force directed against women."[2] So now we know: whereas critics of my generation thought Henry James had been designated "the Master" because of some technical virtuosity or perhaps as a discriminating critic, now we are beginning to wonder instead if he is "the master" in somewhat the same way as is Stowe's infernal Simon Legree (also from the North, remember), by cruelly mistreating those "scribbling women" beneath him in literary bondage, stealing from them the orphan heroine figure, and creating, first, his "masterful" series of canonical texts, then dictating the aesthetic terms for all his subsequent Jacobite critics, beginning with Joseph Warren Beach and Percy Lubbock, to perpetuate them.

Of course, this damning revaluation-scenario of James cannot be all that widespread as yet, for he continues to receive more scholarship every year than any other American author save Faulkner, with whom he remains in a virtual tie: anyone with that thickness of attention is still, at some level, a darling of the academy. Critics of my generation, once again, might have thought that the reason for such continuing attention is that James's corpus is at once extensive, experimentally "phased," and intricately wrought, combining Trollope-like quantity with Joyce-like tapestry. But that very kind of "aesthetic" evaluation of him is precisely the sort of master discourse inimical to serious recanonization, is it not?

Anyone familiar with the history of James criticism knows only too well that his massive corpus, or rather some part of it, comes in for a drubbing at regular intervals, though such attacks are always followed by a resurgence of new scholarship that obliterates the attack. H. G. Wells, Van Wyck Brooks, Vernon Louis Parrington, Maxwell Geismar—all have taken their best shots, but the touchstone of their ultimate impotence can perhaps be measured by the fact that F. R. Leavis's *The Great Tradition* (1948) actually incorporated Parrington's and Brooks's stinging critique of James's late work ("hypertrophy of technique," Leavis calls it) while still affirming nothing less than Jacobite laudation worthy, say, of R. P. Blackmur, the author of the James chapter in the *Literary History of the United States* published the same year. For Leavis, James and the other members of the great tradition exhibited a "registration of sophisticated consciousness," a "classical achievement" producing "an ideally civilized sensibility."[3] In other words, James accomplished all this (and making the "top five" this time) even if we discount what all the other scholars of the same period would call, after F. O. Matthiessen, his "major phase." Clearly James could not help but win for losing; after all, how many authors can have their "major phase" dismissed and still be selected for "the great tradition"? Obviously the sheer quantity of work extending through his career—the early, middle, and late periods—pointed up the possibility of several "canons" within his oeuvre. The more one attends to the long-range history of James criticism, the more one perceives that the early and late James fiction in particular has been treated as if they were two separate canons. The same point comes home when one considers the ongoing dispute about whether James's early or revised texts are to be preferred. I can recall when his revised Scribner's texts were just as canonical as he is. Now we seem to reside in a period in which, far more often than not, editors of textbooks and anthologies seem to prefer printing his early texts.[4]

But as true as this is, I hardly think it will surprise very many readers, certainly not Jamesians. What I really prefer to explore is a vastly different sense in which James contains several canons, a sense that may bring the issue closer to contemporary recanonizers, since such folk are not likely to be much interested in the old early, middle, and late James question, or whether to print his unrevised texts. What I have in mind is rather a remarkable critical morphology found within the most recent history of James scholarship, as well as the very bewildering experience one often has right now in confronting and assessing the trends of James's stock in the academy.

Let me begin by pointing out a configuration in James scholarship that probably even most professional Jamesians are not yet aware of, or at best only vaguely. The criticism of Henry James from its very beginning until the beginning of the last decade, 1980, marks a discernible epoch with regard to approaches, methodology, and thus canonicity. That is to say, despite all the various time-honored disagreements about the meaning of "Daisy Miller," *The Turn of the Screw,* or any of the major novels—and despite the vast difference in assessing James himself as profound cultural anatomist by Stephen Spender, Ezra Pound, Graham Greene, or James Baldwin, or as poet of the novel by R. P. Blackmur, F. O. Matthiessen, Daniel M. Fogel, or Ruth B. Yeazell, or as heroic and troubled psychological specimen of genius by Leon Edel, or as international historian by Joseph Warren Beach, Christof Wegelin, or Alwyn Berland, or as moral-epistemic philosopher by Dorothea Krook, Stephen Donadio, or myself—despite these and all other manner of "Jameses" constructed by literary critics, the James scholarship before 1980 was, so to speak, pre-postmodern. During that period, which I shall henceforth call James's "first wave," the novelist was most frequently the arbiter of New Criticism for the novel, extending his dominion onward from Percy Lubbock's *Craft of Fiction* to Wayne Booth's *Rhetoric of Fiction,* signifying the aesthetic marriage of formalism and reader-response.[5] But the 1980s have seen two important new developments. First, the sheer quantity of work on him has become so massive as to number yearly well over a hundred essays and book chapters, not counting major (or minor) critical books—fifteen in 1989 alone—together with doctoral dissertations, edited textbooks, or bibliographical studies. Such acceleration, to be sure, has simply gained momentum since the 1950s.

The other and more important development in the 1980s, however, is my principal subject for the remainder of this essay. Henry James studies have without question experienced an amazing ideological "second wave," profoundly affecting his canon. This has occurred because, more than any other American writer, poet or novelist, James has become the receptacle for all the divergent, sometimes overlapping, strands of postmodern critical theory—as distinct from "literary criticism" of the sort that originally made his academic reputation during the "first wave."[6] The James of the 1980s is the iridescent prism of John Carlos Rowe's deconstructionist approach, the incandescent object of Paul Armstrong's phenomenological study, the power figure of Mark Seltzer's political and Foucauldian analysis, the subject of Alfred Habegger's feminist critique (as we saw earlier), the principal example in Susan Mizruchi's new historicism, the protagonist in Marcia Jacobson's and Michael Anesko's cultural studies, the prime figure in Paul John Eakin's biographical narratology work, the preoccupation of Donna Przybylowicz's Marxist and Lacanian analysis—and innumerable others.[7] What light has this ideological "second wave" to shed on our knotty problem of recanonization?

Quite a bit, I think. Let me propose something like "four posts" that support James's new canonical bed in the wake of this "second wave" of criticism. The first is one that affects any college teacher, Jamesian or no, when teaching courses in American literature or the American novel: for the two James novels that, initially at least, have not participated—at least with expected proportionality—in the "second wave" are precisely the hitherto "indispensable" ones, the "masterworks" from his canon, *The Portrait of a Lady* and *The Ambassadors*. Whatever may be the case in the classroom, these two classic works—*The Ambassadors* particularly—began to move toward the background in the journals, presses, and conferences while others, as we shall see, came forward to take their places. This is a remarkable development. How many American literature curricula in the past have included, along with *The Scarlet Letter, Adventures of Huckleberry Finn,* and *The Great Gatsby,* the inevitable James contribution, *The Portrait of a Lady?* And yet, its initially diminished attention from theoretical critics is not really so difficult to comprehend, for *The Portrait* is without question a formalist masterpiece, the spacious "house of fiction" of James's famous preface. To recall the quintessential formalism of James's most famous novel, one need not even be a Jamesian familiar with everything from Matthiessen's essay on the textual revisions to, say, Laurence Holland's loving treatment in *The Expense of Vision.* One need only recollect the discriminating formalism of either Dorothy Van Ghent (1953) or Richard Chase (1957), both of whose chapters on *The Portrait* evoke not only an academic critical school but a whole era.[8]

But if a change at first began to take place, perhaps with *The Portrait of a Lady,* think how much more it was the case with *The Ambassadors.* Back in 1918, Joseph Warren Beach had asserted that "the *ideal* of James is clearly a combination, or rather a *fusion,* of good taste with spiritual discernment, and perhaps the most complete, if not the most dramatic, instance of this fusion is . . . Lambert Strether. For him there seems to be no such distinction between esthetic and ethic as perplexes most of us mortals." Percy Lubbock three years later went even further, affirming that Strether's mind is so "fully dramatized" that James's "art of dramatizing the picture of somebody's [inner] experience touches its limits. There is indeed no further for it to go." *The Craft of Fiction* thus fully privileged and canonized both James and *The Ambassadors* at the same time, by applying aesthetic criteria gleaned from James's prefaces and evaluating major classic writers such as Tolstoy and Flaubert by "James" standards. Far more Jamesian than James, his study together with Beach's codified "point of view" and the dramatic method (in fiction), setting the stage for the revival of and continued formalist work on James many years later. In short, the history of formalism and the history of *The Ambassadors* are one and the same. For the recanonizer, this same history—coterminous and coextensive with the great "first wave" of James criticism—is of crucial importance. After all, James *himself* dictated it out of his own prefaces and literary essays, as Lubbock's study testifies. Verily, it is even "worse" than that, inasmuch as James in those prefaces designated only two novels as his best, as in his words exhibiting "superior roundness," and these were *The Portrait of a Lady* and *The Ambassadors!* We could not possibly be back more clearly with the bête noire of the recanonizer, James as mandarin Master, controlling with his sacred texts, the prefaces, the destiny of his own literary history, extending his dominion throughout the "first wave."

Nevertheless the 1980s, as I say, have created in the "second wave" a literary figure drastically different from him who canonized *The Portrait* and *The Ambassadors.* So what is the poor teacher to do? By which I mean the teacher of American literature. By which

I also mean even the professional Jamesian as teacher. What is that teacher to do, if the most vital James texts at the conferences began to become increasingly different from the hitherto "indispensable" James teaching canon? If the reader has followed me to this point and is willing to trust my veracity about the main reconfigurations of James's critical history, perhaps that reader also recognizes here a familiar dilemma experienced by us all (well, most of us) regardless of the particular author or literary subject. That is, how do we begin to reconcile the teaching we do in our class with the scholarship we read and papers we hear at conferences? *The Portrait of a Lady* is a most inviting case: its scholarship remains plentiful enough, despite the trend I here recount; but even were criticism of it to stop altogether, good students would forever love it and teachers continue to feel it a masterpiece to teach.

Perhaps it is fortunate to be able to report that the trend I have just recounted already begins to show certain symptoms of reversing itself—which is why I spoke earlier of *The Portrait* and *The Ambassadors* as "initially at least" not participating in the "second wave." In other words, these two novels, while at first not attracting the theorists, are just now starting to draw them in as if by a magnet: *The Portrait of a Lady,* for example, is being revisited as perhaps his most fertile text for post-Freudian psychoanalysis, and *The Ambassadors* as the locus for his "pluralized masculinity" or else "dialogic knowledge." Indeed, the very fact that James did endorse these two books so directly will probably, eventually, result in a spate of critical studies that employ them as repositories of personal Jamesian gender and psychodynamical issues. Such criticism will not be a case, as in the classroom situation, of returning to those novels largely for their formal beauty and symmetry.[10]

My larger task, however, is to relate what *other* new novels within James's textual amplitude have come to the fore and at least temporarily "backgrounded" those two jewels of the older dispensation, *The Portrait of a Lady* and *The Ambassadors*—to present, that is, the second of James's "four posts" of canonicity. Actually, this new group, appropriate to the "decentered" worldview of the "second wave," constitutes a most diverse group of novels. We might well call several of them "problem novels" after Shakespeare's problem comedies. Most are works that used to be thought of as experiments with greater or lesser success, but always as interesting attempts that merely prepared the way to the great achievements of the "major phase"—much as Michelangelo's slaves give way and usher us into the presence of his *David* at the Academy in Florence. But no longer. Now it is rather those problem works that most engage the postmodernist sensibility of the "second wave." *What Maisie Knew,* for example, has more to tell us about epistemology, sexual curiosity, the coding of manners and morals, cultural orphans, and the enduring condition of very young girls in a manipulative social order than, presumably, *The Portrait* and *The Ambassadors* put together. Another work, *The Princess Casamassima,* dealing as it does with British anarchism in the 1880s, is felt now to be one of James's two major political novels, and perhaps the one that raises the most profound and disturbing questions regarding the relationship of power to the sources of violence and art. Interestingly this same novel, whose neglect yet importance Lionel Trilling and Irving Howe alone had pleaded for in the 1950s, is now riding the "second wave" of James scholarship and already ensconced as one of his major achievements, its "gaps" and virtual absence of formal symmetry all the more indicative of its authenticity.[11] Still another important book for the "second wave" is his other political novel *The Bostonians* ("a very *American* story," James called it). This novel about feminist movements in the 1870s has taken over by virtue of its sexual politics the seat of controversy formerly given to *The Turn of the Screw.* James can be interpreted as either antifeminist or, more broadly anti-ideological (or anti–idée fixe), depending on how much the critic extrapolates through James a severe critique of paternalist ideologue Basil Ransom or else his antagonist Olive Chancellor, the ardent feminist, and possibly lesbian, heroine, as these two battle for the soul of Verena Tarrant. The critical dispute ranges quite literally from James as enlightened compatriot to women, ahead of his time, to James as downright hostile misogynist. In truth, perhaps no novel James ever wrote exhibits a narrative voice that seems to undergo so many sea changes of tone or apparent attitude. But this very feature makes *The Bostonians* all the more appealing to narratologists.

Other novels enjoying prominence after the "second wave" are *The Sacred Fount, The Awkward Age,* and, to a slightly lesser extent, *Washington Square. The Sacred Fount* is another textbook example (pardon the pun) of a once-problem novel that has now taken the spotlight away from the novel it was long supposed to have imperfectly adumbrated, *The Ambassadors,* by virtue of its experimental mode and irreducible ambiguity. The unnamed narrator-busybody who hypothesizes that certain couples at Newmarch House are undergoing vampirism exchanges, whereby the "sacred fount" of youth passes from one party to the other, used to be designated by Jamesians as fundamentally "unreliable," his preposterous claim at best never confirmed, at worst sheer lunacy. Meanwhile, the novel itself, published in 1901, was agreed to have been James's last abortive attempt at first-person narration in a full-length novel just prior to his brilliant solution of alternating "picture" and "scene"—the simultaneity of subjectivity and verification through third-person-focusing "registers"—the method, in other words, of *The Ambassadors* and the other "major phase" novels, the kind of work Lubbock hailed as the triumph of novelistic form. However, James scholarship since the "second wave" perceives *The Sacred Fount* as utterly different. It is not that critics no longer feel the narrator is untrustworthy in his hypothesis about vampirism. It is more as if now such obvious "unreliability" is about the least interesting thing about him, unless it is in some special sense the most glorious! That is, he is no longer condemned for his lack of ethics but is now seen more as a "rival creator" to James himself, and the novel is read increasingly in metafictional terms. Psychoanalytically speaking, his obsessive projections can be understood as a Jamesian rendering of the Lacanian Imaginary.[12] And the first-person method, far from being a liability, now illustrates James's "objective" rendering of the "subjective" state and psychic-interior. In any case, all the old problems with *The Sacred Fount* are what "second wave" scholarship celebrates most in this metanovel. Next, *The Awkward Age* was long felt to be James's fullest experiment with the "scenic" method; i.e., a drama in novelistic form, with acts and scenes, pruned of all save its dialogue, a work that avoids "going behind" his characters, as James put it, to explain or amplify them. But now one can speak of it as "subjectivising" the objective (the obverse of *The Sacred Fount*). Moreover, James's cultural critique and complicated attitude toward adolescent girls like Nanda and Aggie are of considerable interest to cultural-feminist scholars. Furthermore, the same scholars, especially feminists, are taking a fresh look at *Washington Square* and its stolid heroine Catherine Sloper, especially her resiliency and determination once she rejects both the proffered friendship of parasite-lover Morris Townsend and the manipulation of Mrs. Penniman. It is probably the radical difference between James's Catherine and the theatrical heroine of *The Heiress* (played brilliantly on screen by Olivia de Haviland) that interests scholars now, for James's character is far less rigidly vindictive—thus less subject to "perversion" by men like her father and Morris—than the Catherine of play and screen.

James's own caustic, clinical dissection of Catherine's unfeeling paternalistic physician-father, Austin Sloper, also intrigues scholars interested in family relations, especially between father and daughter. Catherine Sloper was invented at the same time as Isabel Archer, but the two could not be more different specimens of the young American woman of the 1870s or early 1880s. Because Catherine's story was not international in theme like Isabel's, it held a somewhat lowly place during the "first wave" James scholarship, especially since he himself rather disparaged the work. But "the Master," as we are learning, can no longer dictate his "top ten" canon anymore, at least not since the 1980s.

In fact, three of the six novels I have been discussing—*Washington Square, The Bostonians,* and *The Sacred Fount*—were omitted from his authorized New York Edition with its sacred-text prefaces. Even granting the fact that James would have liked to have included more novels and tales than Scribner's permitted, the truth remains that the old dispensation followed his apparent lead in judging all three novels lesser works. But no longer. For now that James-as-master is deemed a myth, it is increasingly normal to respond to the six novels above (and one could make a case for a seventh, *Roderick Hudson*) as works of major critical interest.

If the brief retreat of *The Portrait of a Lady,* the short-lived decline of *The Ambassadors,* and the ascension of the novels above constitute two of the four "posts" of James's newer canonical bed, the third is a group of works perhaps best described as already venerable in the old dispensation but rebaptized into the new one on different critical and ideological grounds. The foremost examples here are *The Spoils of Poynton, The Turn of the Screw, The American, The Wings of the Dove,* and *The Golden Bowl. The Spoils of Poynton* has an extraordinary critical history in that, slim as it is, it has long been the focus for examining James's ethical consciousness in the person of Fleda Vetch (the tormented "free spirit," James calls her in his preface) whose unique blending of imagination and altruism critics have forever found fascinating, exalting, or disturbing. Moreover, James explained his "masterly" theory of the "germ" in his preface to *The Spoils*. However, the "second wave" Jamesians love this book as much as their predecessors, but not for the aesthetic-ethical fusion within the "little drama of my 'Spoils,'" combining "picture" and "scene" in interesting artistic ways. They love it instead because both Fleda and Mrs. Gereth are so drastically "marginalized" in the social order; they love it because the pernicious English law of primogeniture, like an absent-present master discourse (like James!) dictates everything that happens; they love it because the spoils themselves are such powerful commodities in the Marxist exchange, all the more so in their having been collected by Mrs. Gereth and her late husband as the fruition of England's colonial empire; they love it because the characters too, especially Fleda, are likewise commodified and compromised. The Maltese cross that has figured so spiritually and symbolically in pre-1980s readings is now perceived at once as very material yet freighted with the bloody history of the Colonial Empire. *The Turn of the Screw,* as all know, has long been the darling of academic controversy, evincing its "irrevocable ambiguity" during James's "first wave" criticism; indeed its scholarship has been so extensive as to compete with the printed work on *Hamlet.* Now, however, it has become something almost unique in the academy, a work whose very interpretive literature has assumed the status of "primary literature" generating its own theoretical analysis: scholars write more frequently on the hermeneutics of the debate than on *The Turn of the Screw. The American* is still a different case. For years it was of great importance by virtue of being James's first attempt at the international novel. But it was also critically salient because of James's celebrated censure in his late preface of its "fatal flaw" of succumbing to "the romantic." Well, to begin with, postmodern criticism of James already celebrates the romantic, or at least dismisses the notion of James as "mere" realist—or else dismisses the notion of realism itself as realistic. In any event, the 1987 volume *New Essays on "The American"* by several fine contemporary literary theoreticians suggests the quiet sea change this always popular book—popular because in part very lively and easy to read—has undergone.[13] Since the last decade, it would be anything but out of place to affirm that James in his famous preface had already "deconstructed" his own earlier novel, *The American,* but that it is now appropriate to deconstruct his critique itself in the New York preface.

The last two novels in this third group are *The Wings of the Dove* and *The Golden Bowl.* Almost everyone knows that once upon a time these two heavyweight novels combined with *The Ambassadors* to form the heart of the "major phase." The three were also felt to be a kind of spiritual or poetic "trilogy" of the late-James's international theme. "Second wave" criticism, however, no longer has any use for the trilogy concept, especially with its overtones of aesthetic formalism. Any slight diminishment of *The Ambassadors* has bequeathed only greater enhancement to both *The Wings of the Dove* and *The Golden Bowl*. Both books were, for the James of the prefaces at least, "problem" novels, although ones whose difficulties were decisively outweighed by the successful resolution of whatever flaws they contain. *The Wings* is now likely to be appreciated as the first major James novel in which he went beyond the narration by one center of consciousness and introduced instead successive centers. Any self-respecting postmodernist knows this is good because the overall effect is, of course, to decenter the world of the novel. Another newly fascinating feature of *The Wings* is the power struggle between Kate Croy and Milly Theale. No longer is it a matter of the spider lady versus the dove, but between two figures of force and power, each in effect delivering to the other a knock-out punch.

The example of *The Golden Bowl* is perhaps the most instructive in all of James criticism. In 1981, exactly sixty years after Percy Lubbock apotheosized *The Ambassadors* as the ultimate in James and in the novel itself, R. B. J. Wilson published *Henry James's Ultimate Narrative,* which formally codified what brilliant commentators like Nicola Bradbury in her intricate reader-response analysis and Ruth B. Yeazell in her discriminating study of James's language previously had just begun to establish: that the *The Golden Bowl* is henceforth James's preeminent work.[14] The reasons are at once the same as those ascribed to *The Wings of the Dove* only more so, as well as several new ones. The "multiple centers" apply once again; the preoccupation by Adam Verver with amassing wealth and power, including buying family members, is another facet. But what is most distinctive about the criticism of *The Golden Bowl* since the 1980s are two additional features. First, the novel is interpreted by virtually everyone now as so profoundly "problematic" in its notional resolution of the Maggie-Amerigo marriage that it calls into question the very institution of marriage itself, which James seems otherwise to be affirming (and which "first wave" critics of the novel assumed he endorsed). This issue has spawned cultural and feminist studies galore with *The Golden Bowl* as prismatic hue. The second feature, inevitably related to the first, is the incredibly breathtaking maneuvering by Maggie Verver in the second half of the novel: her tactics constitute a virtual handbook of survival guerrilla warfare carried on in silence behind the veneer of a high-toned opulent civilization. Maggie's power plays to save her marriage are enacted with a subtlety, toughness, and passion probably unmatched by any heroine in fiction. The result is that she is now both greatly praised or else greatly damned by James critics, almost as if, like *The Bostonians*, we have once again *The Turn of the Screw* type of debate, but no longer addressed to the somewhat attenuated realm of the quasi-supernatural. In sum, no novel by James has received the sheer heft of analysis during the 1980s as has *The Golden Bowl.* As I have said elsewhere, this book has by its mass, intricacy, power, and critical attention probably become James's *Ulysses.*

The last of the "four posts" in James's new canon are his nonfictional writings. To begin with, the prefaces and literary essays are no longer read primarily to understand and clarify the Master's definitive meaning for the novels and tales they address, or to piece together the mosaic of his "poetics of the novel." Instead the prefaces in particular are now more and more probed and deconstructed for the anxieties of influence they may reveal, the mastery they would impose, or simply (though this is never simply) the psychological needs they disguise with a capacious hieroglyphic idiom. Second, the memoirs and travel works, especially *The American Scene* and the autobiographical volumes, have already been significantly "recanonized" from the status of interesting adjunct specimens of Jamesian "sensibility" to that of cultural critique and biographical narrative, yet also sometimes as disguise and evasion. Intertextuality thus meets up with psychoanalytic methodology and cultural studies as "second wave" Jamesians seek to extend Leon Edel's older Freudian analysis of the James family pathology, or else examine James's cultural analysis alongside documents like H. G. Wells's *The Future in America.* One finds new and complex biographical theory by way of the reciprocal relation between James's autobiography and biographical study of him.[15] Still a third body of nonfictional works, it might surprise some readers to hear, are James's *Notebooks,* recently reedited and published by Leon Edel and Lyall H. Powers.[16] Martha Banta points out that his notebooks are diametrically opposed to Hawthorne's nutshell entries. James allows us real access to his writing workplace, with his self-talk, indeed his self-flagellation and self-coercion replete with crisis, goading, and concern for marketability; yet he also reveals the seat of communion with his genius—"mon Bon." To Banta, James's alchemical process resembles, instead of Hawthorne's, Thoreau's journal with its "frightening principle of rank organicism let loose upon the world."[17] Postmodernist preoccupation with discourse theory will, I suspect, continue to make James's *Notebooks* increasingly relevant to the issue of his canonicity.

I have said nothing about James's tales other than *The Turn of the Screw,* yet teachers of James no less than professional scholars obviously seek to know where to cast about these days within his rich corpus of tales. More times than not, however, we all end up with some portion of the great old chestnuts, "Daisy Miller," "The Real Thing," "The Pupil," "The Beast in the Jungle," "The Jolly Corner." It is hard to gainsay these inevitably anthologized texts (along with "The Art of Fiction," no doubt), because they *are* truly great short works; and there is no way, however the new desert winds of critical theory rearrange the sand dunes of academic discourse, that these tales will ever be otherwise. Indeed, "Daisy Miller" (like *The Portrait,* or *The Ambassadors,* never forgotten) is the latest James selection to the Twayne Masterwork Studies.[18] All the same, it is now a story like "The Figure in the Carpet" that elicits all the attention by the same metafictionist scholars similarly intrigued by *The Sacred Fount;* it is *In the Cage* that draws the admiration of those scholars also enmeshed with *The Princess Casamassima* and *What Maisie Knew;* it is James's fable "The Great Good Place" that inevitably beckons to a postmodernist mentality when the tale contains passages like these: that the Place is "for that matter, anything in the world we like—the thing, for instance, we love it most for being."[19] At the same time, though, a wonderful used-to-be-formalist tale like *The Aspern Papers* has, very like *The Spoils of Poynton* among the novels, made the transition from "old" to "new wave" James popularity by being reinvestigated psychoanalytically, by responding to newer theories of textuality (just begin thinking, say, of Aspern's papers eventually consumed as the "rival text" to that of the specious narrator's, and both texts as made and unmade by James's text), or to feminist analysis beyond victim theory focusing especially on the development of resourceful Miss Tina.

I believe anyone who has followed this argument might rightly ask: What will the James canon look like in, say, twenty years? If by then there is a "third wave" of Jamesian criticism, I only hope some academic wag does not begin calling it "the major phase." The question of James's canon obviously is not easy, precisely as the question of the canon itself during the realist period is not easy: the foregoing essays in this volume testify amply to that. All the same, one simply cannot get around the *fact* of corpulent James's corpulent corpus, its mass and diversity, even if one successfully puts to rest, or at least negotiates, the whole business of "the Master." Some readers may recall that the problem of James's massive canon actually came up late in his own life, in 1913, when Mrs. George Prothero, wife of the editor, asked James on behalf of Stark Young for guidance in what works of his to read. The novelist prepared two lists of five novels each, one of which he called "somewhat more 'advanced.'"[20] The episode if not the lists themselves (which overlap several novels) is deeply emblematic of the entire ethos of James's "first wave." Nobody wishes such an encore of James as majestic impresario of his own canon; criticism since 1980 has seen to it that such dominion is neither in our nor James's own lasting interest. But the problem still remains: it is just as hard to discover "Henry James" as it is to discover and settle upon all the others being discovered. As Cary Nelson argues in the *Columbia Literary History of the United States,* writing literary history is a different affair from canon building.[21] Correspondingly, a canonical figure like James, albeit one of the old "Eight American Authors," is the other side of the moon from a monolith.

Notes

1. See *Eight American Authors,* ed. Floyd Stovall (New York: W. W. Norton, 1956); revised edition, ed. James Woodress, 1971. Also *Eight American Writers: An Anthology of American Literature,* ed. Norman Foerster and Robert P. Falk (New York: W. W. Norton, 1963). The "top eight" are Poe, Emerson, Thoreau, Hawthorne, Melville, Whitman, Clemens, and James.

2. Alfred Habegger, *Henry James and the "Woman Business"* (New York: Cambridge University Press, 1989), 230. Another less hostile discussion of James as maker of his literary history can be found in John Carlos Rowe, *The Theoretical Dimensions of Henry James* (Madison: University of Wisconsin Press, 1984), 29–83.

3. F. R. Leavis, *The Great Tradition* (Garden City, NY: Doubleday, 1954), 1, 16.

4. See for example the 3rd ed. of *The Norton Anthology of American Literature,* ed. Nina Baym et al., 1989, or *Tales of Henry James,* ed. Christof Wegelin (New York: Norton, 1984), or the novels published thus far in the James *Library of America* as examples of editors opting for one of the early versions of a given James text as opposed to the New York edition.

5. The critics listed in the order of my citations are: Stephen Spender, *The Destructive Element* (London: Jonathan Cape, 1935); Ezra Pound and Graham Greene in *Henry James: Twentieth-Century Views,* ed. Leon Edel (Englewood Cliffs, NJ: Prentice-Hall, 1963), 27–31, 111–23; David A. Leeming, "An Interview with James Baldwin on Henry James," *HJR* 8 (Fall 1986): 47–56; R. P. Blackmur, *Studies in Henry James,* ed. Veronica A. Makowsky (New York: New Directions, 1983); F. O. Matthiessen, *Henry James: The Major Phase* (New York: Oxford University Press, 1944); Daniel M. Fogel, *Henry James and the Structure of the Romantic Imagination* (Baton Rouge: Louisiana State University Press, 1981); Ruth B. Yeazell, *Language and Knowledge in the Late Novels of Henry James* (Chicago: University of Chicago Press, 1976); Leon Edel, *The Life of Henry James,* 2 vols. (London:

Penguin, 1977); Joseph Warren Beach, *The Method of Henry James* (New Haven: Yale University Press, 1918); Christof Wegelin, *The Image of Europe in Henry James* (Dallas, TX: Southern Methodist University Press, 1957); Alwyn Berland, *Culture and Conduct in the Novels of Henry James* (Cambridge: Cambridge University Press, 1981); Dorothea Krook, *The Ordeal of Consciousness in Henry James* (New York: Cambridge University Press, 1967); Stephen Donadio, *Nietzsche, Henry James, and the Artistic Will* (New York: Oxford University Press, 1978); Richard A. Hocks, *Henry James and Pragmatistic Thought* (Chapel Hill: University of North Carolina Press, 1974); Percy Lubbock, *The Craft of Fiction* (New York: Viking Press, 1921); Wayne C. Booth, *The Rhetoric of Fiction* (Chicago: University of Chicago Press, 1961).

6. Inasmuch as I shall use the phrase James's "second wave" so frequently throughout this essay, I wish to acknowledge Jennifer Wicke, "Henry James's Second Wave," *HJR* 10 (Spring 1989): 146, although her article and subject have nothing in common with this essay.

7. Rowe's *Theoretical Dimensions* deconstructs not only James but the major schools of postmodern theory by using James as its prism for investigation. The other scholars listed in the order of my citations are: Paul B. Armstrong, *The Phenomenology of Henry James* (Chapel Hill: University of North Carolina Press, 1983); Mark Seltzer, *Henry James and the Art of Power* (Ithaca: Cornell University Press, 1984); Habegger, *James and the "Woman Business"*; Susan L. Mizruchi, *The Power of Historical Knowledge: Narrating the Past in Hawthorne, James, and Dreiser* (Princeton: Princeton University Press, 1988); Marcia Jacobson, *Henry James and the Mass Market* (University, AL: University of Alabama Press, 1983); Michael Anesko, *"Friction with the Market": Henry James and the Profession of Authorship* (New York: Oxford University Press, 1986); Paul John Eakin, "Henry James's 'Obscure Hurt': Can Autobiography Serve Biography?" *NLH* 19 (1988): 675–92; Donna Przybylowicz, *Desire and Repression: The Dialectic of Self and Other in the Late Works of Henry James* (University, AL: The University of Alabama Press, 1986).

8. Matthiessen's "The Painter's Sponge and Varnish Bottle" appears as an appendix in *The Major Phase;* Laurence Holland, *The Expense of Vision: Essays on the Craft of Henry James* (Princeton: Princeton University Press, 1964); Dorothy Van Ghent, *The English Novel: Form and Function* (New York: Rinehart & Co., 1953); Richard Chase, *The American Novel and its Tradition* (Garden City, NY: Doubleday, 1957).

9. Beach, *Method,* 155; Lubbock, *Craft,* 156, 171.

10. See William Veeder, "The Portrait of a Lack," Beth Sharon Ash, "Frail Vessals and Vast Designs: A Psychoanalytic Portrait of Isabel Archer," and Alfred Habegger, "The Fatherless Heroine and the Filial Son: Deep Background for *The Portrait of a Lady"* in *New Essays on "The Portrait of a Lady"* (New York: Cambridge University Press, 1990), 95–121, 123–62, 49–93; see also William Veeder, "The Feminine Orphan and the Emergent Master: Self-Realization in Henry James," *HJR* 12 (1991): 20–54. For *The Ambassadors* see Jeanne Campbell Reesman, *American Designs: The Late Novels of James and Faulkner* (Philadelphia: University of Pennsylvania Press, 1991); Susan M. Griffin, *The Historical Eye: The Texture of the Visual in Late James* (Boston: Northeastern University Press, 1991); and Leland S. Person, Jr., "Henry James, George Sand, and the Suspense of Masculinity," *PMLA* 106 (1991): 515–28.

11. See Lionel Trilling, "The Princess Casamassima" in *The Liberal Imagination* (New York: Viking Press, 1951), 58–92, and Irving Howe, "Henry James, the

Political Vocation" in *Politics and the Novel* (New York: Horizon Press, 1957), 139–56.

12. See, for example, Przybylowicz, *Desire,* 39–87.

13. See *New Essays on "The American,"* ed. Martha Banta (New York: Cambridge University Press, 1987). The contributors are Banta, Peter Brooks, John Carlos Rowe, Carolyn Porter, and Mark Seltzer.

14. R. B. J. Wilson, *Henry James's Ultimate Narrative: "The Golden Bowl"* (Brisbane: University of Queensland, 1981); Nicola Bradbury, *Henry James: The Later Novels* (New York: Oxford, 1979); Yeazell, *Language and Knowledge.*

15. Discussions of these nonfictional works exhibiting the methodologies I describe can be found in Paul John Eakin, Mark Seltzer, or Donna Przyblyowicz. See also James M. Cox's "The Memoirs of Henry James: Self Interest as Autobiography," *SoR* 22 (1986): 231–51; also Ruth B. Yeazell's "Henry James" chapter in the *Columbia Literary History of the United States,* ed. Emory Elliott et al. (New York: Columbia University Press, 1988), 668–89.

16. *The Complete Notebooks of Henry James,* ed. Leon Edel and Lyall H. Powers (New York: Oxford, 1986).

17. Martha Banta, "'There's Surely a Story in It': James's Notebooks and the Working Artist," *HJR* 9 (1988): 157.

18. See Daniel M. Fogel, *"Daisy Miller": A Dark Comedy of Manners* (Boston: Twayne Publishers, 1990).

19. *The Novels and Tales of Henry James* (New York: Charles Scribner's Sons, 1909), 16: 238.

20. A convenient place to examine James's letter to Mrs. Prothero and the two lists for Stark Young is *The Wings of the Dove: A Norton Critical Edition,* ed. J. Donald Crowley and Richard A. Hocks (New York: W. W. Norton, 1978), 456–57.

21. See Emory Elliott, *Columbia Literary History,* 913–36.

From Painful Cult to Painful Realism: Annie Ogle's *A Lost Love* and W. D. Howells's Ben Halleck and Penelope Lapham

ALFRED HABEGGER

IN chapter 19 of *A Modern Instance,* just before Ben Halleck's first visit to the Hubbards' apartment, Olive is talking with her brother about Boston's fashionable single women. Suddenly she makes a teasing allusion to an unexplained event from the past: "But what difference does it make to you, Ben? You dont want to marry any of those girls as long as your heart's set on that unknown charmer of yours." The charmer, Howells at once tells us, was an attractive young woman seen years ago by Ben while he was amusing himself in a small Maine town with some college friends. On impulse, he "bribed the village photographer to let him have the picture of this young lady, which he . . . sent home to [his sister] Olive, marked, 'My Lost Love.'" Howells reveals this transaction with a minimum of explanation. There seems no reason to suppose that Ben's romantic caption was anything other than lightheartedly humorous or that it offers a significant clue to his character. Ben was simply carrying out a "freak"[1] with his friends, Howells disingenuously tells us.

But as so often happens in Howells's fiction, the freakish act has a freakishly lingering effect. In the immediately following chapter Howells arranges for Ben to meet his lost love for the first time since that brief momentary sight of her years ago. The meeting takes place in the Hubbards' small apartment, where Ben is dismayed to see that his pretty Maine girl has become Bartley's wife. Not only that, but she is pregnant, as her "dark robe" intimates. In the hands of a popular writer, this rediscovery of the lost love would no doubt be played for all it is worth. Howells, however, obscures Ben's realization to such an extent that many readers may not realize (if I may extrapolate from my own original failure to catch on) that this *is* a discovery scene. Narrating the visit chiefly from the Hubbards' point of view, Howells allows us to observe Ben only from the outside. All that we see is that he is "visibly dazzled" and "quite abashed," and that after Bartley has taken his cane the visitor "limped helplessly about" (215). We do not get any authorial disclosures or interior views of his real feelings, and if we have not attended to the hint Howells casually dropped in the preceding chapter, we probably assume, mistakenly, that Ben is overwhelmed by Marcia's beauty, or perhaps by the domestic contentment the unworthy Bartley apparently enjoys. That is to say, we may misread Ben's behavior as badly as the self-flattering Bartley does.

It is only much later, in chapter 27, that Howells enables dull readers to correct their misapprehension of this oddly veiled discovery scene. The key fact is disclosed following the picnic at Equity, where the spectacle of Marcia's jealous misery deeply distresses Ben. Once again it is Olive who brings up the photograph, not joking now but speaking with somber anxiety:

> "Did you ever fancy any resemblance between Mrs. Hubbard and the photograph of that girl we used to joke about—your lost love?"
>
> "Yes," said Halleck.
>
> "What's become of it—the photograph? I can't find it any more; I wanted to show it to her, one day."
>
> "I destroyed it. I burnt it the first evening after I had met Mrs. Hubbard. It seemed to me that it wasn't right to keep it."
>
> "Why, you don't think it was *her* photograph!"
>
> "I think it was," said Halleck. (300–301)

It may well be that the disclosure of this coincidence strikes many readers as hackneyed or adventitious or undeveloped. Certainly, few of Howells's critics or biographers have given much thought to the revelation that Ben's lost love turns out to be Marcia Gaylord Hubbard. But Howells's treatment of the coincidence is well worth paying attention to, particularly if we notice the similarity between what happens to Ben and what happens to his creator. Just as the character's casual freak grows into a full-blown, late-nineteenth-century monomania, so Ben's fixation invades Howells's own attention, to the point where he seems to forget that his story is basically about Marcia and Bartley's troubled relationship. This threadbare lost-love business, introduced so casually into both Ben's life and the novel itself, merits the closest attention.

1

The chief complication has yet to be mentioned. Ben's caption for the schoolgirl's photograph alludes to the title of a British novel that many American, English, and French readers had taken to heart, *A Lost Love,* by Annie Ogle.

First published in 1854, this now entirely forgotten book enjoyed a surprisingly long shelf life in both England and the United States. It had gone through at least two American editions by the time Howells began composing *A Modern Instance,* the first in 1859 by T. J. Crowen of New York, the second in 1865 by A. K. Loring, the not-very-distinguished Boston publisher who in 1864 compelled Louisa May Alcott to rewrite *Moods.* Loring published Ogle's novel under a title conventionally highlighting the heroine's name, *Georgy Sandon; or, A Lost Love;* in 1871 he brought it out under its original title. In 1883, one year after the publication of *A Modern Instance,* T. B. Peterson, a Philadelphia publisher, brought out his own edition under the deceptive title, *Her Second Love,* no doubt hoping to catch the eye of purchasers seeking a second Ogle. If this was the strategy, it appears to have been successful, at least in the Clemens household: in 1884 Mark Twain entered into a notebook the title, publisher, and place of publication of Peterson's imprint. Interestingly, two cancelled words, <A Lost>,[2] indicate that Mark Twain had Ogle's one big hit, now thirty years old, on his mind.

A quiet and elegiac narrative, *A Lost Love* seems to have given cultivated nineteenth-century American readers one of the kinds of reading experience they desired—distinguished pathos free of the taint of vulgar sentimentality. The novel's protagonist, Georgy Sandon, an orphan, lives with a dull uncle and aunt in a Northumberland town devoid of activity or interest. She is engaged to a man she scarcely knows who has gone to South Africa for three years. She is shy, unassertive, isolated, and depressed, and evidently has no clear idea how trapped and unhappy she is. When she makes the acquaintance of a young man named James Erskine, she begins enjoying herself for the first time in her life. Not even suspecting that she is falling in love, she suddenly rebels, informs her uncle she cannot marry her fiancé, and runs away to London. Her stated purpose is to find her great-aunt. An accidental encounter with James (an episode closely resembling the scene in which Marcia finds Bartley in the train station after running away from Equity) shows Georgy that the man she loves regards her only as a casual friend. More depressed than ever, she again sets out for the great-aunt. But the address has been lost and Georgy ends up wandering in a daze through London. Once again, she is found by James and this time she is taken to his home, where she spends a month recuperating. He now pays attention to her, falls in love, proposes. Georgy had not imagined that life held such happiness, but unfortunately events conspire to delay the announcement of her engagement. Then she learns that a friend, the charming and brilliant Constance, had formerly loved James but had been alienated from him by a misdirected letter. Overcome by scruples and "the excitement of self-sacrifice," Georgy resolves to give James up to the woman who loved him first. Her heart breaking with misery, she marries her original fiancé, now back from South Africa. But she soon grows "tired with life" and dies. Although James marries Constance, he often thinks of Georgy and before long seems "worn and tired to the heart's core."[3] The lassitude that so pervades the beginning of the novel thus returns in force at the end.

In 1877 and 1878, Howells ran two brief anonymous essays on *A Lost Love* in the *Atlantic Monthly's* "Contributors' Club." This monthly feature offered writers the opportunity to express their "intellectual grudges of every sort"[4] without signing their names. To get the thing going, Howells solicited his friends for contributions and probably also wrote several himself.

The first of the two essays, in the March 1877 *Atlantic,* appeared at a time when the Contributors' Club was in its third month and still getting off the ground. The point the anonymous essayist wished to make was that *A Lost Love* had acquired a

> curiously enthusiastic *following*—worship, cult— . . . among certain refined American women. . . . My observation is that it was expressly written for some ten or a dozen ladies of my acquaintance, who read it fifteen or twenty years [ago] in the English edition, and who have ever since gone about proselyting people to it.

The writer was recently persuaded to read the novel and now professes to regard his former indifference to it as "heathen." He knows of "no other book so simply and merely and just sufficiently touching." According to a friend, the book has "a real gulp." It also has a fine, understated artistry:

> What should be so wonderful about a young girl's not getting the man whom she loves, and who loves her as much as, if not more than, he loves the brilliant woman who does get him? That is the author's secret, and you are made to know that it is a very great matter,—a matter of life and death. The little book is truth and life, treated with consummate, unfailing, uninsistent art.

The writer calls attention to a scene "forlorner" than any other, which made him feel "incomparably homesick and forsaken."[5] Offering a brief list of cult books, he concludes by asking whether the editor has another correspondent who could add other titles to it—a query that neatly coincides with Howells's own hope that the Contributors' Club would generate replies from readers and become self-perpetuating.

Although it is always risky to propose an attribution on internal grounds alone, it is hard not to suspect Howells of writing the three paragraphs that compose this essay. They betray a suspiciously acute sense of his editorial requirements; they focus on questions known to be of concern to him; and the language and sentiments seem typically Howellsian.[6] Another reason Howells comes to mind as the possible author is that in *The Rise of Silas Lapham* (1885) he invented an imaginary cult novel, *Tears, Idle Tears,* that is popular with women and has the same plot as *A Lost Love.* He created several characters, such as Miss Cotton in *April Hopes* (1887), who are passionately devoted to romantic visions inspired by fiction. In 1895, when he organized an account of his own life as a reader, the leading idea was "my literary passions." Forlorn homesickness was to be a prominent motive in his early letters, his autobiographical writing, and the relatively few fictional narratives drawing on his Ohio boyhood, such as *The Flight of Pony Baker* (1902). There is a typically Howellsian ambivalence in the essayist's tone towards *A Lost Love,* for while he praises its pathos and restraint and humbly repents of his own "former hardness of heart and darkness of mind"[7] concerning the book, his irony suggests he still has some private reservations. All told, the essay displays many signs of being written by its editor. Pending firm external evidence, however, we cannot take Howells's authorship for granted.

The second brief essay on *A Lost Love* in the *Atlantic* was obviously written by one of the novel's admirers. This anonymous contributor had read the book ten years earlier "with wonder at its searching power, its terse strokes, its pathos of suggestion rather than word." Lending it to others, though without daring to praise it as it deserved, the contributor was delighted to learn from the first essayist that others also prized the novel. This contributor offered several favorite extracts, one of which has an obvious relevance here:

> A fine touch of nature is that in which Erskine, turning to leave the room just after his engagement to Georgy, looks, by chance, at a picture bought long ago for its strong resemblance to Constance, his first love. "Now he felt provoked with himself for putting it there."[8]

In this passage, which passed under Howells's editorial eye two or three years before he dusted off his old *New Medea* manuscript and composed *A Modern Instance,* we have the germ of Ben Halleck's acquisition of the photograph of his own lost love.

2

Manuscript evidence, Howells's correspondence, and the text of the novel all indicate that Ben Halleck came into *A Modern Instance* well after the book had begun to take shape. Howells originally set to work on the novel in September, 1876, shortly before creating the Contributors' Club. By all accounts he did not make much progress on the book at that time. He put the manuscript away, and it was not until 1881 that he set to work in earnest on it. Whether he was able to redeploy what he'd written five years earlier is open to conjecture.[9] The brief prospectus he drafted in February 1881, which focuses on the leading couple, makes no mention of Ben or most of the other secondary characters. Howells admitted in this statement that he still had only a very sketchy idea of his characters and episodes.

The surviving manuscript, which breaks off with chapter 15, makes it clear that Howells devised fundamental elements in the novel only after he had already composed the opening chapters. As the editors of the Indiana edition point out, schoolteaching, not journalism, was to be Bartley's occupation in what was first called Long Plain and then Bassett before finally getting the name of Equity.[10] Unfortunately, this edition does not convey the scope of the changes Howells made in the manuscript. The moment one pays attention to the revisions that concern Ben Halleck, one makes some major discoveries about Howells's creation of the novel as a whole.

Although Ben does not make an appearance in the first fifteen chapters, mention is made of him in paragraphs five, six, and eight of chapter 3 and near the end of chapter 13. In the last of these mentions, Marcia and Bartley are in their Boston hotel room discussing the future: "[h]e asked Marcia whether she would look up his friend Halleck if she were in his place" (p. 142). Turning to sheet 590 of the manuscript, we find the identical passage. The implication is obvious: by the time Howells composed this segment of his narrative on 13, 14, or 15 August 1881,[11] he had invented Ben and planned to bring him and Bartley together in Boston.

But if we flip forward to chapter 3 and compare that with the manuscript version, we find that the *early* mentions of Ben were added as an afterthought. Howells used purple ink when he first composed the early chapters. Later, he changed to black ink, which he continued to use when he turned back to the first chapters for revision. Hence, some of the later modifications are easy to detect (provided one has access to the original manuscript and not a black and white photocopy). As first composed, sheet 88, in purple ink, ended in midsentence—"But it had been a question of bread and butter, which was to be solved by this"—and was then followed by sheet 89, beginning "means, or by that experiment of the [illegible word] West, upon which even the [illegible word] poor boy of New England enters reluctantly and with misgivings of a traditional barbarism. . . . " Howells then continued writing in purple. At some later time, however, when he was using black ink, he cancelled both passages and inserted five new sheets numbered 2=89, 3=89, 4=89, 5=89, 6=89. (Sheet 7=89, written in purple and originally numbered 78, was evidently shifted from an earlier position.) The original number 89 was then renumbered 8=89. This was the standard numbering system in use when writers wished to insert pages without going to the trouble of renumbering all the following sheets. The key fact is this: the first mention of Ben occurs in these added, black-ink sheets. There can be no doubt that Howells first introduced this character into his novel after having gotten well into it.[12]

If we look at the manuscript version of the last paragraph of chapter 3, where Halleck is again mentioned, we find that the passage that mentions Holcombe, as Halleck was originally called, is once again in black ink, on a sheet numbered 2=96. This mention, too, must have been added later.

Although many questions about Howells's composition of the first fifteen chapters will have to await a thorough analysis of the manuscript, it is apparent that it was at some time *after* the two Contributors' Club essays on *A Lost Love* crossed his editorial desk in 1877 and 1878 that he decided to introduce the tormented character of Ben Halleck into *A Modern Instance.* That is to say, it was after the contours of his novel had taken shape, and the early chapters were written in preliminary form, that Howells tried to work in a belated preoccupation—the dangerously hypnotic power of poignant love stories. This relative chronology of his compositional steps is crucial, not simply because it partly accounts for the adventitious feel of the lost-love episode, but because it marks the first appearance of a prominent feature of the writer's fiction and criticism in the 1880s—his massive attack on popular reading. Thus, when Howells created one of his most unstable characters by joining irrational "psychological" behavior (obsessive interest in an unavailable woman) with high literary/cultural practice (regarding novels as sacred cult objects), he was making what can be seen in retrospect as a fateful swerve in his career.

If the invention of Ben was prompted by Howells's notice of a cult novel favored by women, the question immediately arises: why did Howells make his sickly Lost Lover a *man,* when those who cherished Ogle's novel (according to the first *Atlantic* essayist) were chiefly "certain refined American women." The answer to this question brings us to one of the more interesting twists in this intertextual story—Howells's mistaken assumption about the gender of the cult-author he was dealing with. Ogle had brought her book out under a pseudonym, "Ashford Owen," a name that looked masculine without strictly mandating this assignment of gender. In this respect her disguise resembled those chosen by her contemporaries, the Brontë sisters, for neither were "Acton," "Ellis," and "Currer" standard male Christian names. The author's mask apparently remained intact until the Murray edition of 1920. Certainly, the two Contributors' Club essayists took for granted that Ashford Owen was a man. Indeed, everyone on the first contributor's list of cult-authors happens to be male: George William Curtis, Paul Ferrol, Bjørnstjerne Bjørnson, Robert Browning, Ivan Turgenev, and Henry Taylor. If the silent assumption here is that books with a following are written by men, that is perhaps because the writer (Howells?) is anxious about what it means to be a *male* writer.

Another aspect of Ogle's pseudonym that is of interest here is the apparent ethnic identity of "Ashford Owen." In *Years of My Youth* we learn that Howells's father's Welsh origins were considerably more salient for the writer than was his mother's so-called Pennsylvania Dutch background. He thought of himself as Welsh, in fact, and when he drew on his own experience to create the timid male lead of *A Fearful Responsibility* (1881), he gave him a Welsh name, Owen Elmore.

These considerations tell us that Howells had good reasons for regarding the *Lost Love* cult, not simply as an affair among women, but as something that could seriously implicate certain men. Men, too, might be swept away by this perilously sad book, might even write it if they weren't careful, particularly if they found themselves on the margins of American life. To all appearance, the editor of the *Atlantic,* the friend of Mark Twain, the biographer of presidents, the rising novelist now entering his prime was anything but marginalized, but as biographers have made clear, Howells was haunted by a feeling of not really belonging to the highbrow Boston literary world he had conquered.[13] Also, and quite aside from this latent forlornness, he had shown an obsessive interest in female victims—the seduced girl his mother once took into their home, the drowned prostitute in *Suburban Sketches* (1872), the broken-down daughter in *A Counterfeit Presentment* (1877). In addition, in the early 1880s his wife Elinor and his daughter Winifred suffered from severe and mystifying afflictions. These matters, and others, prompted Howells's creation of the demasculinized Ben Halleck, who, like the refined readers who cried over *A Lost Love,* surrenders to a passionate fixation on a woman destroyed by love.

Thus, Ben's introduction into *A Modern Instance* added a remarkable complication to Howells's writing. Now, in addition to telling the story of a female victim of love, he was also telling the story of a male spectator who becomes wholly absorbed in this victim. This double focus was troublesome because it prompted, in fact compelled, the author to reflect on his own motives, private as well as professional—to scrutinize those interests that had been an implicit part of his writing and his audience's reading. The novel turned out to be not just about female blues, but about why female blues fascinate and what should be done about this. It implicitly questioned the cultural status of novels about suffering heroines, but at the same time it *was* one of these novels.

Given this paradoxical turning on itself, the book's subject became excruciatingly complicated and painful for Howells to work out. An author who prized simple truthtelling found himself tangled in a vexedly involuted narrative.[14] Ben's wretched obsession with Marcia began to interfere with Howells's representational difficulties: it was as if the author's struggle to finish his novel had been undermined by the character's futile struggle for self-control. These connections become evident if we take a closer look at what Howells reveals about Ben's obsessiveness.

Ben's primary motive for destroying the photograph is no doubt to show a proper respect for Marcia. He feels that what began as a "freak"[15] and a private running joke with Olive may be shameful intrusion into the sanctity of a marriage. To continue to dwell on the pregnant Maine beauty would be to commit a kind of spiritual adultery. But it is too late for Ben to regain control of himself: his imagination has already been seduced by an image, and events conspire to place this image before him again and again. He finds the image riveting and enervating, so that the more he lingers over it, fingering it with his caressing imagination, the less strength of will he can muster to tear himself away. Ben slowly turns into the classic, self-indulgent fetishist.

Burning the photograph does not help, for when Ben brings the drunken Bartley home and struggles to explain his condition to his wife, he acquires a *mental* image of her a good deal more indelible than the photograph. This image is engraved on his mind at the moment when he helplessly reveals to Marcia why her husband does not need a physician. As her "innocence was beginning to divine the truth," "her head began to droop, and her face to turn away in a dawning shame too cruel for him to see"[17] (275). In this configuration, the expression on Marcia's face is hidden from Ben and the only indication of the slow onset of shame is the position of her head. Instead of effectively concealing her embarrassment, however, her averted, drooping head inflames the man's imagination. When Ben next sees her, he is helplessly embarrassed: he cannot stop making conjectures about what Marcia was thinking and feeling as she turned away from him, and he talks the episode over with his friend Atherton in order to get his interpretation. When Ben says, "I don't know how she looked *then:* I couldn't look at her," he seems to have convinced himself that he refrained from gazing at Marcia, as his sense of decency mandated. But in fact he must have looked, for in the next sentence Howells tells us that "he stopped [talking], as if still in the presence of the pathetic figure, with its sidelong, drooping head" (284).

By this point in the narrative, Ben has become addicted to a certain kind of picture. When he is advised not to "idealize the victim," he breaks out:

> "Atherton, it makes me sick at heart to think of that poor creature. That look of hers haunts me! I can't get rid of it!"
>
> Atherton sat considering his friend with a curious smile.
>
> "Well, I'm sorry this has happened to *you*, Halleck." (286)

The smile signifies Atherton's recognition of Ben's well-known disease, as does the demonstrative pronoun *this*, whose missing referent is clearly understood by both men. Hoping to cure Ben by demystifying Marcia, Atherton proposes, alternatively, that she is "obtuse" (284) and that her shame over her husband's public drunkenness was shortlived. But Ben cherishes his "melodramatic compassion" (283). Marcia's half-concealed shame has become a fetishistic object to be touched and retouched, revisited and restored. Walking home from Atherton's, Ben goes out of his way to pass the Hubbards' house, which he gazes at from the street:

> He wished to rehabilitate in its pathetic beauty the image which his friends' conjectures had jarred, distorted, insulted; and he lingered for a moment before the door where this vision had claimed his pity for anguish that no after serenity could repudiate. The silence in which the house was wrapped was like another fold of the mystery which involved him. The night wind rose in a sudden gust, and made the neighboring lamp flare, and his shadow wavered across the pavement like the figure of a drunken man. This and not that other was the image which he saw. (288)

Ben is so addicted to the image of Marcia's "drooping" and "pathetic beauty" that it is no exaggeration to compare him, as here, to someone suffering from chronic alcohol intoxication. As the last sentence suggests, he himself is fully aware of his predicament. In addition to being the victim of his fetishism, he also suffers from the agonies of helpless self-condemnation. If he looks at Marcia's shame out of the corner of his eye, he looks at his own directly. But he remains helpless.

Earlier American writers had shown an interest in the bachelor who fixes his attention on the sorrows of a married woman—Ik Marvel in *Reveries of a Bachelor,* Henry James in "Madame de Mauves"—but to my knowledge no one before Howells had attempted a full psychological study of this condition. In Ben Halleck, the author was trying to objectify a cultural activity that had eluded conscious scrutiny. He was trying to watch a certain kind of watcher, to understand a certain kind of self-condemning spectatorship. Just as the second essayist in The Contributors' Club praised and quoted the saddest parts of *A Lost Love,* and just as the first essayist's friend loved the book for providing "a real gulp," so Ben loves to torment himself with the image of Marcia's dawning matrimonial sorrow. The painful pleasure the Lost Lovers derived from the novel's "pathos of suggestion rather than word" corresponds to Ben's absorption in a drooping head whose expressive features are turned away from him. Similarly, the Hubbards' house fascinates and tortures Ben because of "the silence" that enfolds a woman's sorrow. The married woman's inaccessibility makes the bachelor's painful cult as issueless as it is delicious.

This cult was closely related to the pleasure of novel-reading and the labor of novel-writing. As critics have noted, while *A Modern Instance* begins as a study of Marcia and Bartley's doomed relationship, the narrative seems to become decentered as it goes, as if taken over by centrifugal forces. Loose ends are not tied together; minor characters remain on stage too long; problems of moral judgment pressed on us by the narrative seem out of place or misleadingly posed. (Why dwell so exorbitantly on Ben's effort to decide whether he has the right to propose to Marcia, when it's obvious she wouldn't have him?) The author's apparent loss of mastery has generally been explained by reference to his history of mental instability.[16] But as with many other writers, life-problems are closely tied to certain problems inherent in the writer's novelistic material—fiction's sinister involutions. Like Ben Halleck, Howells could not resolve how closely he should look at his female lead or how sorry he should feel for her. Ben was free to tear up the photograph, but Howells was committed to the photography of realism. If he provided a glancing, indirect, "artistic" view of Marcia's misery, he would end up creating one more pleasing fetish of a woman's half-seen misery. (This is partly what we get in *The Portrait of a Lady.*) But if he offered a full and frank exposure of her gradual and painful disillusionment, his demystifying realism might turn out to be an unprecedented kind of "indelicacy."

Contrary to what some Foucauldian readers have suggested, Howells's realistic practice does not afford a good example of a superior's all-surveying, penal gaze. The point of his essay on the Boston police court is that it is profoundly corrupting to be a spectator of misery.[17] Much of his fiction actually questions the gaze, "interrogates" it, so to speak (if I may adopt, for this sentence only, the strangely inquisitorial usage that has become so widespread).

Closely related to the spectatorial quandary is the unresolved question of moral responsibility. Is Marcia the victim of a man's predatory nature, as the novel variously suggests, or is she "almost equally to blame"[18] for her misery, as Howells originally claimed in his prospectus?

Deeply implicated in these two problems was a matter that would become central in the novels Howells wrote after 1882, the demystification of female character, to attempt which was to risk assaulting the novel itself (which might be regarded as the cult of the heroine). In 1881–1882 Howells was on the verge of a newly aggressive and self-conscious realism, one that would feature a highly critical representation of certain widely idealized types of femininity. The insertion of Ben Halleck into *A Modern Instance* marks the crucial moment when the author shifts from the old to the new. Without having imagined his way very far into his book, Howells had promised his publishers to secure "the reader's sympathy" for Marcia—"because she inevitably suffers most"[19]—and thus to provide the public with the reading experience it expected. But as he wrote the novel he learned that to provide this experience was to invite the very fetishism Ben can't renounce—a delicious sort of pity for an obscurely perceived and helplessly suffering female lead.[20]

Such considerations help explain why Ben becomes a kind of loose cannon in the second half of the novel. At the same time that the book lavishes an extraordinary amount of attention on this character, it fails to explore his key problem—his *reading*, the formation and operation of his literary imagination. What was his reaction to *A Lost Love?* What exactly did the phrase he borrowed for a caption mean to *him?* Why did the photograph get such a hold on his imagination *before* he met Mrs. Hubbard? The last question, which is central and important, remains unanswered in the novel. With his intense focus on Ben's moral dilemma, Howells gives too little attention to the nature and history of his imagination. Not until the creation of Penelope Lapham in 1884-85 did the writer succeed in showing how a certain kind of reading led to a loss of soundness or sanity. And it was by going back to the English cult-novel that had somehow entrapped Ben that Howells was able to work out a critique of the culture of fiction-reading and to integrate this critique with his own newly-defined practice as a realist writer.

3

Tears, Idle Tears is Howells's name for the book that exerts a strangely retentive hold on Penelope Lapham's imagination. As is well known, the title comes from a lament sung by one of Ida's maids in Tennyson's long poem, *The Princess:*

> Tears, idle tears, I know not what they mean,
> Tears from the depth of some divine despair
> Rise in the heart, and gather to the eyes,
> In looking on the happy autumn-fields,
> And thinking of the days that are no more.
>
> . . . .
>
> Dear as remember'd kisses after death,
> And sweet as those by hopeless fancy feign'd
> On lips that are for others; deep as love,
> Deep as first love, and wild with all regret;
> O Death in Life, the days that are no more![21]

When Howells was a boy, this poem meant a great deal to him. He memorized the first stanza, and one summer, when riding with his older brother Joseph, recited it from memory. He quoted it in a letter of 1859 to this same brother, and quoted it yet again the following year. "Tears, idle tears" was a powerful, talismanic phrase for the aspiring young writer, who carried his "dear old Tennyson in [his] coat-pocket" when he first landed in Liverpool in 1861. Oliver Wendell Holmes helped him grow up by criticizing one of his poems for being "rather Tennysonish."[22] By 1885 "tears from the depth of some divine despair" seemed almost as bogus to the mature Howells as "Shall I Never See Thee More Alas" and "Yes, crush, cold world, this breaking heart" did to the creator of Emmeline Grangerford and the Duke of Bilgewater.

But of course Tennyson was not an author of novels, and the information we are given about the plot and characters of *Tears,*

Idle Tears is far more detailed than the hazy suggestions in the last stanza of the lyric from *The Princess.* Even allowing that self-sacrifice was a common motif in Victorian novels, it seems obvious that Howells must have had *A Lost Love* in mind as he composed *The Rise of Silas Lapham.* There is the same fond circle of women readers and the same basic story and heroine—a woman who renounces the man she loves (who loves her) so that the woman who loved him first can have him. Tom Corey calls *Tears, Idle Tears* "a famous book with ladies" and adds, "They break their hearts over it."[23] The book is said to be making a "sensation" at the time of the novel, the middle 1870s—just before the two Contributors' Club pieces appeared. Clara Kingsbury praises the book in her characteristically unrestrained manner: "It's perfectly heart-breaking, as you'll imagine from the name; but there's such a dear old-fashioned hero and heroine in it, who keep dying for each other all the way through and making the most wildly satisfactory and unnecessary sacrifices for each other." Charles Bellingham has not read the book, and although Nanny Corey has, she thinks it "ought to have been called 'Slop, Silly Slop.'" Reverend Sewell disapproves on moral grounds of "old-fashioned heroes and heroines" (197): the exaltation of "self-sacrifice" is "nothing but psychical suicide." After the minister has made his controversial denunciation of the exaggerated interest novels arouse in "the whole business of love," Howells offers an authorial endorsement by giving him the triumphant last word with Clara Kingsbury and also revealing that "Lapham wanted to make some open recognition of his good sense" (198).

The only detail in the dinner conversation about *Tears, Idle Tears* that doesn't match up with *A Lost Love* is Clara's implication that the hero and heroine *both* die for each other. In fact, while Georgy dies for James's sake, James lives on into an uninspired connubiality (as happens in James Joyce's "The Dead," where the genders are reversed). But literal accuracy is not to be expected from the giddily enthusiastic Clara, who speaks with her usual hyperbole in praising the novel. Penelope undoubtedly gives the more trustworthy account of its plot, which she considers

> "very natural till you come to the main point. Then the naturalness of all the rest makes that seem natural too; but I guess it's rather forced."
>
> "Her giving him up to the other one?"
>
> "Yes; simply because she happened to know that the other one had cared for him first."

With her appeal to naturalness,[24] Penelope would seem to be a less sophisticated reader than Clara, whose delight in older forms of sentiment reflects a consciousness of fashion and artifice that is beyond the Laphams. But Howells regarded the ability to dismiss outworn tastes in sentiment as a sign of both modernity and good sense; he shared this perspective with Mark Twain. For both writers, fiction-reading was the sort of activity in which one was well-advised not to forget what one had learned from the rest of one's experience. Self-taught Penelope turns out to be a better reader than Clara:

> "Why should she have done it? What right had she?"
> "I don't know. I suppose that the self-sacrifice—"
> "But it *wasn't* self-sacrifice—or not self-sacrifice alone. She was sacrificing him, too; and for some one who couldn't appreciate him half as much as she could. I'm provoked with myself when I think how I cried over that book—for I did cry. It's silly—it's wicked for any one to do what that girl did." (217)

A realist's resisting reader, Penelope shares Howells's view that the heroine's self-sacrifice is harmful as well as preposterous. Yet she also gets so much pleasure from the novel that she lingers and cries over it; in fact she is reading it at the beginning of the scene in which Tom Corey proposes. Thus, in spite of her heated dismissal of the book, her response turns out to be as ambivalent as Ben's: the lost-love idea seems attractive and powerful almost because of its absurdity. Precisely as in *A Modern Instance,* a crazy artifact of popular culture takes on an insidious life of its own, like a casually acquired object that is found to be a live parasite one cannot shake off. The instant it is revealed that Tom loves her rather than Irene, Penelope begins imitating Georgy Sandon, declaring that she cannot accept a suitor on whom another woman supposedly has a prior claim. Penelope loses her humor, self-assurance, and common sense, has crying spells, utters lofty sentiments about death, goes through unpredictable changes of tone and mood. The forthright talker and family entertainer is now coy and inconsistent and at a loss for words, as when she labors to compose a brief note to Tom.

One of the reasons Penelope goes to pieces in spite of her sound judgment is that she has the fluid subjectivity characteristic of those who live through their imagination. Her gift for mimicry not only makes her a keen listener to voices; it also turns her into an imperiled reader of novels. As such, she is the perfect vehicle for Howells's critique of an older kind of fiction, which deliberately invited readers to leave their personalities in abeyance and temporarily assume that of a hero or heroine. Howells's tactic is to show what this kind of fiction can do to a mercurial temperament.

But Penelope is much more than a vehicle for literary criticism. She takes her place with Howells' other highly imaginative and often rather weak-willed characters, such as Don Ippolito in *A Foregone Conclusion* (1874), Easton in "Private Theatricals" (1875), Colville in *Indian Summer* (1886), Putney in *Annie Kilburn* (1888), and Angus Beaton in *A Hazard of New Fortunes* (1890). All of these characters exhibit the same mimetic vulnerability we see in Penelope: that is, they lose themselves in their impersonations. This predisposition, an extremely important one in Howells's fictional universe, clearly reflects the writer's own combined instability and protean creativity. For that reason, it is a matter of the utmost importance that Penelope's nickname happens to be "Pen."

Considered as a mark on the page rather than a linguistic sign, *Pen* is virtually identical to *Ben:* add the lower semicircle to her name and you get his. Equally arresting is the accident of rhyme, especially when one remembers that Howells became a novelist after dreaming of being a poet, and that the book that holds Pen's attention takes its name from the phrase that formerly captivated her maker. And just as Ben's trouble originates in a "freak" in which he humorously applies a cult-narrative to his own life ("*my* lost love"), so Pen gradually and unconsciously acquires a parasitical selfhood quite unlike her real one (now perhaps merely "real") by heedlessly getting cozy with a novel she considers *un*real. It is not too much to say that Ben is a rough, early version of Pen, that what is unexplained and underdeveloped in Howells's treatment of *him* is fully worked out with *her.* Both characters, furthermore, were created partly in response to one and the same Victorian novel: it is Ben's lost love that causes Pen's idle tears.

Then there is the fact that Penelope's nickname designates the instrument with which her author wrote—with which, indeed, he fathered Ben and her. Not only does "Pen" name the most important part of her highly productive author, but the narrative of her collapse and recovery recapitulates his *own* professional development since creating "Ben." Thus, just as Pen's imitative vulnerability reflects Howells's retrospective assessment of his dreamily literary youth, so her sharp insights into the mimetic and moral flaws of *A Lost Love* embodies his mature convictions about the importance of resisting literature. Just as Pen slowly wins her way back to "common sense," so Howells painfully reconstructs himself into a realist. To trace a line from Ben to Pen is to see an author not simply moving from a character who is out of control to one who struggles for understanding and self-mastery, but *through* that movement becoming conscious of the invasive potential of his chosen genre and of a need to create a new kind of novel, one that would be nonparasitic, tool like, and modern, and that would help readers liberate *them*selves.

4

We can understand *Silas Lapham* without having even heard of *A Lost Love*. Because Howells's novel does not require us to catch an indispensable allusion, later generations of readers can construe the book without undertaking any historical excavations. In this respect it resembles "Daisy Miller," with its mention of *Paule Méré:* We don't have to know anything about Victor Cherbuliez's novel in order to follow James's story. At the same time, we cannot grasp the contemporary and intertextual significance of these narratives if we ignore the texts that provided Howells and James with what Adeline R. Tintner aptly calls their "templates."[25]

A Modern Instance, on the other hand, remains slightly obscure as long as we don't know about "Ashford Owen's" *A Lost Love* and the Contributors' Club and the state of the manuscript. In order to make sense of Ben's obsession, we need certain facts external to the novel and not in general circulation. That's because the author had only recently begun to reflect in a newly critical way on the activity of novel-reading; he wasn't really in control of Ben's involvement in the lost-love business. By the time he created Penelope, his sense of popular reading had become integrated with his redefinition of his own craft as realist. He had learned how to extract Pen from Ben.

Even so, some readers may wonder whether Howells's controlled analysis of reading in *The Rise of Silas Lapham* is finally preferable to the explosive confusion of *A Modern Instance* (or to that of *A Hazard of New Fortunes,* which is messy in different but still interesting ways). *A Modern Instance* and *Hazard,* both of which end with a character's nervous admission of uncertainty, were the author's own favorites, perhaps because, with all their raggedness, they allow a space for human tragedy, as *Silas Lapham* does not. The latter novel works so hard to get Penelope and Silas to do the right thing that their final resolutions may seem more disturbing than the predicaments they clear up. Maybe it would have been less costly for Howells to lose his struggle against "psychical suicide." It is dismaying to compare his dismissive treatment of self-sacrifice with Joyce's in "The Dead." To recall how the image of Michael Furey standing in the rain powerfully reorganizes our sense of the Conroy's marriage is to ask whether Howells may have labored too hard to make sure there would be no place in modern fiction for wild romantic regret.

Notes

1. W. D. Howells, *A Modern Instance* (Bloomington: Indiana University Press, 1977), 206.

2. *Mark Twain's Notebooks & Journals* (Berkeley: University of California Press, 1979), 3:50. The entry was made between 7 March (48) and June (55), 1884. By this time there had been at least three British editions of *A Lost Love,* and also a French translation for the Bibliothèque des chemins de fer under the title *Georgy Sandon: Histoire d'un amour perdu.* Although the *National Union Catalog* attributes to Ogle another provably different book, *The Story of Catherine* (London: Macmillan, 1885), the foreword she wrote in old age for *A Lost Love* spoke of the latter as her only novel.

3. Annie Ogle, *A Lost Love* (London: J. Murray, 1920), ch.19 and 22.

4. Philip B. Eppard and George Monteiro, *A Guide to the* Atlantic Monthly *Contributors' Club* (Boston: Hall, 1983), xiv.

5. "Books with a Following," *Atlantic Monthly* 39 (March 1877): 362–63.

6. Another possible candidate is Thomas Bailey Aldrich, who in 1881, after assuming direction of The Contributors' Club, complained that people "send me nothing but book-notices"; similarly, the March 1877 essayist disowned any intention to "review" the novel, since "I suppose your Club is not the place for that" (Eppard and Monteiro, p. xvi; "Books with a Following," 362). A third and more remote possibility would be Mark Twain.

7. "Books with a Following," 362.

8. "A Lost Lover Once More," *Atlantic Monthly* 42 (1878): 505.

9. See William M. Gibson, "Introduction," *A Modern Instance* (Boston: Houghton Mifflin, 1957), v–vi.

10. George N. Bennett, "Introduction," *Modern Instance,* xix; David J. Nordloh, "A Note on the Manuscript," *Modern Instance,* 490.

11. As he began chapter 13, Howells penciled in the date of composition, 13 August (574). The next penciled date, in the middle of chapter 14, was 16 August (611). Ms. at Houghton Library (MS Am 1577.2). By permission of the Houghton Library, Harvard University.

12. There are many more complications than I have space to deal with here. The black ink pages show that Ben's last name was originally Holcombe. At some later time, when Howells had gone *back* to using purple ink, he changed this to Halleck (sheet 3 = 89).

13. See Edwin H. Cady, *The Road to Realism: The Early Years 1837–1885 of William Dean Howells* (Syracuse, NY: Syracuse University Press, 1956); Kenneth S. Lynn, *William Dean Howells: An American Life* (New York: Harcourt Brace Jovanovich, 1971); and John W. Crowley, *The Black Heart's Truth: The Early Career of W. D. Howells* (Chapel Hill: University of North Carolina Press, 1985), 110–24.

14. For an interesting study of the way paradoxes of the type, "This sentence is false," entered into the structure of some of Shakespeare's plays, see William O. Scott, "Self-Undoing Paradox, Scepticism, and Lear's Abdication," *Themes in Drama* 12 (1991): 78–85. *A Modern Instance* has long been seen as a novel in which Howells dramatically raised the level of his work; in the words of his first biographer, "the old self-consciously poetic hypersensitivity and temptation to pose are gone" (Cady, *Road to Realism,* 201). What should be added is that Howells simultaneously achieved a new kind of self-consciousness.

15. This word reappears later in the novel, again in connection with Ben's irrational behavior, when we are informed that Clara Kingsbury "had been greatly shocked by Ben Halleck's sudden freak" (374). Presumably, she has in mind some aspect of his obsession with Marcia. But the reference is obscure, because we have not been informed just how much Clara knows about Ben.

16. This has been a leading theme with the novel's critics, who often invoke a psychological explanation of his unidentified illness to explain why the novel got away from him. Cady attributed Howells's illness or breakdown to his inability to maintain "direct vital contact" with "the profound suffering of Marcia or the sinful self-destruction of Bartley" (211). See also Lynn, *Howells,* 251–66. Crowley, *Black Heart's,* 124–49, offers the outstanding presentation of this general view.

17. "Police Report," *Atlantic Monthly* 49 (January 1882): 1–16.

18. Howells, *Modern Instance,* xxix.

19. Howells, *Modern Instance,* p. xxix.

20. My argument should be distinguished from the frequently encountered claim that a given character in a novel is a metonymic figure for the author. I am talking not about figuration but about resemblance, or common membership in a set: the character's circumstances, desires, dilemmas, and choices coincide to some extent with those of its creator, and these shared elements end up interfering with the author's original plans for the narrative. This interference results in a paradox or loop that implicates the entire narrative in what happens to the character.

21. *The Complete Poetical Works of Tennyson* (Cambridge: Houghton Mifflin, 1898), 134.

22. W. D. Howells, *Selected Letters: Volume 1: 1852–1872* (Boston: Twayne, 1979), 39–40, 57, 95, 74.

23. W. D. Howells, *The Rise of Silas Lapham* (Bloomington: Indiana University Press, 1971), 217.

24. Because the older praiseworthy quality of "naturalness" has been replaced in current critical thought by the very suspect activity of "naturalizing," Penelope's critique looks more naive than Howells intended. But Penelope has more of a feel for what the realists were up to than we do. Even Henry James was preoccupied with naturalness in his notebook entries for *The Portrait of a Lady:* "Oh, the art required for making this delusion natural!" "To make it natural that she should have brought about Isabel's marriage to her old lover—this is in itself a supreme difficulty." "That, I think, is perfectly natural." *The Complete Notebooks of Henry James* (New York: Oxford University Press, 1987), 13–15.

25. *The Pop World of Henry James* (Ann Arbor: UMI Press, 1989).

Is *Huckleberry Finn* Politically Correct?

TOM QUIRK

As with so many questions one may put to *Huckleberry Finn,* Twain has anticipated my topic here. The implicit contradiction of the author's "Notice" and his "Explanatory" is one of the several paradoxes of his book. The Explanatory insists upon a certain cultural diversity, and upon Twain's own meticulous and painstaking efforts to render several Mississippi River Valley dialects and thus to give voice to those who speak them. His characters (most of them disenfranchised in one way or another) are to speak for themselves, and we, his readers, are not to suppose that all these characters are trying to talk alike and not succeeding. So instructed, we may approach his heterogeneous narrative with impunity so long as we yield also to the unequivocal Notice that we not attempt to find motive, moral, or plot in it. What other novel has ever made such difficult claims upon the reader? We are to listen to its voices and resist (on pain of prosecution, banishment, or execution) even so slight a temptation to interpret this series of adventures as purposive or instructive or even useful. *Huckleberry Finn* thy tongue is diversity, thy authority is the long arm of the law, G. G., Chief of Ordnance.

I do not intend to answer the question my title poses. Indeed, I suspect that neither the book's most avid partisans nor its most vocal detractors would wish to deem *Huckleberry Finn* a politically correct novel. True, we are sometimes told that the novel is an "attack on racism" without ever being told, precisely, why we should believe this. But by and large we prize *Huck* for its incorrectness; it is an incorruptibly incorrect book in nearly every particular. But the issues my title raises are delicate ones, and I hope you will indulge me if I approach the subject with a certain eager wariness and stalk it in a roundabout way. What I hope to offer in return for this indulgence is not, I hasten to add, a new reading of *Huckleberry Finn.* God forbid. Still less do I mean to infuse the novel with an ideological perspective. Quite the reverse. I hope to show that ultimately *Huckleberry Finn* resists, in fact refuses, ideology itself.

About a dozen years ago, Leslie Fiedler came to my campus to deliver a lecture. I can't recall the title, but I do recall that he observed that the customary Euroamerican response to the Klansmen's revenge scene in D. W. Griffith's *Birth of a Nation* is disturbingly positive, and that this fact testifies to the deep and abiding racist character of our culture. I am ashamed to say that I have never seen *Birth of a Nation* and therefore do not know what my own reaction to this controversial scene might be. But I have seen a few movies in my time.

As a child I used to go to the Westerns every Saturday afternoon. I grew up in a rather unique community called McNary, Arizona. It was a company lumber town and had originally been McNary, Louisiana. But when the yellow pine of Louisiana played out around the turn of the century, old man McNary picked up his town lock, stock, and barrel and moved it to Ponderosa pine country, smack dab in the middle of the White Mountain Apache Reservation. It was a town of about four hundred souls. We, that is the families of the white company men, lived on the hill; the Chicano families lived just to the north of us, almost in the forest; the blacks lived down the hill in what was called the "Quarters"; the Apaches, of course, lived all around the town, but not in the town itself.

Despite these well-understood boundaries, all the kids converged at the movie house on Saturday afternoons. There were separate drinking fountains at the entrance, and the black kids had to sit in the balcony. (Most of us kids, brown and white alike, usually said that they "got to sit" in the balcony and begrudged them their good fortune.) At any rate, we watched the newsreel, and the Batman serial, and a couple of Westerns every Saturday. At the age of four or five, I unthinkingly accepted, or rather never questioned, this segregated arrangement. On the other hand, every time the cavalry came to save the settlers from the Indians, which was every week, we all cheered; and I was sufficiently aware of race at that age to ask my Native American friends why they, too, cheered for the cavalry and not the Indians. The explanation was irrefutable: "Those aren't Apaches; they're Navajos."

I put this anecdote up against Mr. Fiedler's observation about the subterranean racist nature of American culture. The only point I wish to make is so simple that I am somewhat embarrassed to make it: Our response to works of the imagination has a great deal less to do with political or social realities as such than with an imaginative identification with heroism, courage, nobility, and so forth. We cheer for the good guys in white hats, not because they and their hats are white, nor, for that matter, because they are guys, but because everything within the fictional world they inhabit marks them as good.

Identification, I confess, is a flimsy basis upon which to build any convincing reply to those who find *Huckleberry Finn* a racist book.[1] Ralph Ellison once confessed that when he read the novel, he identified with Huck, not Jim, and justified this natural response by observing that a black person is likewise heir to "the human experience which is literature, and this might well be more important to him than his living folk tradition."[2] Now I am not so benighted that I do not know that Ellison is much out of favor these days—one thing that Jerry Falwell and Terry Eagleton can agree upon is the danger and evil associated with anything that passes for humanism. We live in an era of linguistic naturalism, which is to say that prevailing critical ideology has it that we no longer think our language, our language rather thinks us. Values, literary or other, are thus vanities, and discussing, adopting, or pursuing them is utter foolishness.

Nevertheless, I can sympathize with a fiction writer interviewed on National Public Radio some time ago. He had written a short story about a marriage breaking up. The husband, a fireman, was a callous clod, and the story was meant to dramatize his unthinking cruelty. The author, a few months after the story was published, received a letter from a firefighters organization demanding a public apology for so maligning the character of firemen. Literature, the author complained, is in the process of being paradigmed to death, and this writer was both amused and annoyed to discover that he had written so politically incorrect a story.

The problem, of course, is not with reading but with interpretation, though, again, prevailing critical opinion has all but collapsed this distinction. For the last ten or fifteen years I have taught Willa Cather's *O Pioneers!* as often as I could, and I have noticed that none of my white male students has any difficulty whatsoever identifying with Alexandra Bergson, not only as the hero of that novel, but as the mythic embodiment of an American pioneering spirit that is unquestionably female. Some, however, do balk when I point out that by implication that same figure repudiates such time-honored assumptions as that the history of America is the history of rugged individuals preserving the force of personality by escape to the frontier, or that the East represents the Past, and the West, the Future. For *O Pioneers!* calls both these assumptions, and many others as well, into question.

Now, *Huckleberry Finn* has always been something of a subversive book. In the beginning it was banned because it encouraged mischief in America's youth. I have heard that it was for a time banned in China because it undermined a culture devoted to ancestor worship—Huck does not display a proper reverence for his father. Then there is the apochryphal story that a public librarian removed the novel from the shelves because of the homosexual elements in it—and I can imagine Leslie Fiedler, if he ever heard this story, saying, "That's not what I meant at all." The trouble, as I say, is with interpretation, not with reading.

The more recent banning of *Huck Finn* on the basis of, on the one hand, the rendering of Jim as an unflattering portrait of a black man, and the excessive, perhaps obsessive use of the word "nigger" on the other, is a far more serious charge, but not because previous critiques were incidental, even superficial complaints. If, indeed, *Huck Finn* was in any way subversive to late Victorian American culture or to the whole notion of a republic of virtue populated and ruled by slightly overgrown Good Boys routing out and punishing Bad Boys, it was subversive indeed. If, for the Chinese, Huck's cagey defiance of his father discredited a politically altered but still lively sense of ancestor worship, he is, in fact, a dangerous character. What makes the charge of racism far more serious is that, if true, it serves to damn all those (mostly white male) critics who have for decades defended the book, if not as a potently antiracist book, at least as a profoundly moral one. Moreover, unlike the other charges, this one unsettles our conviction about what Twain was trying to do in his novel. (Twain meant to disturb the prevailing American ethos, he meant nothing at all about China or the Chinese, and he meant and probably thought he had effectively damned race prejudice.) In contemplating the political correctness of *Huckleberry Finn,* we are willy-nilly caught up in such questions as: What is the relation of the author to his or her book? What is the social function of literature? Is the canonical status of this novel evidence of cultural hegemony and racist myopia?

Insofar as we appropriate our past and make it serve the uses of our present, the question of *Huckleberry Finn* becomes a very simple one, expressed in the obnoxious vernacular of our own day: Do we want a book that makes Euroamericans feel bad about themselves or one that makes African Americans feel good about themselves? The questions have an inevitable corollary: Is literature in some way humanistic in the sense that it presupposes the possibility of moral vision and an attendant willingness to "do the right thing?" Or is it rather a signifying chain that somehow thinks us and therefore, in the interests of a certain political objective, must be condemned or, more likely, construed in such a way that (through the auspices of an instructed vision that we may call criticism) alters not the understanding but the structure of thought itself.

Now whites have been feeling bad about themselves for centuries; in fact, I rather suspect that we enjoy feeling bad about ourselves and are sometimes inclined to designate the more effective forms of this self-torture *The Arts*. Coincidentally, I was recently serving on a college committee with the peculiar title "The Ethnic Civility Task Force." This moral SWAT team was comprised of several diverse and well-meaning sorts, but I must confess that I became tired of hearing my white colleagues say, "Hey, I'm a sensitive guy!" One of the black members put his finger on the problem when he observed that "sensitivity" has its own mysterious logic to it: "Pretty soon, we'll have to be sensitive to the needs of left-handed people, and bald headed people, and clumsy people, and blacks will be put on the back burner once again."[3]

I can recall my own most embarrassing moment of sensitivity. I was teaching a composition course to a group of Navajo women many years ago. I was determined to be relevant, and one day brought copies of the Navajo Night Chant for discussion. But discussion was not forthcoming; instead there was whispering and muttering among the students. "Did I do something wrong?" I asked. "No," they assured me. "But that song is sacred to us." "Oh, then I shouldn't talk about it?" "Oh you can talk about it all you want to," they insisted, "but we can't listen to you."

The fictional epitome of sensitivity, I suppose, is Bigger Thomas's lawyer, Boris Max. *Native Son* was of course hailed as a powerful indictment of white racist culture, and so it is. However, my sampling of reviews of the novel in African American periodicals does not square with the standard reaction of white readers and reviewers. For many blacks, Max, his political commitments and sensitivity nothwithstanding, was just another white man giving a black man the run around.[4]

As Kenneth Burke once observed, capitalist societies, stressing as they do the individual, nevertheless achieve some degree of social cohesion by two antithetical means—war and charity. Both, of course, excite and promote feelings of superiority, racial and other. Our devastation of Iraq brings us together, and our contribution to the United Way brings us together. Sensitivity, it seems to me, is but a noninstitutionalized form of charity, or worse, pity; and it is as welcome an ally in institutions of political correction as it is in our now kinder and gentler republic.

As a critical principle, at any rate, it is chaotic and pernicious. One can, indeed some readers do, feel pity for each and every character in *Huck Finn*—Pap because he hasn't a decent pair of shoes, Huck because he was pestered by the Widow and abused by his father, the Wilks girls, the Shepherdsons, the Grangerfords, the drunken Boggs, well-meaning, God-fearing Silas Phelps, even the Duke and the Dauphin. The sensitive guy who reads this book is apt to be paralyzed by the superabundance of his good and charitable feelings.

Now, and here at last I begin to move in on the subject at hand, Twain presented in Huck and Jim twin images of nobility, images contrary to what he knew or thought he knew about the ways of the world and of human possibility. Whatever else they may be, Huck and Jim were for their author metaphors, metaphors of their own human possibilities, nothing more, and certainly nothing less. And Twain wished to believe in them. The desire to believe in a metaphor, observed Wallace Stevens, "is to stick to the nicer knowledge of / Belief, that what it believes in is not true."[5] Of course we know, and I'd hazard that Twain did as well, that Huck and Jim are not true: it was more realistic, even probable, that Jim should have gotten lynched or that Huck would have turned Jim in than otherwise.

Actually, I am little interested in protecting Twain from the charge of racial prejudice. By nearly any reckoning Samuel Clemens was something of a racist, though the form it took was typically paternalistic rather than actively prejudicial. However, I might extenuate this charge by claiming that the imaginative self who created *Huckleberry Finn* ought not be confused with the ordinary self who, on the one hand, wrote abundant racist remarks in letters to his mother, or, on the other, as one who paid a black man's tuition to Yale. The question of whether or not Samuel Clemens was a racist seems to me urgently, even crucially unimportant. I am far more interested in protecting Twain from the charge of being a sensitive guy.

The record of Twain's strivings with his novel indicate that his manifold purposes and accidental effects fall away as Jim nudges his way to the center of the novel's concerns. Jim refuses to be put on the back burner, and it is Twain's imaginative courage, not his political or moral courage that, by allowing to Jim speak for himself, finally claims our admiration.[6] We become less and less interested in the anti-Southern, anti-sentimental, anti-aristocratic, anti-everything-under-the-sun elements in the novel, and more and more concerned with its affirmations, which is to say we become more and more concerned with Jim—Jim not as a representative of the black, the oppressed, or the wretched, but as Jim.

Two of the most conspicuous objects of Twain's satire are war (or organized violence) and charity (or sentimentality). But if one could magically subtract from the book all the instances of violence—not merely the feud chapters or the Boggs shooting but the proposed lynching of Sherburn or whatever happened to Pap on the floating house or even the desire to ransom the Sunday School girls to death—and then if one could take from the remainder all instances of charity—the slave hunters' forty dollars acquittal of their responsibility to Huck and his supposed father with small pox, or the determination of the Judge to make a new man of Pap, or the Widow Douglas who wishes to save Huck (the poor lost lamb!) or Emmeline Grangerford's insufferable odes—if, as I say, one could perform this sort of higher mathematics, what would be left? Not much, I'd guess, but that "community of misfortune," Huck and Jim. And they, as outcasts and runaways, are happily exempt from the need for social cohesion.

Yet they are hardly pure. Twain's realism works by a kind of mean averaging of experience; or perhaps a more fashionable way of putting it is that it contains and announces its own ambiguities, it deconstructs itself before a critic lays a glove on it. *Huckleberry Finn* was a book motivated by multiple intentions and it achieves diverse, even contradictory effects. Jim is a coward aboard the *Walter Scott* and a hero when Tom gets shot; he is alternately obsequious and insistent, curious and bullheaded, boastful and self-recriminating, credulous and shrewd.[7] As for Huck, I doubt that he is any more inconvenienced by the moral dilemma he faces in his desire to help Jim than he was by wearing starched collars or mumbling over his victuals. His decision to help Jim is as trivial and immediate as an itch that has to be scratched or a sneeze that has to be sneezed. As for deciding to go to hell, we know from the very first page of the novel that he wasn't much interested in playing the harp anyway.

The beauty, the sheer magnificence of Huck's moral decision is how very small it is. Unlike his earlier decision to help Jim Turner aboard the *Walter Scott,* there is no sense of adventure in the prospect. Unlike his decision to help the Wilks girls, there is no pity in it. And despite his own fears, Huck is in no real danger of becoming a low-down abolitionist. He is absolutely incapable of abstracting from his own experience a general principle, and had he been allowed to reach his majority and thereby given to such generalizing, Huck would likely have become as shiftless as Pap, as indeed Twain predicted he would.

We know that the curious genesis of *Huckleberry Finn* introduced several textual peculiarities and ruptures. However, a far more serious rupture, it seems to me, occurs right after the raft is hit by the riverboat at the end of chapter 16.[8] When Huck surfaces, he calls out for Jim "about a dozen times," but he never really worries about him. Instead, Huck climbs ashore and is soon involved in other adventures. For all Huck knows, Jim is dead or injured, but his creator had drifted from the so-called moral center of his book and was so eager to get to a satire of Southern aristocratic pretension that he was for the moment no longer much interested in Jim or his flight.

By chapter 18 Huck and Jim are rejoined, however, and soon they are once more on the river. As much as Twain might have wanted to get shed of Jim, he couldn't. Jim unnecessarily complicated his plot, for not only was it absurd to have a slave escaping into the deep South, but the two had to travel at night and avoid the river communities. Jim's mere existence imposed all sorts of limitations on his author. After Jim's early appearance in the novel Twain seems to have pretty much forgotten about him. Yet Jim turns up again on Jackson's Island. The river might have drowned him, but he survives to repair the raft and wait for Huck. The "Working Notes" for the novel indicate the possibility that Twain contemplated having Jim lynched, but he missed every opportunity to do so.[9] The King and the Duke sold him (to Abram Foster they say) but Huck finds him again at the Phelps farm. Twain made a note to himself to "*Blow up* cabin,"[10] but he did not indicate whether Jim would be in it at the time. And even after Twain had manufactured a conclusion to the novel and had set Jim free, the image of Jim still nagged at him it seems. At any rate, Twain interpolated half of chapter 12 and all of chapters 13 and 14, chapters that dramatize Jim's native capacity to reason regarding Frenchmen who refuse to talk like men and his moral indignation at King Solomon as the sort of biblical patriach who prefers the "bo'd'n house" of a million souls to sensible and dignified employment.

Even then Twain was not through with Jim (or perhaps it was the other way round). For he planned a lecture tour to make some cash and to promote the book, and when he sent proof sheets of *Huck* to his fellow lecturer, George Washington Cable, asking for suggestions about what he might read on the tour, Cable particularly recommended the "King Sollermun" episode and "How Come a Frenchman doan' Talk Like a Man" (a title Cable recommended over the needlessly offensive "You can't learn a nigger to argue").[11]

Jim stalked his creator. The author gave him his voice, but not even Mr. Mark Twain was going to shut him up. The novelist Fay Weldon makes the distinction between characters that are "described" and those that are "invented." When an author describes a character, she observes, all of the prejudices and prepossessions one has about the world and its people go into that character. But when an author invents a character, the character takes on its own life and speaks its own world.[12] Huck, virtually from the beginning, was an invented character. By degrees, Twain ceased to describe Jim and began to invent him.

Whether or not Twain the man was a racist (a charge that seems oddly superfluous in this context), his imaginative parts created a character who challenged Twain's own moral nature (or more accurately called it forth), just as he had Huck's. Houston Baker once observed that he made a living by telling people things they don't want to hear but that they know are true. This, I submit, was the method of Twain's realism in *Huck Finn,* with the important difference that Twain was rendering truths, particularly in and through Jim, that perhaps he himself did not want to hear but that he knew were true. Uncharacteristically, Twain had the human decency to keep his mouth shut and listen, but he wisely knew that he might have to call in the Chief of Ordnance to have us do the same.

Notes

1. The whole process of identification is a mysterious one. One thing we may say about it, though, is that however fully one's emotional and moral states tally with those of a created character, there is always a critical faculty at work in the process of reading. No reader no matter how naive, I think, ever took *Huckleberry Finn* as a literal recipe for moral heroism. If this were so, there would be hundreds

of fourteen year old white boys searching out and linking their fortunes with black adult male fugitives. Nor, I suppose, has any young woman reader decided, after reading *The Scarlet Letter,* that the path to moral greatness is to marry an older man, have an adulterous relation with her minister, keep the baby, and linger in a contemptuous community. If this were the practical result of imaginative engagement, there really would be a hue and cry from white America to ban both novels.

2. Ralph Ellison, *Shadow and Act* (New York: New American Library, 1966), 72–73.

3. Not long ago an editorial writer in *Time* sardonically remarked that perhaps we ought refer to short people as the "vertically challenged." By extension, I suppose, we ought call tall people "vertically gifted." And one of the most absurd instances I can recall is the objection of a School Board to the use of the word "bitch" in one of Laura Ingalls Wilder's *Little House* novels. In the novel the word is applied not to a woman (which might be cause for complaint) but to a female dog. Sever the relation between signifier and signified and introduce sensitivity to fill the vacancy, and our language can think us in peculiar directions, it seems.

4. A recent National Public Radio interview emphasized the uncompromising courage of Richard Wright as it was so palpably represented in *Native Son.* No one, I think, could question the moral and imaginative courage of Richard Wright. However, perhaps it should be pointed out that Wright acceded to the request of his publishers that he excise portions of the manuscript that were deemed too explicitly sexual. And as courageous and damning of white racist America as the novel is, *Native Son* was nevertheless a Book of the Month Club selection.

5. Wallace Stevens, "The Pure Good of Theory," in *The Collected Poems of Wallace Stevens* (New York: Alfred A. Knopf, 1968), 332.

6. Twain's "Working Notes" for the novel show a preoccupying and continuing concern with Jim's dialect; they also reveal that the author had contemplated giving Jim an instant education, presumably with the intent of outfitting the runaway slave for a larger and more vocal role in the several conversations that take place particularly in the latter half of the book. Twain considered having Huck teach Jim to read and write, instruct him in history and even astronomy. See "Mark Twain's Working Notes" and "Mark Twain's Marginal Working Notes" in the California/Iowa edition of *Adventures of Huckleberry Finn,* ed. Walter Blair and Victor Fischer (Berkeley and Los Angeles: University of California Press, 1988), 711–64.

7. For Ralph Ellison, these same ambiguities are a tribute to Twain's moral vision, a quality he insists that moderns such as Hemingway, anxious to emulate his technical improvisations, have been all but blind to: "Jim is drawn in all his ignorance and superstition, with his good traits and his bad. He, like all men, is ambiguous, limited in circumstance but not in possibility." *Shadow and Act,* 48–49.

8. Until the recent discovery of the first half of the *Huckleberry Finn* manuscript, it had been supposed that after he wrote this episode, Twain dropped the ms. for some time and that when he returned to it he had other things on his mind than the comradeship of two outcasts. Now it appears that Twain's first burst of composition during the summer of 1876 ran through chapter 18. Nevertheless, it is clear that he was excited by the new satirical possibilities of a Southern feud and, even in so brief a time, may have altogether forgotten Jim until he revived the character at the end of chapter 18.

9. For the evidence for this supposition, see my "'Learning a Nigger to Argue': Quitting *Huckleberry Finn,*" *American Literary Realism* 20, no. 1 (Fall 1987): 18–33.

10. See the "Working Notes" C-9, 755 of the California/Iowa edition of the novel.

11. See editorial comment in *Mark Twain and George W. Cable: The Record of a Literary Friendship,* ed. Arlin Turner (East Lansing: Michigan State University Press, 1960), 47.

12. See Fay Weldon, *Letters to Alice on First Reading Jane Austen* (New York: Carroll and Graf Publishers, 1984), 88.

Whatever Happened to Bret Harte?

GARY SCHARNHORST

In the midst of a literary reformation whose most radical protestants decry the very notion of a canon, something rather curious has occurred: Bret Harte's works have disappeared from the textual landscape like books banned in Boston. Neither the *Heath* nor the *Harper*—the most inclusive and unabashedly decentered of the new college anthologies of American literature—contains a single word by Harte, and he receives scant attention in the new *Columbia Literary History of the United States*. The Signet paperback edition of *The Outcasts of Poker Flat and Other Tales,* the collection of Harte's stories best-suited for classroom adoption, has recently lapsed from print. At this writing, no volume on Harte has appeared among the six hundred studies in Twayne's United States Authors Series, one of the most ambitious critical projects of the past thirty years, which includes monographs on such otherwise obscure figures as Will Harben, Sherwood Bonner, and Adelaide Crapsey. That is, the *re*canonization of American literature in recent years has led to a virtual *de*canonization of Harte for reasons that are problematic at best in the present climate of literary studies.

It was not ever thus. Harte's story "The Luck of Roaring Camp," published without signature in the July 1868 issue of an upstart California magazine, "startled the Academists on the Atlantic Coast," as Kate Chopin remembered later.[1] From the first, his work, so different in tone and texture from the genteel tradition of Emerson, Hawthorne, and the Fireside Poets, challenged the established canon. Mark Twain thought him at the time "the finest writer" in the West[2] and turned to him for help and advice as he was revising *The Innocents Abroad.* Harte, he allowed, "trimmed and trained and schooled me patiently until he changed me from an awkward utterer of coarse grotesquenesses to a writer of paragraphs and chapters that have found a certain favor."[3] In 1871, after earning a national reputation with a half-dozen or so memorable stories and poems in the *Overland Monthly*—e.g., "The Outcasts of Poker Flat," "Tennessee's Partner," "The Idyl of Red Gulch," "Miggles," "Plain Language from Truthful James"—Harte was lured east by the promise of wealth and literary success. W. D. Howells later compared his journey across the continent to "the progress of a prince" in the "universal attention and interest" it received in the daily press.[4] According to Twain, Harte "crossed the continent through such a prodigious blaze of national interest and excitement that one might have supposed he was the Viceroy of India on a progress, or Halley's comet come again after seventy-five years of lamented absence."[5] In Boston, Harte signed the most lucrative contract that had ever been offered an American writer—ten thousand dollars—by the firm of James R. Osgood & Co., the publisher of the *Atlantic Monthly* (whose stable included Emerson, Thoreau, Stowe, Hawthorne, Longfellow, Lowell, Whittier, Holmes, and Howells) for all the poems and sketches he might produce over the next twelve months. For that one year, it may be fairly said, Harte was both the highest-paid and the best-known writer in America.

He was not, however, the most widely read writer in America that year, largely because he published very little under the terms of the contract. He "was in the midst of new and alien conditions," Howells explained, "and he had always his temperament against him, as well as the reluctant if not the niggard nature of his muse."[6] Harte's career went into a tailspin that lasted most of a decade, but it is simply not true that, as Eric Sundquist remarks in the *Columbia Literary History,* his career was "brief."[7] In fact, Harte published at least one new book of fiction each year, fully two-thirds of his collected works, between 1883 and his death in 1902. By 1893, moreover, he was earning a reported fifteen thousand dollars annually, more than he had received while under contract to Osgood in 1871–1872.[8] To be sure, late in his career Harte was especially popular in England and Germany. In 1890, Havelock Ellis ranked him with Hawthorne, Poe, and Mark Twain among American "imaginative writers . . . of worldwide significance,"[9] and at his death the London *Spectator* claimed he had "probably exerted a greater influence on English literature than any other American author."[10] No less a luminary than Henry Adams regarded Harte as one of "the most brilliant men of my time,"[11] and as late as 1914 his books had appeared in more German editions than had Twain's.[12]

His standing in the canonical pecking order may be inferred from the comments about his work in high school and college textbooks and the frequency with which it has been anthologized over the years. Julian Hawthorne and Leonard Lemmon in *American Literature: An Elementary Text-book* (1891)—issued, ironically, by the D. C. Heath Co.—hailed Harte as "a brilliant innovator" who spoke in "a new voice." His "first half-dozen stories were his best"—such has been the critical consensus since the 1870s— but it "would be difficult to praise these half-dozen stories too highly. It is difficult to see how they would have been done better."[13] Fred Lewis Pattee echoed the point in his *History of American Literature* (1903): Harte's early stories for the *Overland* "were works of literary art worthy to be compared with the rarest products of American genius."[14] Similarly, Eva March Tappan contended in 1906 that, while Harte reached his peak in those first tales, "no one can help seeing that within his own limits he is a master."[15] Brander Matthews asserted the next year that Harte "had a finer sense of form" than Dickens,[16] and John Erskine argued in 1910 that Harte was one of six American writers of fiction whom "time has sifted . . . for special remembrance."[17] Charles Swain Thomas edited a selection of Harte's *Poems and Stories* published expressly for schools and colleges by Houghton Mifflin—the successor firm to Osgood & Co.—in 1912,[18] and William MacDonald edited a collection of Harte's *Stories and Poems* published by the Oxford University Press three years later.[19] Mary E. Calhoun and Emma L. MacAlarney reprinted one of Harte's poems in their *Readings from American Literature: A Textbook for Schools and Colleges* and lamented that space prevented them from excerpting more of his work.[20] Meanwhile, "The Luck of Roaring Camp" and "The Outcasts of Poker Flat" became staples in anthologies of short fiction.[21]

Harte was clearly at the height of his modern popularity during the second quarter of this century. Though never in the first rank of American writers, he was a major minor figure, certainly more canonical than marginal. His grandson compiled a collection of his letters for publication by Houghton Mifflin in 1926, and the scholar George Stewart both edited *The Luck of Roaring Camp and Selected Stories and Poems* for Macmillan in 1928 and wrote the standard biography, *Bret Harte: Argonaut and Exile,* issued in 1931. Meanwhile, the gold regions of central California had begun to be known as "Bret Harte country" in deference to the writer's role in romanticizing the exploits of the redshirted miners. "Of all the Californias that men have invented for their delight or their profit, Bret Harte's is the most charming," or so the travel writer Mildred Adams claimed in 1930.[22] Not even Joseph Stalin was immune to Harte's appeal: In 1927, the Soviet leader inaugurated a policy to encourage mass migration to Siberia "after reading Bret Harte's novels about the California Gold Rush"—or so he claimed.[23] Moreover, every American literature anthology published in the thirties, forties, and fifties included at least one story by Harte. More typically, they contained generous selections from his writings. Both *American Poetry and Prose* (Houghton Mifflin, 1939), edited by Norman Foerster, and *A College Book of American Literature* (American Book Co., 1939), edited by Milton Ellis, Louise Pound, and George W. Spohn, reprinted "The Luck of Roaring Camp," "The Outcasts of Poker Flat," "Plain Language from Truthful James," and one or two other Harte texts. The *Oxford Anthology of American Literature* (1939), edited by William Rose Benét and Norman Holmes Pearson, contained "Outcasts" and four of Harte's poems, including "Plain Language." Two major postwar anthologies—*The Literature of the United States* (Scott, Foresman, 1947), edited by Walter Blair, Theodore Hornberger, and Randall Stewart, and *American Heritage* (Heath, 1955), edited by Leon Howard, Louis B. Wright, and Carl Bode—reprinted "The Luck," "Tennessee's Partner," and "Plain Language"; and *The Rise of Realism* (Macmillan, 1949), edited by Louis Wann, featured both "The Luck" and "Outcasts," one of Harte's parodic "condensed novels," and eight of his poems. *The American Tradition in Literature* (Norton, 1956), the most popular college anthology of all, edited by Sculley Bradley, R. C. Beatty, and E. Hudson Long, included "Outcasts" and four of Harte's poems. Even the immediate predecessor to the *Heath* anthology, the survey-text *American Literature* (Heath, 1969), edited by Harrison T. Meserole, Walter Sutton, and Brom Weber, contained another of the "condensed novels," Harte's story "The Idyl of Red Gulch," and his comic poem "Miss Judge Jenkins." Less than a generation ago, Harte was still a standard, if not a vital, figure in the canon, his stories and poems a part of the established curriculum in American literature.

So what happened? Why has Harte in recent years suffered a sort of critical eclipse? First, he seemed to represent for the New Critics all that was wrong with American fiction. Cleanth Brooks and Robert Penn Warren excoriated "The Outcasts of Poker Flat" and especially "Tennessee's Partner" in *Understanding Fiction* (1943; rev. ed. 1959), one of the most influential of all New Critical texts. According to Brooks and Warren, Harte was "straining for a highly emotional effect," one of the "surest symptoms that one is dealing with a case of sentimentality." In the latter story, he was "so thoroughly obsessed with the pathos of the partner's loyalty that he has devoted no thought to the precise nature of the basis of that loyalty."[24] Never mind that Harte subtly mocks the popular-sentimental conception of friendship Brooks and Warren believe the story affirms; despite their vaunted critical acumen and the very title of their book Brooks and Warren oversimplify and misread the text.[25] Never mind that they would reprint "Tennessee's Partner" in their own anthology *American Literature: The Makers and the Making* (St. Martin's, 1974). The damage to Harte's critical reputation was irreparable, however misdirected their attack may have been. Brooks and Warren made it possible, even fashionable, for academic formalists to denigrate Harte. Roy R. Male, for example, complained in *Types of Short Fiction* that Harte "strains for effect," that his fiction exhibits an "uneven, insecure, and facile tone."[26] Bradley, Beatty, and Long excerpted Harte's work in the Norton anthology notwithstanding their lament it "was often sentimental, melodramatic and mawkish."[27] And Jay Gurian charged in the *Colorado Quarterly* that Harte's verse was marred by "trite rhyming, intrusive rhythm, topical reference, and lack of idea."[28]

Harte has also suffered in recent years from a number of invidious comparisons with Mark Twain. As in a zero-sum game, Twain's star has risen as Harte's has fallen, the success of one coming at the expense of the other. Their rivalry has historical roots, of course: Despite their early friendship, despite Harte's early patronage, despite their collaboration on the play *Ah Sin,* the two men were estranged in 1877 and never spoke again. Harte believed that Twain had conspired with Elisha Bliss of the American Publishing Company of Hartford to cheat him out of royalties he had earned on sales of his novel *Gabriel Conroy.* On his part, Twain thought Harte had insulted his wife. As early as January 1878, at any rate, Twain publicly but anonymously alleged that "Harte was absolutely devoid of a conscience. If his washerwoman had saved $500 by long years of careful industry, he would borrow it without the slightest intention of repaying it."[29] When he learned a few months later that Harte was angling for a diplomatic appointment, Twain vilified him in a letter to Howells as "a liar, a thief, a swindler, a snob, a sot, a sponge, a coward" and asked "what German town he is to filthify with his presence" so that he could "write the authorities there."[30]

In Australia in 1895, he declared Harte "sham and shoddy," with "no pathos of the real, true kind."[31] He fulminated about Harte again in 1906, in autobiographical dictations Bernard De Voto edited and published in 1940 in *Mark Twain in Eruption.* Harte "was an incorrigible borrower of money" who "deserted his family" and "never sent them a dollar" all the years he was abroad. Harte walked with a "mincing" gait, Twain recalled, thus insinuating he was homosexual. In all, he was

> one of the unpleasantest men I have ever known. . . . He hadn't a sincere fiber in him. I think he was incapable of emotion, for I think he had nothing to feel with. I think his heart was merely a pump and had no other function. . . . He was bad, distinctly bad; he had no feeling, and he had no conscience.[32]

Never mind that none of these allegations is strictly true: for example, by his own estimate, Harte sent his wife a total of sixty thousand dollars over a period of twenty-four years.[33] The labels stuck nevertheless. Ever loyal to his master, De Voto dismissed Harte in *Mark Twain's America* as "a literary charlatan whose tales have greatly pleased the second rate."[34] Twain scholars, who can scarcely be accused of dispassionate objectivity in this matter, have without exception rallied to the side of the greater writer. Dixon Wecter claimed that "Harte burned himself out early" and "left a wake of personal unpopularity such as few other American writers have ever achieved."[35] According to Edward Weeks and Emily Flint, Harte "became jealous and vindictive" when Twain succeeded him.[36] Twain's blast was "about the bitterest denunciation one American writer ever made of another," Edward Wagenknecht observed, though it was tempered by Twain's generous "estimate of Harte's work."[37] Ironically, in the most thorough review of the extant evidence, Margaret Duckett revised the jaundiced assessment of Harte's star-crossed relations with Twain. The only scholar of note to specialize in Harte's writings since Stewart published his biography in the early 1930s, Duckett readily conceded her "belief that for too long a time the scales have been heavily weighted on the side of Harte's damnation." Far from "jealous and vindictive," Harte simply "remained silent" on the subject of Twain during the last twenty-five years of his life "in the face of considerable provocation."[38] Unfortunately, Duckett's *Mark Twain and Bret Harte* (1964) was received with unvarnished hostility by most critics, especially those employed in the Twain industry. Wilson O. Clough toed the orthodox line in *American Literature,* asserting that "Twain had some ground for impatience" with Harte,[39] and G. A. Cardwell carped that Duckett "gives Harte the benefit of the doubt but not Mark Twain."[40] Hamlin Hill, a Twain biographer, detected "the strong odor of whitewash" about the book,[41] as if Duckett were merely imitating one of Tom Sawyer's boyish pranks. Twain, it seems, will always be the plaintiff, Harte the defendant whose guilt is presumed.

Ironically, Harte has been marginalized—or, more accurately, simply ignored—during a canon debate that has served to rehabilitate the reputations of literally dozens of nineteenth-century American minority and women writers. Like the gatekeepers at a trendy nightclub, the editorial board of the *Heath Anthology of American Literature* admitted to its pages only those writers who fit a certain profile in dress and appearance. As general editor Paul Lauter explains, the board reviewed the hundreds of texts recommended for inclusion by the profession at large, "made an initial cut, and then in a series of meetings over three years narrowed the selections to what could fit within the covers of two large volumes." Like brands of house paint or car wax that have been test-marketed (text-marketed?), the reprinted works ostensibly reflect the "new scholarship developed by leading specialists in the fields."[42] Harte was omitted from the anthology not because he lacks merit but because he lacked sponsors. What the New Critics began in the 1940s the anthologists-by-committee finished in the 1980s. Or are we to assume that such figures as Sui Sin Far, Mary Antin, and Alice Dunbar-Nelson are included because each of them really was a more significant writer than Harte? The same forces that have rehabilitated the reputations of minority and women writers have not touched Harte: they have produced what is, in effect, a conspiracy of silence to exclude him. The editorial board of the *Heath* now proposes to delete *The Scarlet Letter, Huck Finn,* and *Daisy Miller*—texts that are "inexpensively available in paperback" and which were included in the first place, as one of the editors confided to me, only at the insistence of the publisher—to make room "for additions to the Second Edition" of the anthology, a process that may be likened to replacing the chestnuts with the Chesnut(t)s, Mary and Charles.

Even more ironically, the case against Harte (i.e., that his fiction is marred by excessive sentimentality) mirrors exactly the old argument for excluding such women writers as Elizabeth Stuart Phelps and Harriet Beecher Stowe from the canon. As Herbert Ross Brown opined half a century ago, the sentimental novelists "were escapists, artfully evading the experiences of their own day. . . . They fed the national complacency by shrouding the actualities of American life in the flattering mists of sentimental optimism."[43] De Voto summarizes the consensus view of Harte's tales in remarkably similar terms: "The syrupy tales that he spun out . . . drifted opportunely before a public relieved of war and facing westward. They were prettily written, between laughter and kind tears. They informed readers enamored of sentiment that even in the Sierras the simpler virtues were imperishable and that humanity remained capable of sweetness on the Pacific slope."[44] To their credit, Jane Tompkins and others have recently attempted to redress the charge that sentimental fiction "presents a picture of life so oversimplified and improbable" that "only the most naive and self-deceiving reader could believe it."[45] They contend, with good reason, that the formalist bias against sentimentality was often invoked merely to exclude popular fiction from the canon and from serious critical discussion. Unfortunately, the argument has never been made in defense of Harte's fiction. Lora Romero, while conceding that women's novels are not "necessarily different from men's novels," nevertheless argues that because "women novelists have been excluded" from the canon "*as a class,* feminist literary histories must include them *as a class.*"[46] That is, works by men writers may encode an ideology as subversive as those by women writers, but Harte's tales—and, for that matter, the novels of Sinclair Lewis or James Branch Cabell or Richard Harding Davis (who is now known, if at all, as the son of Rebecca Harding Davis)—may be ignored precisely because as "dead white males" they fall outside the parameters of gender. A recent collection of Harte's early California essays was panned by reviewers who groused that it appealed only to "San Franciscans and buffs of California memorabilia,"[47] that "interested readers (as opposed to scholars)" will have "to wade through soporific passages about politics and religion in order to get to nuggets of interest."[48] I daresay the book would have escaped such cavils had the essays been written, say, by Jessie Benton Fremont or Ina Coolbrith. Harte had published one of these essays earlier in the weekly paper the *Golden Era* and he would collect it in the first edition of *The Luck of Roaring Camp and Other Sketches* as well as in his collected works. Are we now to conclude that its appeal is slighter because he also published it during his literary apprenticeship in the pages of the Boston *Christian Register?*[49]

By any reasonable criteria, whether aesthetic or historical, let alone ideological, Harte deserves to be resurrected from the footnote. Not only did he write some fine and influential tales and poems, he was remarkably liberal on issues of race, class, and gender; that is, he was/is "politically correct," a point in his defense that is, regrettably, germane to the ongoing debate on the canon.[50] As a young journalist in Humboldt County, California, in 1859, Harte risked life and limb by editorially condemning a massacre of Native Americans, and in 1866 he publicly defended the right of African Americans to march in a Fourth of July parade through San Francisco. In addition, his story "Miggles," published in the *Overland* in 1869, is an exploration of gender-role reversal comparable to Charlotte Perkins Gilman's "If I Were a Man." Much as he satirized racial chauvinism and the stereotype of the inscrutable Oriental in "Plain Language from Truthful James," his 1874 story "Wan Lee, the Pagan," based on the murder of a Chinese child in San Francisco in 1867, was a powerful indictment of racial hatred. In such late allegorical tales as "The Crusade of the Excelsior" and "Three Vagabonds of Trinidad" he condemned American imperialism in Latin America and the Caribbean and the doctrine of manifest destiny that sanctioned military adventurism. Throughout his career, in short, Harte made repeated and sustained attacks on ignorance and prejudice and discrimination.[51] 'Tis a pity on every count that he was so long misunderstood and then forgotten.

Notes

1. Kate Chopin, "Development of the Literary West," *St. Louis Republic,* Sunday magazine (9 December 1900): 1; rpt. in *American Literary Realism* 22 (Winter 1990): 70–73.
2. *Mark Twain's Letters,* ed. Harriet Elinor Smith and Richard Bucci (Berkeley: University of California Press, 1990), 2: 359.
3. *Mark Twain's Letters,* ed. A. B. Paine (New York and London: Harper & Bros., 1917), 1:182–83.
4. W. D. Howells, *Literary Friends and Acquaintance* (New York: Harper & Bros., 1900), 290.
5. *Mark Twain in Eruption,* ed. Bernard De Voto (New York and London: Harper & Bros., 1940), 265.
6. Howells, *Literary Friends,* 301–302.
7. Eric Sundquist, "Realism and Regionalism," in the *Columbia Literary History of the United States,* ed. Emory Elliott et al. (New York: Columbia University Press, 1988), 516.
8. Mabel Percy Haskell, "Bret Harte in London," *San Francisco Examiner* (12 February 1893) 17:4–5.

9. Havelock Ellis, *The New Spirit* (London: George Bell & Sons, 1890), 86.
10. "News of the Week," *Spectator* (10 May 1902): 715.
11. *Letters of Henry Adams 1892–1918,* ed. Worthington Chauncey Ford (Boston and New York: Houghton Mifflin, 1938), 391.
12. Grace Isabel Colbron, "The American Novel in Germany," *Bookman* 39 (March 1914): 47–48.
13. Julian Hawthorne and Leonard Lemmon, *American Literature: An Elementary Text-book* (Heath, 1891), 244, 247.
14. Fred Lewis Pattee, *A History of American Literature* (New York, Boston, Chicago: Silver, Burdett and Co., 1903), 398.
15. Eva March Tappan, *A Short History of America's Literature* (Boston and New York: Houghton Mifflin, 1906), 115.
16. Brander Matthews, *The Short Story* (New York: American Book Co., 1907), 253.
17. John Erskine, "Bret Harte," in *Leading American Novelists* (New York: Henry Holt, 1910), 325–69.
18. *Poems and Stories by Bret Harte,* ed. Charles Swain Thomas (Boston: Houghton Mifflin, 1912).
19. *Stories and Poems by Bret Harte,* ed. William MacDonald (London: Oxford University Press, 1915).
20. *Readings from American Literature: A Textbook for Schools and Colleges,* ed. Mary Edwards Calhoun and Emma Leonora MacAlarney (Boston and New York: Ginn and Co., 1915), iv.
21. *Short Stories,* ed. C. Alphonso Smith (Boston: Ginn and Co., 1916); *The Great Modern Short Stories,* ed. W. D. Howells (New York: Boni and Liveright, 1920); *Representative American Short Stories,* ed. Alexander Jessup (Boston: Allyn and Bacon, 1923).
22. Mildred Adams, "Glamour Clings to Bret Harte's Hills," *New York Times Magazine* (31 August 1930): 12–13. See also "Gold Rush in Reverse," *Time* (31 August 1992): 15–16, which mentions the "scenic small towns" in central California which were "once made famous by Mark Twain and Bret Harte."
23. "That Russian Gold," *Time* (15 May 1964): 108.
24. *Understanding Fiction,* ed. Cleanth Brooks and Robert Penn Warren (New York: Appleton-Century-Crofts, 1943), 214–20, 230; rev. ed. 1959, 181–84. Brooks and his fellow editors, including Warren, reiterated the critique of "The Luck" in *An Approach to Literature* (New York: Appleton-Century-Crofts, 1952), 86–87.
25. Charles F. May, "Bret Harte's 'Tennessee's Partner': The Reader Euchred," *South Dakota Review* 15 (Spring 1977): 109–17; William F. Connor, "The Euchring of Tennessee: A Reexamination of Bret Harte's 'Tennessee's Partner,'" *Studies in Short Fiction* 17 (Spring 1980): 113–20.
26. Roy R. Male, *Types of Short Fiction* (Belmont, CA: Wadsworth, 1962), 304.
27. *The American Tradition in Literature,* ed. Sculley Bradley, R. C. Beatty, and E. Hudson Long (New York: Norton, 1956), 2:483.
28. Jay Gurian, "The Possibility of a Western Poetics," *Colorado Quarterly* 15 (Summer 1966): 71.
29. *Cincinnati Gazette* (10 January 1878), 5:4.
30. *Mark Twain–Howells Letters,* ed. Henry Nash Smith and William M. Gibson (Cambridge: Belknap Press of Harvard University, 1960), 1:235–36.
31. Sydney *Morning Herald* (17 September 1895).
32. De Voto, ed., *Mark Twain in Eruption,* 254–92.

33. Bret Harte to Anna Harte, 15 September 1901, Alderman Library, University of Virginia.
34. Bernard De Voto, *Mark Twain's America* (Boston: Little, Brown, 1932), 164.
35. Dixon Wecter, "Mark Twain and the West," *Huntington Library Quarterly* 8 (August 1945): 373.
36. *Jubilee: One Hundred Years of the Atlantic,* ed. Edward Weeks and Emily Flint (Boston: Little, Brown, 1957), 88.
37. Edward Wagenknecht, *Mark Twain: The Man and His Work* (Norman: University of Oklahoma Press, 1961), 89.
38. Margaret Duckett, *Mark Twain and Bret Harte* (Norman: University of Oklahoma Press, 1964), 333, viii.
39. Wilson O. Clough, "Book Reviews," *American Literature* 37 (January 1966): 491.
40. G. A. Cardwell, "Book Reviews and Book Notes," *Social Studies* 57 (January 1966): 36.
41. Hamlin Hill, "Mark Twain and His Enemies," *Southern Review* ns 4 (Spring 1968): 521–22.
42. Paul Lauter, "To the Reader," *Heath Anthology of American Literature* (Lexington, MA: D. C. Heath, 1990), 2:xxxiv.
43. Herbert Ross Brown, *The Sentimental Novel in America, 1789–1860* (Durham, NC: Duke University Press, 1940), 360.
44. De Voto, *America,* 162. See also Kevin Starr, *Americans and the California Dream 1850–1915* (New York: Oxford University Press, 1973), 49: Harte "fixed the Gold Rush into formula and made it serve as California's mythic history. Harte depicted the Gold Rush as quaint comedy and sentimental melodrama."
45. Jane Tompkins, *Sensational Designs: The Cultural Work of American Fiction 1790–1860* (New York: Oxford University Press, 1985), 152.
46. Lora Romero, "Domesticity and Fiction," *The Columbia History of the American Novel: New Views,* ed. Emory Elliott et al. (New York: Columbia University Press, 1991), 111.
47. P. J. Perroza, *Choice* 28 (April 1991): 1308.
48. Joe Boe, "When Harte & Twain Went Mining for Literary Gold," *San Francisco Review of Books* 15 (Fall 1990): 21.
49. *Bret Harte's California* (Albuquerque: University of New Mexico Press, 1990), 155.
50. I know of no more explicit rationalization for the politicization of the canon debate than Tompkins's (201): "The struggle now being waged in the professoriate over which writers deserve canonical status is not just a struggle over the relative merits of literary geniuses; it is a struggle among contending factions for the right to be represented in the picture America draws of itself."
51. See Margaret Duckett's essays "Plain Language from Bret Harte," *Nineteenth-Century Fiction* 11 (March 1957): 241–60; "Bret Harte's Portrayal of Half-Breeds," *American Literature* 25 (May 1953): 193–212; "Bret Harte and the Indians of Northern California," *Huntington Library Quarterly* 18 (November 1954): 59–83; and "The 'Crusade' of a Nineteenth-Century Liberal," *Tennessee Studies in Literature* 4 (1956): 109–20.

Notes on Contributors

ELIZABETH AMMONS is Professor of English and of American Studies at Tufts University. She is the author of *Edith Wharton's Argument with America* and *Conflicting Stories: American Women Writers at the Turn into the Twentieth Century.* She has edited *Short Fiction by Black Women, 1900–1920, How Celia Changed Her Mind and Selected Stories by Rose Terry Cooke,* and *Critical Essays on Harriet Beecher Stowe.*

ALFRED HABEGGER is Professor of English at the University of Kansas. He is the author of *Gender, Fantasy, and Realism in American Literature* and *Henry James and the "Woman Business"*. At present he is completing *The Father: A Life of Henry James, Sr.*

SUSAN K. HARRIS is Professor of English at Pennsylvania State University. She is the author of *Mark Twain's Escape from Time* and *19th–Century American Women's Novels: Interpretative Strategies.*

RICHARD HOCKS is Professor of English at the University of Missouri. He is the author of *Henry James and Pragmatistic Thought* and *Henry James: A Study of the Short Fiction.* He is also the author of the Henry James chapters in *American Literary Scholarship,* the current president of the James Society, and has coedited the Norton critical edition of *The Wings of the Dove.*

KENETH KINNAMON is the Ethel Pumphrey Stephens Professor of English at the University of Arkansas. He is the author of *The Emergence of Richard Wright* and monographs on James Weldon Johnson and James Baldwin. He compiled *A Richard Wright Bibliography* and has edited collections of essays on *Native Son* and James Baldwin. He is the coeditor of *Black Writers of America* and *Conversations with Richard Wright.*

AMY LING is Associate Professor of English and Director of the Asian American Studies Program at the University of Wisconsin, Madison.

She is the author of *Chinamerican Reflections: Poems and Paintings*, *Between Worlds: Women Writers of Chinese Ancestry*, and coeditor of *Imagining America: Stories from the Promised Land*, *Visions of America: Personal Narratives from the Promised Land*, the *Heath Anthology of American Literature*, and *Reading the Literatures of Asian America*.

SANFORD E. MAROVITZ is Professor of English and former chair of the department at Kent State University. He has served as associate editor of *Studies in American Jewish Literature;* and he has coedited *Artful Thunder: Versions of the Romantic Tradition in American Literature;* and co-authored *Bibliographical Guide to the Study of the Literature of the U.S.A.*, 5th edition.

PATRICIA OKKER is Assistant Professor of English at the University of Missouri. She has recently completed a manuscript on Sarah Hale and the tradition of nineteenth-century women periodical editors.

TOM QUIRK is Professor of English at the University of Missouri. He is the author of *Melville's Confidence Man: From Knight to Knave*, *Bergson and American Culture: The Worlds of Willa Cather and Wallace Stevens*, and, most recently, *Coming to Grips with "Huckleberry Finn"*. He coedited *Writing the American Classics*.

GARY SCHARNHORST is Professor of English at the University of New Mexico. He is the author of *The Lost Life of Horatio Alger, Jr.* and books on Charlotte Perkins Gilman and Bret Harte. He coedits *American Literary Realism* and is the editor in alternating years of *American Literary Scholarship*.

CHERYL WALKER is Richard Armour Professor of English at Scripps College. She is the author of *The Nightingale's Burden: Women Poets and American Culture Before 1900* and *Masks Outrageous and Austere: Culture, Psyche, and Persona in Modern World Poets*. Her anthology of nineteenth-century American women poets was published in 1992.

NANCY A. WALKER is Professor of English and director of Women's Studies at Vanderbilt University. She is the author of *A Very Serious*

Thing: Women's Humor and American Culture, *Feminist Alternatives: Irony and Fantasy in the Contemporary Novel by Women*, and *Fanny Fern*. She has also edited *Redressing the Balance: American Women's Literary Humor from Colonial Times to the 1980s* and prepared a critical edition of Kate Chopin's *The Awakening*.

Index